THE GAME OF
HUMOR

THE GAME OF HUMOR

A Comprehensive Theory of Why We Laugh

Charles R. GRUNER

TRANSACTION PUBLISHERS
New Brunswick (U.S.A.) and London (U.K.)

First paperback printing 2000

Copyright © 1997 by Transaction Publishers, New Brunswick, New Jersey 08903.

Library of Congress Catalog Number: 97-2825
ISBN: 1-56000-313-8 (cloth) 0-7658-0659-2 (paper)
Printed in the United States of America

Library of Congress Cataloging-in-Publication Data

Gruner, Charles R.
    The game of humor : a comprehensive theory of why we laugh / Charles R. Gruner.
       p. cm.
    Includes bibliographical references and index.
    ISBN: 0-7658-0659-2 (paper : alk. paper)
    1. Laughter. 2. Wit and humor—Psychological aspects. I. Title.
BF575.L3G78   1997
128'.3—dc21   97-2825
                                                              CIP

Contents

Introduction

In 1955 I was a first-year graduate student in desperate need of a topic on which to do a major research/lecture assignment at Southern Illinois University. With the kind help of an educational psychologist named Leslie Malpass I began a life-long study of humor, wit, and laughter. This fascination with why and how we humans laugh has enabled me to produce a number of term papers during my graduate education, a doctoral dissertation, one book, and a sizeable clutch of scientific studies published in scholarly journals and/or presented at professional meetings.

Early in my studies I encountered the *superiority theory of humor* advanced so forcefully by philosopher Thomas Hobbes and explained so lucidly in human evolutionary context by Albert Rapp. This explanation of why we laugh gave birth to a *gestalt* which made my understanding of humor and wit crystal clear. For forty years hence, I have been able to explain to myself and others in "superiority theory" language each and every instance of humor I have encountered.

But many humor "experts" and researchers, while admitting that "superiority" explains much humor, resist the notion that it can explain all humor. In my discussions with these folk the common plaint I hear is something like, "I just don't feel superior to anyone or anything every time I hear or tell a joke."

I have concluded that this statement reveals the fact that such people do not really understand the ramifications of the theory. I suspect that they, like those who argue for the validity of the "Adam and Eve" tale without ever having carefully read Genesis, have not scrupulously read the relevant literature on the superiority theory.

I further suspect that the social pressure on us humans to be kind, understanding, and charitable (or, at the very least, civil) to all our fellow human beings conflicts with the idea that the pleasant, warm, fuzzy comfort that humor provides can always be explained in the negative terms of "superiority," "aggression," "hostility," "ridicule," or "degradation." These folks, I guess, do not agree with comedian Jay Leno, host of The Tonight Show. He was queried in "Walter Scott's Personality Parade" (*Parade*, 19 May 1996): "Why is it that Jay Leno, who doesn't hesitate to make fun of everyone else, never tells any jokes about his wife?"

Jay's answer: "*Jokes have to be demeaning to be funny* [emphasis mine]...and I have a lot of respect for my wife, Mavis. We don't argue. Fighting makes me uncomfortable. If I talk about Mavis on *The Tonight Show*, it's to tell a funny story that happened to *us*, not to pick on her."

So: this book is my second major effort (first: *Understanding Laughter*) to explain the superiority theory of humor in socially acceptable language. I wish for the reader to think of all humor as a succession of *games*. The very idea of a game implies fun, leisure, entertainment, recreation, affable human interaction; but it also implies *competition, keeping "score"* and a *winner* and a *loser*.

To paraphrase what was recently pronounced in neighboring Atlanta, Georgia: "Let the explanation of the games begin."

1

Win Or Lose: The Games We Play

Sign outside a church:

Next Sunday: "Do You Know What Hell Is?"
Come in and hear our organist.

The time: 12 March 1996; the place: Terrell Hall 214, University of Georgia. Event: my lecture to the members of SPC 490, "Wit and Humor as Communication."

I wanted to quickly communicate to the students the central theme of this book. I told this story:

George Ostermeyer went into the operating room with a critical illness and for a surgical procedure that he knew in advance he very well might not survive. When he awoke, he found himself lying in a large sumptuous bed in a huge bedroom. On the walls hung priceless old masters paintings, and gorgeous antique tapestries; exotic oriental rugs covered the floor; beautifully haunting music cascaded softly from all sides. A manservant stood attentively at the side of George's bed. "Could I get you anything, Sir? Anything at all?" he asked.

"I must have died," replied George.

"Yes, Sir, you certainly did," answered the manservant. "Can I get you anything to make you comfortable?"

"Why, yes," said George. "How about a large, very dry, very cold martini?"

"Done," said the servant, and George instantly held in his hand the biggest, coldest, driest martini he had ever sipped.

As George finished his martini the servant again asked if he wanted anything. George replied, "Well, I *am* famished. How about a big, thick steak, medium rare, with baked potato and Caesar salad, and a bottle of your very best champagne."

"Certainly, Sir," said the servant, and the bountiful repast was suddenly spread before the amazed gentleman.

After George finished his dinner, the servant once again asked if he could bring his master anything. George thought for a moment, then brightened: "I'd really like a woman. A blonde. Say—how about a young Marilyn Monroe."

"Of course, Sir." And suddenly a nubile Marilyn Monroe was under the sheet next to George, wearing nothing but perfect makeup and a smile, throatily saying through her smile, "Dear George—I am totally yours!"

"Wow," interjected our hero. "I always dreamed of going to Heaven, but I had no idea I would find it this great!"

"Oh, but Sir," interrupted the servant, "I fear you have the wrong impression. You did not go to *Heaven*."

As the story ended, there was a long, puzzled silence in the classroom.

I continued. Let's suppose that I am the servant and you are the "Georges" and I could grant each of you any and everything that any of you could possibly desire: suppose I could provide it instantly and completely, without reservation or condition. Would you really enjoy that?

After another pause, one student opined that such instant gratification could get pretty old pretty fast.

I asked if anyone present played golf. Three young men held up their hands. I turned to Craig, the golfer in the front row: "Suppose I could grant that you would play perfect golf each time you hit the links. How (and what) would you do at 'perfect golf'?"

"Eighteen straight holes-in-one," was the reply.

"OK, Craig. I grant you perfect golf for life. You now will score a perfect eighteen each round you play. Will you now enjoy the game more?"

Without even thinking about it he said, "Heck no. I'd quit the game."

I knew that Omari played on the UGA Bulldog football team. I turned to him. "Omari, what would be perfect football for the 'Dawgs?'"

"Well," he said, "Each offensive play is drawn on the board to go for a touchdown on each play."

"What about defense?" I queried.

"Each defensive play gets drawn on the board as stopping the other team for no gain or else intercepting a pass."

"OK, then," I said. "I decree that the Bulldogs will now play nothing but perfect football. Each offensive play they run will result in a touchdown; every defensive play will either throw the opposition for a loss, or recover the ball for us. So Georgia ought to win all their games by several hundred points to none. Wouldn't you like that, Omari?"

"Shoot, I can't see any fun in that!"

Scanning the entire class, I continued: "How about you fans? Wouldn't you enjoy the game better if Georgia played perfectly?"

They all literally or figuratively held their noses.

"But don't you always want to *win*?" I asked.

Of course, they did. But it had to be a *contest*. The synonym for a truly boring game came out: "No contest."

So I asked for examples of truly interesting, exciting, fun games to win. One student recalled the football game over at Georgia Tech in the 1980s. Georgia was down by four points with just over two minutes to play when they got the ball on their own twenty-yard line. Quarterback Andy Johnson brought the team down the field with short down-and-out passes to stop the clock since the Bulldogs had no more timeouts left. Finally, with seconds left on the clock, Johnson crashed over the goal line in a quarterback draw play. The Georgia fans went ballistic in their gleeful celebration.

Another recalled the great comeback by Duke's basketball team in the 1992 NCAA tournament. Duke was trying for its second consecutive national championship, but found themselves behind by one point with only 2.7 seconds left in the game. After a timeout, Duke's Grant Hill threw a baseball-type pass the length of the floor where stood center Christian Laettner at his foul line, his back to the basket. Laettner faked left, dribbled once right, and lofted a perfect shot through the net as the buzzer sounded. The entire Duke half of the Coliseum erupted in a hurricane of cheers, laughter, screams, back-pounding, and high-fives.

Other students gave accounts of close games of chess, bridge, Parcheesi, poker, Monopoly, even *solitaire* in which they had joyously pulled out victories.

I presented somewhat contrasting examples from my hometown experience. It had been a tremendous thrill for tiny Pinckneyville to win the Illinois state basketball championship in 1948, although the championship game became so lopsided that the seniors watched the last two minutes from the bench while the second-stringers (including myself) got onto the floor to take a small part in the 65–39 score, a record differential for a championship game.

On the other hand, when Pinckneyville once again became an Illinois state basketball champion (1994), this time as a Class A school, it was with a last second heartstopping drive by all-stater Shane Hawkins, ending in a leaping pass-off to forward Ryan Bruns, who dropped through a six-foot jumper to break the tie as the buzzer sounded. The result was crowd pandemonium!

Other dull, boring victories came up in the discussion. Perhaps the biggest yawner must have been the most uneven score in football history, according to the *Guinness Book of World Records*:

> Georgia Tech's thrashing of hapless Cumberland University. That scoreboard read 222–0 at the game's merciful end.

So: in order to be fun, in order to provoke a big emotional high at it's conclusion, a game must (1) be close-must involve a conflict that keeps tension high until (2) a *sudden* conclusion, resulting in a *victory* for the winner and a *defeat* for the loser. (One is tempted to remember ABC's "The thrill of victory, the agony of defeat.")

But, of course, there *are* "laffers," where you or the home team is assured of victory long before the game's end. But at the conclusion of those "no-contests," the squeals, the shouts, the celebration of victory becomes much subdued. Oh, you enjoy those wins, but not as ecstatic, blood-pounding highs; instead, more as warm, pleasant, satisfying inward glows. We call it "gloating."

This same formula that operates in sports and games (tension built up, then suddenly released) also accounts for humor. Let us consider one of my favorite jokes:

> Old Zeke was in poor health, but he liked to play the lottery, and had done so for years. One day Zeke's family learned by way of TV that Zeke had won $100,000 in the lottery. They were concerned about how to convey this information to dear ole Zeke because of his bad ticker. They feared that the sudden good news would trigger a heart attack and kill Zeke.
>
> They conferred with their minister, who was naturally good with words, and asked him if he would break the news to Zeke in a gentle and life-preserving fashion. The minister agreed.
>
> The minister began his conversation with Zeke:
>
> "Zeke, I understand you like to play the lottery."
>
> "Yep, shore do," Zeke replied.
>
> "Well, tell me, Zeke, did you ever win any money?" the minister asked.

"Nope, never won a dime," said the gambler.

"Well, Zeke," replied the preacher, "Tell me. Have you ever considered what you would do if you did win some money? For instance, let's just suppóse that you won, say, $100,000. That's a lot of money. What would you do with that much money, Zeke?"

Zeke replied immediately. "Well, first, I'd give half of it to the church."

Whereupon the minister dropped dead of a heart attack.

In the story of Zeke and the minister we have a subdued microcosm of a close, hard-fought, suddenly won game. Zeke's good fortune, as well as his poor health and thus his family's concern, first engage our interest (read: "develops tension"); then the enlisting of the wordsmith minister to help solve this touchy, dangerous problem heightens our concern. We notice that the minister starts out doing a good job of approaching the subject matter in an emotionless manner. He gradually leads up to a nonthreatening *hypothetical* illustration of what Zeke might do *if* he had won a large sum. Zeke's quick reply *suddenly* "turns the tables," as the minister immediately suffers a fatal heart attack. Let's retell the "joke" without the tension-building.

Old Zeke ran into his minister on the street one morning, says to him, "Hey Parson, I just heard on TV that I won $100,000 in the lottery. I'll be giving the church half of it when I git it." The minister drops dead of a heart attack.

Not as funny, right? Let's tell it again and take out the sudden turning of the tables: The minister has just asked his hypothetical question of Zeke, and Zeke replies,

"Well, first I'd give half of it to the church." At this news the minister falls silent. After a moment: "Please excuse me, Zeke, but I don't feel well. I think I had best get home." At home, the minister complains to his wife of chest pains. Despite his protestations that it's probably only "heartburn," his wife calls an ambulance and insists that he go to the hospital. There, in the emergency room, the minister is diagnosed as having had cardiac arrest. He is put on artificial life support; the city's leading heart surgeon is called in, and she performs a triple bypass operation on the minister. But to no avail. After a coma lasting four days, the minister "Graduates to Glory."

Again, not very funny, eh what? Slow, agonizing deaths are funny only to one's meanest, most spiteful enemies.

What I have just illustrated here is the major thesis of this book: laughing at something that is "funny" is basically the same thing as our reactions to winning in sports and games, even the "game*s* of life" (and I emphasize the plural in "games" because we play so many such in this existence).

In sports or games, the amount and duration of our outward expression of joy and happiness is, at least in gross measure, proportional to the amount of tension built up by the closeness of the contest, and then to the suddenness of perception of *winning*. With humor, our behavior indicating pleasure (usually laughing, smiling, grinning, sometimes screaming with joy or applause) varies with the amount of emotional involvement with the subject of the humor and the abruptness or *suddenness* of the surprising outcome. The desired resolution of the game, as well as that of the joke, must pleasantly surprise us to evoke the strong "thrill of victory." (More on "the agony of defeat" later.)

To put that thesis more succinctly: *laughing equals winning*.

Now, lest you prematurely reject that thesis, let me define what I mean by "winning." I do not mean the mere "beating" of someone else, as in a formal or informal game in which a score is kept, although "beating someone" comes into play (again, later, with the "agony of defeat"). Of course, I do include "winning" to mean coming out first in a contest between individuals. But I mean far more, too. The dictionary helps us.

Winning also means succeeding at "reaching a specified condition or place," such as to "win freedom from bias and prejudice" or "win free from a pressing crowd." It also means having success in a dispute or argument; perhaps being proved "right" or "correct." To win also can mean to prevail upon, to persuade, as in "to win over a convert" or "to win sympathy" from another; you might "win" someone as your own, to marry. Or you might "win" from nature some treasure, such as minable ore, or gold, or oil.

In short, I use "winning" here in its broadest sense: *Getting what you want*. For it is "getting what we want" that makes us happy, isn't it? We say that we *enjoy* getting what we want. And it is *not* getting what we want that makes us unhappy.

We experience, not joy, but frustration or sadness when we do *not* get what we want.

And getting what we want *suddenly*, as a surprise, exhilarates us far more than receiving the same as a simple matter of course. Being born into and growing up with great wealth would please but not *excite* us; but hearing from Ed McMahon that we just won ten million dollars for answering his letter sends our emotions soaring to the stratosphere. Helping to plan your own birthday party will hardly thrill you; but the lights suddenly coming on, and everyone jumping up from behind furniture and shouting "Happy Birthday" and "Surprise!" provides an emotional jolt long to be remembered.

The rest of this book is devoted to demonstrating that enjoyment of successful humor, like enjoying success in sports and games (including the games of life), must include *winning* ("getting what we want"), and *sudden* perception of that winning.

Subtheses include the following:

1. For every humorous situation, there is a *winner*.
2. For every humorous situation, there is a *loser*.
3. Finding the "winner" in every humorous situation, and what that "winner" *wins*, is often not easy.
4. Finding the "loser" in every humorous situation and what that "loser" *loses*, is often even *less* easy.

But, that having been said,

5. Humorous situations can best be understood by knowing *who* wins *what*, and *who* loses *what*,

and,

6. *Removal* from a humorous situation (joke, etc.) what is won or lost, or the suddenness with which it is won or lost, removes the essential elements of the situation and renders it humorless.

I will try to demonstrate the validity of my thesis and subtheses by considering a wide range of different humorous situations. Eventually we will return to the story of Old Zeke and the minister and see who "won" (I think we can already agree that the loser was the preacher!) and *what* was "won." But before diving into the nuts and bolts of applying the "laugh/win" theory to various kinds of laughter-provoking situations, let me try to explain why I think we humans engage in the business of joking and laughing at all. In order to seek this explanation, we have to consider just what kind of animal we humans have developed into, *and from what*.

* * *

Lots of people have theorized about why humans laugh. In a book entitled *A Study of Laughter in the Nursery School Child*, Blatz, Allen, and Millichamps (1936) list a total of *thirty-seven* different theories of humor. But in *The Psychology of Laughter and Comedy*, J.Y.T. Greig (1923) listed a total of *eighty-eight* "different" theories of laughter and comedy. However, Mr. Greig judiciously points out that many of these theories borrow heavily from one another and, thus, do not really represent all that many "different" theories. In the same vein I have a book on my shelf entitled *The Psychotherapy Handbook: The A to Z Guide to More Than 250 Different Therapies in Use Today* (1980); it does actually summarize over 250 "different" psychotherapies in use today; but, as with humor theories, they borrow heavily from one another, and many have common bases.

Theories are very useful to human inquiry. A theory postulates how and why things are. It tells researchers what to look for in order to see if the theory actually "fits reality."

Theories are neither "true" nor "false." They are merely more or less *useful*. A theory is useful to the extent that it meets two criteria: *Explanatory comprehensiveness*: a theory should offer a set of logically consistent statements that explain each and every phenomenon which the theory purports to cover. *Verifiability*: a theory should lead to the discovery of new knowledge that confirms the validity of the theory. This new knowledge can come from either empirical, observational research (as, in experiments or field studies) or through the stimulation of other statements or propositions that should or should not logically agree with the theory's statements (this latter is often called the theory's "heuristic influence").

Once *explanatory comprehensiveness* and *verifiability* of a theory are established, scientists generally opt among competing theories for the "law of parsimony" which states that the simpler explanation or theory is to be preferred over the more complicated and involved. Let's look at these criteria in a little more detail.

If a theory lacks explanatory comprehensiveness, then there are some phenomena it cannot explain. For instance, the theory must specify *sufficient* causes for the phenomena, not merely *necessary* causes for the same events. Consider: being a female is a *necessary* cause for becoming pregnant; but it is not a *sufficient* cause. It is *necessary* for a person to be thirty-five years of age to become president of the United States; it is not sufficient.

Another aspect of a theory's explanatory comprehensiveness is that there should be no events specified in the theory that cannot be found, ultimately. For instance, Sigmund Freud (1905) postulated that there were two kinds of wit (humor), "tendency wit" and "harmless wit." "Tendency wit" is the common humor directed *at* a *butt*, making fun of someone or some institution. "Harmless wit" was described as humor directed *at* no one or thing, but which merely relies for its laughter-evoking on its verbal form. The important point here is that Freud was unable to provide a single example of "harmless wit."

Theories are constantly tested for their *verifiability*, and are thus indispensable for the researcher. The theory tells the researcher *what* to test for. For instance, suppose that your humor theory states that, since men and women have different attitudes toward sex, then their reactions to or appreciation of sexual humor should also differ. Then, if you should expose random samples of men and women to sexual humor and ask them to rate it on, say, "funniness," you should find that men and women *do* differ in their ratings of the humor. If they do, your findings would tend to support your theory. Then you could publish your results in some scholarly journal and avoid "perishing," academically.

If you were to find that the men and women in your study did *not* differ in their funniness ratings of sexy humor, you would have to go back to the drawing board: either revise your theory (hypotheses), your experimental procedures, or both. If only *some* men and *some* women in the study did *not* rate the humor as did their same-sex fellows in the study, these would be "exceptions that prove the rule (theory)," meaning exceptions that *test* the rule (the original meaning of "prove" in this old saying). In this case you would have to revise your theory to take into account not just averages, but individual differences!

A further test of verifiability for the sex-related theory, above, would be information on preferred recreational choices of men and women. Are men more inclined to read "sexy" (some would say "pornographic") material, attend xxx-rated movies, use more sexual slang in same-sex conversations, and/or view "date rape" as a lesser crime than would women? If so, then these other findings would comprise further data to support the verifiability of the sex-related humor theory.

So as we look at theories here, let's keep in mind these two criteria: explanatory comprehensiveness, and verifiability. And we will also want to consider *parsimony*.

Much of what I see as "scholarship" is antiparsimonious.

Scholarship that takes the ordinary and transforms it into the near-incomprehensible in order to make it "sound scholarly" irritates me as puffery. For example, in my own field, communication, a perfectly good concept that everyone understands as "stage fright" has been transformed into "communication apprehension." The existence of some people who "talk about themselves a lot" has given birth to the mouth-filler, "conversational narcissists." We no longer study "lying" or "deceiving," but experiment with "information manipulation" (under the rubric of "Information Manipulation Theory," or IMT). No more do we "end conversations"; instead, we practice "conversational retreat." The study of "persuasion" sounds old hat; so we get dissertations on "compliance-gaining strategies."

OK, now. Let's get back to those thirty-seven, or eighty-eight, or whatever number of theories of humor we think viable. As implied above, many of these theories borrow from and resemble each other in various ways.

Raskin (1985) summarizes the various theories as belonging to one of three main categories:

1. Cognitive-perceptual, usually associated with *congruity*;
2. Social-behavioral, usually associated with *disparagement* (and wherein our laugh/win theory would fall);
3. Psychoanalytical, concerned with release from suppression/repression, concepts popularized by Freud (1905: 31).

Raskin then presents his own theory of humor, based on semantics, which he seems to claim is "neutral toward" the above three classes of humor theory, but which also resolves the conflicts among the three classes of theories and provides a "unifying basis" for all of them (131–32). He refers to each of these three classes of theories as merely "partial" theories of humor.

In this book I expect to "prove" that the laugh/win theory can explain *all* occasions for laughter. It is not "partial" at all (Raskin's theory, on the other hand, *must* be considered "partial"; being *semantic*, it refers only to *verbal* humor, leaving out discussion of the "practical joke," slapstick, most of "clowning," "the uproarious laughter of triumph," etc.). In fact, the final chapter will apply the laugh/win theory to Raskin's (and others') own examples of so-called "innocent" or "neutral" or "nontendentious" humor, demonstrating the greater degree of parsimony to be found therein.

I tend to agree with author Anthony Ludovici, who stated in his book *Secret of Laughter* (1932) that all of these theories can be classified into two groups: those that do, and those that do *not* agree with the theory of seventeenth-century philosopher Thomas Hobbes. I further agree with Ludovici that those theories that *don't* agree with that of Hobbes can be consigned to oblivion.

What did Hobbes (1840) say about humor? He states in his *Treatise on Human Nature* the following:

> Men laugh at mischances and indecencies, wherein there lies not wit or jest at all.... Also men laugh at the infirmities of others...I may therefore conclude that the passion of laughter is nothing else but *sudden glory* arising from a sudden conception of some *eminence in ourselves* by comparison with the infirmity of others, or with our own formerly: for men laugh at the *follies* of themselves past, when they come suddenly to remembrance, except they bring with them any present dishonor.

He further explains this simple point in *Leviathan*:

> *Sudden glory* is the passion which maketh those *Grimaces* called LAUGHTER, and is caused either by some sudden act of their own, that pleaseth them; or by the apprehension of some deformed thing in another, by comparison whereof they suddenly applaud themselves.

What Hobbes has said here is that, basically, when we find humor in something, we laugh at the misfortune, stupidity, clumsiness, moral or cultural defect, suddenly revealed in *someone else*, to whom we instantly and momentarily feel "superior" since *we* are *not*, at that moment, unfortunate, stupid, clumsy, morally or culturally defective, and so on. To feel superior in this way is "to feel good"; it is to "get what you want." *It is to win!* To refer back to our joke about Old Zeke and his minister: ordinarily, the death of a preacher is not considered very funny. But, in the context of the joke "play frame," the sudden demise of the minister allows us to "win" over the crafty religious wordsmith who (much to our consternation and guilt) constantly covets our purse.

And Hobbes plainly tells us that we can momentarily feel superior *to ourselves*. We can recall and laugh at our own past or present misfortunes, mistakes, and embarrassments because they are behind us and we are now much "better off." One part of a person can laugh at another "part" of that same person. The "adult man" in me can laugh at the little boy in me for wanting a new "toy," such as a new firearm or a sports car that I don't "need," and the little boy in me can laugh at my "stuffy professor" persona as I extol upon the great value of abstract knowledge, when I am never really sure whether the gems of wisdom I drop before my students will be worth a plugged nickel to them or not. As Fry (1963) put it, "we understand that a man laughing alone in a room is engaged in intrapsychic 'interpersonal behavior. One portion of his personality is joking with another portion" (10).

Now, this way of thinking might seem pretty inhuman, or at least inhumane. Must we laugh only at our own sudden sense of superiority over someone else (including ourselves)? Well, yes, basically. As Zillmann, Bryant, and Cantor (1974) put it, "In various conceptions of the motivational bases of humor appreciation, the expression of aggression has been considered to be an important component of humor responses, if not the most critical component."

Arthur Koestler, whom I consider an intellectual giant, stated the "superiority" theory more eloquently than most:

> The more sophisticated forms of humour evoke mixed, and sometimes contradictory, feelings; but whatever the mixture, it must contain one ingredient whose presence is indispensable: an impulse, however faint, of aggression of apprehension. It may be manifested in the guise of malice, derision, the veiled cruelty of condescension, or merely as an absence of sympathy with the victim of the joke—a "momentary anesthesia of the heart," as Bergson put it. I propose to call this common ingredient the *aggressive-defensive* or *self-asserting* tendency.... In the subtler kinds of humour this tendency is so faint and discreet that only careful analysis will detect it, like the presence of salt in a well-prepared dish—which, however, would be tasteless without it. (1964: 52)

We will see in the chapter on "puns" and, especially the final chapter, how that "careful analysis" will detect the "salt in the well-prepared dish."

And, remember, we almost always couch our "aggression or apprehension" within a kind of "play frame"; we know "it's just a joke" and nothing "serious." Whoever we "laugh at" is in a sense a "victim," but not a real, flesh-and-blood victim who actually suffers loss or pain. Again, I quote Bill Fry (1963): "First, humor is play. Cues are given that this, which is about to unfold, is not real. There is a 'play frame'...created around the episode" (138).

This "play frame" often so obscures the expression of aggression that even the person appreciating the humor remains unaware of the "ill will" implied. Davies (1990) continually makes this point regarding *ethnic* humor, as do Zillmann and Cantor (1972): "It is not implied, however, that the decoder of humorous materials is in any way aware of any categorizations [of persons ridiculed] in his interpretation of a communication."

> A patient standing inside the fence of the State Hospital notices a truck parked at the curb nearby. He speaks to the driver: "What you gonna do with that load of manure, Mister?" The driver replies: "I'm takin' it home to put on my strawberries." "Gee," the inmate responds, "You oughta live here. We get to put *milk* and *sugar* on *our* strawberries!"

We might laugh at this little anecdote because of the sudden revelation of the inmate's stupidity, but we know in our heads that the poor guy can't really be so moronic as to believe that anyone would deliberately sprinkle manure on his strawberries before eating them. This is just a playful little example of hyperbolized idiocy leading to a false inference. If the "story" had actually happened, and one of *us* had been the truck driver, the hospital inmate would have probably been more a recipient of our sympathy (or, embarrassment) than our laughter. And a jokester who tell this story would ordinarily "set the stage" for play with an introduction of something like, "I just heard a good one..." or "Did you hear the one about..." or even, "I read a good joke in *Playboy* the other day. It seems that..."

The opening content of a joke often tips the listener(s) that a joke is forthcoming, also. How often do we talk about mental patients staring out from the fence of the asylum? Consider how transparent are joke openings such as "There were these two drunks leaving a bar, see..."; "A Jew, an Irishman, and a German were eating dinner together..."; "Do you know the difference between..."; "Did you hear about the Little Moron who..."; "Knock, Knock"; "A paraplegic and a diabetic were arguing one day over..."; or "What do you say to a Pollock who..."

In addition to the "warning" of a joke's imminent appearance through a formal verbal introduction or stock opening "joke language" in the opening, the jokester usually provides a wealth of nonverbal cues that we should prepare to be amused. As Fry puts it:

> Usually these [play] frames are established at the beginning of the humorous episode. A wink, a smile, a gurgle in the voice will set the stage before the joke begins its evolution. The joker may communicate the message by the posture of

his body or an *almost* unnoticed movement of his arm. His nose may wriggle; he may emphasize various sounds or frequencies in his voice.... The implicit meanings of the total situation themselves contain the cue-message. (1969: 141)

But why must we experience sudden *superiority* in order to laugh? It's because of the kind of animal we humans have become. How did Man (and Man, capitalized, includes Woman) rise to the top of the food chain and become the masters of the earth? Simply by the most successful combination of aggression, competitiveness, curiosity, and resourcefulness of any of the planet's living species.

Let me warn the reader at this point that my explanation now turns to the theory of how Man evolved. That means the theory of evolution through natural selection, the "theory" that virtually every reputable scientist who works with it every day (biologists, zoologists, botanists, geneticists, anthropologists, bacteriologists, epidemiologists, etc.) no longer even consider it a *theory*, but an established wealth of fact and data necessary to explain their professional subject matter. Some of my students refuse to "believe in evolution." I tell them that the reason for their "disbelief" is the set of religious tenets they acquired long ago, before they could read. Further, I point out that, since no empirical evidence supports any one set of religious beliefs over another (religion must rest solely on *faith*), I do not argue religious beliefs. This position has saved me much grief over the years.

Anyway, as Man was evolving over the two to four million years (the exact number is still argued) of history and prehistory, he had to fight for everything he got, like all the other creatures of the earth. Life was difficult. We still today "struggle" for food, shelter, security, and the right to reproduce ourselves sexually, but our contemporary efforts are nothing compared to what they were a million years ago. Our grandpas who brag to us of the hardship of walking to school through miles of knee-deep snow could hardly outdo our primordial ancestors in the "we-really-had-it-tough-in-the-old-days" tales. Early Man had to hunt, dig, and gather for his food; then through his ingenuity he had to learn to plow and plant, and hope for good weather and a harvest. He had to defend himself from wild animals that were larger, stronger, and swifter than himself, as well as fight off others of his species.

In his struggles for survival, Man went through the process of building up tension in his contests, then suddenly achieving "victory," and then releasing that tension with a hearty laugh of triumph, what philoso-

pher Albert Rapp (1951) called "thrashing laughter." Countless generations built up this oft-duplicated tension/win/tension-release behavior
reaction into an inborn human trait, what Carl Jung (1970) called "a
groove in the collective unconscious." The creatures that eventually became *homo sapiens* absorbed the "win syndrome" into its genes. Laughter became the natural reaction to "winning," especially if that "win"
came suddenly, and after a mighty struggle.

We humans chauvinistically like to tout our big brains and capacity
for *reasoning*; but we all too often neglect our animal heritage. Zoologist
Desmond Morris (1967) and others urge that we exchange that neglect
for concern, and that we need to try to retrieve some of our "[lower]
animal humility."

In a new book (*Shadows of Forgotten Ancestors*), Carl Sagan and
Ann Druyan (1992) explore what is reason and what is "animal instinct"
in human behavior. They point out how little our intellect might influence us:

> Among the many human feelings that, although culturally mediated, may be fun-
> damentally preprogrammed, we might list sexual attraction, falling in love, jeal-
> ousy, hunger and thirst, horror at the sight of blood, fear of snakes and heights and
> "monsters," shyness and *suspicion of strangers*, obedience to those in authority,
> hero worship, *dominance of the meek*, pain and weeping, *laughter*, the incest ta-
> boo, *the infant's smiling delight at seeing members of its family*, separation anxi-
> ety and maternal love. [Note: all italics mine (CRG)]. There is a complex of
> emotions attached to each, and thinking has very little to do with any of them.
> Surely, we can imagine a being whose internal life is almost wholly composed of
> such feelings, yet nearly devoid of thought. (169)

Man's brain outgrew that of other mammals, and he eventually discovered, then developed, language. This marvelous new skill, language, the
most human of attributes, enhanced to a quantum degree the opportunity
for mutual cooperation in the struggle for survival. Slow, weak and small,
humans could band together and, through cooperation, gang up on the rest
of nature and begin to overcome it. Humans lived in groups for common
defense, shelter, and overall survival. Probably back in the Pleistocene,
men left to the women and kids the gathering of roots, berries, and nuts and
to keep the home fires burning, and went off hunting. To ensure sexual
fidelity and the passing of his genes on to future generations, Man invented
monogamous pair-bonding, where one male and one female would fall in
love and remain faithful partners in creating and maintaining a family.
This arrangement was highly successful both socially and economically.

With the organization of humans into societies (villages, tribes, etc.) the amount of interpersonal conflict was reduced. Tribe members might fight the members of other tribes, but tribal living also soon made clear just who could best whom, and who was the strongest or fastest in the tribe. The strongest, boldest, or fastest became the ruling bureaucracy, and everyone "learned his place" in the social scheme of things.

With "civilization" came more leisure time for Man. Man the Fierce Competitor, Man the Warrior, Man the Inquisitive, Man the Explorer found he could become bored sitting around the village, the hunt finished for the time being, food for a few days stored away, and the threat of an enemy tribe attacking merely a distant probability. What can he do? Where's the action? How can he expend his aggressive, competitive, in-born curiosity?

Man first probably figured out that he need not actually beat up on a fellow tribesman in order to get that "thrill of victory" feeling (and a hearty laugh). Just the *sight* of a compatriot hobbling into sight, nursing a black eye, a sore leg, and a number of bruises and contusions could set him off. His reaction: "Hey, look at this poor slob. He (and, *not me*) got really clobbered!" Ho Ho Ho! The laughter of ridicule is born. Early Man, and today, Modern Man, can get a real kick out of perceiving his sudden superiority to another human that is lame, halt, blind, accident-prone, stupid, clumsy, illiterate, socially inept, excessively fat or skinny, ugly, embarrassed, and so on.

Scientists and their research are not universally agreed that smiling and laughter are either inborn or learned (Apte 1985); however, the bulk of the evidence indicates that the smile is probably inborn, and the vocalized laugh, which begins very early in life, results from specific outside stimuli (249). But what seems sure about this research is that infants do not smile or laugh when *not getting what they want*. Indeed, smiling and laughing always occur when the baby is experiencing pleasure; that is, when he or she *is* getting what he/she wants. We might even say, when he/she is *winning*.

Children usually exhibit their first real "laugh" at the age of about six months (more on this later); this kind of laughter persists as simple "plea-sure" up to about the age of three years, according to researcher Ernest Harms (1943). Children that young cannot verbalize to an adult "what is funny." But at that age (three years), still having difficulty *saying* what is considered funny, children can *draw* what they think is funny. When researcher Harms asked three-year-olds to "draw something funny," they almost invariably drew a picture of some person with a grotesque physical oddity: an ugly face, a long, crooked nose, an excruciatingly thin or generously obese body, and so on. In other words, the first *object* of the child's laughter is the person physically very much *unlike* the child!

You readers who have had the experience of raising children no doubt have been embarrassed at one time or another when a child of yours has encountered someone physically *different*, who elicited loud, spontaneous laughter from the kid. (I know I have!) As parents, we have to teach children to suppress this kind of behavior, since it does not belong in "polite society." But such behavior is probably an inherent biological part of us humans, buried deep within the small, reptilian part of our brain down near the brain stem. We ascended to the top of the food chain by being able to instantly recognize potential friend from potential foe. Babies achieve this skill at the age of about six months, when, as pointed out above, they laugh for the first time.

Desmond Morris has documented baby's first laugh and the reasons for it, first in his early best-seller *The Naked Ape* (referring, of course, to Man) and more recently in *Babywatching* (1992).

It happens like this: a baby, by the age of six months, can easily recognize its mother's face. Then, when the mother *startles* the baby (as, with a sudden face-to-face confrontation, of the "peekaboo" kind) the infant gets two disparate signals: first, "there's *danger* here," but also "it's not *real* danger, because it's only *Mommy*!" In Morris's (1967) words,

> she can give the double signal: "There's danger but there's no danger." Or, to put it another way: "There may appear to be danger, but because it is coming from me, you do not need to take it seriously". The outcome of this is that the child gives a response that is half a crying reaction and half a parental-recognition gurgle. The magic combination produces a laugh. (Or, rather, it did, way back in evolution. It has since become fixed and fully developed as a separate, distinct response in its own right). (84)

This built-in tendency for humans to make crucial positive/negative evaluations upon meeting other creatures (extant in babies at six months!) can be amply documented. Ellen Berscheid, opening her chapter on "Interpersonal Attraction" in the encyclopedic *Handbook of Social Psychology* says, in part:

> For a species to survive, its members need to find food, to avoid injury, to reproduce, and, for higher animals, to rear the young. These adaptive behaviors not

only engage issues of interpersonal attraction for the individual but also present vital concerns for all of human society.... Because our feelings of attraction and repulsion for other people are rooted in our most basic and fundamental biological needs, it is not surprising that sentiment for others is often regarded as the theme of interpersonal relations. (1985: 413)

She then quotes Osgood, May, and Miron (1957) at the University of Illinois, who found the evaluative factor (good/bad) to be the primary theme of human language; the Illinois group gave an evolutionary inter- pretation to the ubiquity of *evaluative* behavior in language:

We humans are still animals at base. What is important to us now , as it was back in the age of Neanderthal man, about the sign of a thing, is, first, does it refer to something *good* for me or *bad* for me (is it an antelope or a saber-toothed ti- ger?).... Survival, then and now, depends on the answers. (395)

Dr. Berscheid follows this quotation from Osgood et al. with further explanation:

As a consequence, humans are among the most social creatures in the animal kingdom, and our evolutionary development has led to a hair-trigger disposition for making discriminative judgments along the attraction dimension. Those early humans who were either indifferent to or incapable of making evaluative judg- ments of other humans—who could not differentiate between friend and foe—did not survive. The result over evolutionary time is an animal who can and will make such judgments, even in circumstances in which the exposure to the stimulus is so brief that the individual cannot even tell precisely what the stimulus was, only whether he or she likes it. (414)

She then illustrates by way of example the classic and oft-quoted study done by Eugene Hartley (1946), wherein college students were asked to rate for "social desirability" a large number of classes of human beings, identified by racial, ethnic, religious or nationality grouping. Included in this list of peoples were three entirely *fictitious* groups, the Pireneans, the Wallonians, and the Danierions, whom these college student respon- dents had no possible way of knowing. But the ratings revealed one very clear finding: these students did not at all *like* those Pireneans, Wallonians, and Danierions! Peoples who, of course, were mere figments of Profes- sor Hartley's own imagination.

Man's newfound ability to get a laugh out of the misfortunes of others (ridicule) became greatly enhanced by his invention of language. He quickly found that he could *deliberately ridicule* his fellow creatures.

Why should our aggressive, competitive humanoid have to wait for one of his acquaintances to come out second-best in a fight in order to exercise his pleasure in ridicule? With language he could *recall*, even invent or *exaggerate* upon some past shortcoming of a colleague.

> Hey, guys, remember when Klug came back to the village last year with that certain air of his? He *would* be dumb enough to have to learn at his advanced age the difference between a puppy and a skunk!
>
> Did you see the new bride Crull dragged home the other day? I've seen ugly women before, but her face can curdle coconut milk!

If such crudities as the above sound childish to you, the point is intentional. These are the kind of vulgarisms which today's least civilized of humans employ early in their humor repertoires. I refer to human *children*.

Language allowed our forbears to actively utilize their competitive instincts in another manner, and without the least danger of physical harm coming to them-in contests of *wit*. A great deal of historical and literary evidence points to the fact that early man put great stock in the back-and-forth question/answer games in which one person tries to "stump" the other for an answer, the successful wit-worker laughing at his defeated opponent, of course.

Our contemporary barbarians (children, again) love to "play school" in question/answer format. They delight in finding out who the dumb kids are, and love to demonstrate their mental superiority over them through raucous (and cruel) laughter.

Contests of wit in general became formalized as "riddle contests." And, as those of us who have raised or otherwise spent much time around small children know, riddles are one of their earliest and most eagerly exploited forms of verbal play.

But someone eventually figured out that words can sound alike but have different meanings, and some words *are* the same but have different meanings in context. And this someone invented the first *conundrum*, or "punning riddle."

> Why is Samson like a comedian? Because he brought down the house.
>
> Who was the first man to bear arms? Adam. He had two.

Early inventors of conundrums had come up with a "new" game. Not only did the punning riddler *defeat* the person to whom he addressed it (who had no answer), he *tricked* him by employing a meaning for a word which the *victim* could not even suspect. Such early underhanded trickery may well have earned the clever punster a poke in the nose.

The punning riddle, of course, is the humor staple of the young child new to reading. Urchins delight in following a parent around with a child's riddle book, asking such things as "What's the difference between a man from Mars and a tiger taking a bath?"

And it was only a very short evolutionary step from the punning riddle to the pun, which is a punning riddle with the question/answer format removed.

Samson was a real comedian; brought the house down.

Adam was the first man to bear arms; had two of 'em.

We no longer punch out the guy who *defeats* and *tricks* us with a punning riddle or pun (by demonstrating to us his superior verbal cleverness). We merely attempt to punish the punster with a groan.

As noted above, man evolved to his high estate by development of a high capacity for curiosity and exploring behavior. Morris (1967, 1984) devoted an entire chapter to man as "an exploring creature." By necessity, early man developed keen interest in his surroundings and the breadth and depth of his abilities to solve the problems of survival. His inquisitiveness allowed him to exploit his habitat and to enlarge it. He learned to eat a wide variety of foods and exist in nearly every nook and cranny of the globe-from the mountain heights to the deserts below sea level, from the arctic to the antarctic circle. He became a master of adaptation, and thus a *generalist*. The *specialist* panda bear might become extinct because its one food, bamboo shoots, disappear from his habitat; and the *specialist* dinosaurs might all die out when the nature of the earth changed drastically (for what reason we still argue); but Man the Explorer continues to solve the problems of survival as they crop up whether individually or in a cluster.

So here is the theory we will be applying in the rest of this book. It has been called the "superiority theory"; it has been called the "derision" theory, the "hostility" theory, or the "superior adaptation" theory. Leonard Feinberg (1978) subsumed all these concepts in his name for the reason for laughter, "playful aggression." Feinberg's "playful aggression" is very close to what I mean here, also; I certainly emphasize the "playful" nature of wit and humor. But I prefer the "laughing is winning" metaphor. Humor is a *game*.

Another similar theory is that put forth by Morreall (1983). After "refuting" the "superiority," the "incongruity," and the "relief" theories, he proposes his own—"A New Theory." Simply stated, he says that "laughter results from a pleasant psychological shift" (39). And, of course, this statement is correct. My basis for disagreeing with Morreall's position is twofold; first, he fails to utilize the nature of man, as evolution has decreed it, to explain *why a psychological shift is pleasant*; that is, he does not *operationally define* what he means by "pleasant psychological shift." Secondly, he (falsely, I believe), dismisses "superiority" as a theory for its supposed inability to explain *all* laughter and humor. His theoretical position would be more difficult to refute had he not offered *examples* of "non-superiority" humor. But, alas, he did offer such, and, as we shall see in this book's final chapter, superiority cannot be dismissed from those examples. Like Freud, he could provide no illustrations of "harmless wit."

Morreall clarified his stance later (Morreall 1989). In his *Humor* article he claims that "incongruities" can have one of three psychological results in humans: (1) *negative emotion* results from incongruity between what one wants and what one gets; (2) *puzzlement* results from a vital, unsolvable incongruity; and (3) any other (apparently) incongruity which makes us laugh. Morreall himself, by the way, also admits elsewhere that "incongruity is not sufficient for amusement, though it is necessary" (1987, 224). He cites one example of supposed incongruity that *does* cause amusement:

A *New Yorker* cartoon shows a downhill skier who has just "passed" a large tree; his ski tracks go completely around *both sides* of the tree. A puzzlement! In fact, Morreal reports that, when the cartoon appeared in Germany, several people wrote in their "explanations" of the puzzle. What Morreal apparently does not realize is that this cartoon, which also appears in the Mindess et al. "Antioch Humor Test" and in his later book (1987), gets its *humor* from another figure therein. A man who is trudging uphill on his skis is looking backwards, over his shoulder; he has *seen* the amazing skier zip around/through the tree! And the look on his face is of utter horror/shock! We laugh at his amazed inability to believe the extraordinary event he has actually witnessed! What Morreall has failed to see in this cartoon is that the amazed/baffled/mystified/*horrified* poor devil of a *witness* is prominently in the *foreground* of the cartoon (the loser!) while the miracle-working skier is heading downhill from the encircled tree *in the background*. It is this unfortunate *spectator* and his reaction at which we laugh; apparently the Germans who offered "solutions" to the "incongruity" also failed to see the horrified onlooker.

In his book, Morreall gives many examples of humor arising out of "pleasant psychological shifts;" in the final chapter we will see what *actually makes* them pleasant-winning and losing.

What about those "other" theories? Those others that do *not* agree with Thomas Hobbes? Most can be disposed of easily.

Probably the most popular competing theory is the so-called incongruity theory. This theory specifies that when two highly disparate ideas or entities are juxtaposed, especially suddenly, the result is laughter. The rebuttal here is simple: incongruity is not *sufficient cause* for laughter. Incongruity can produce other emotions (or, none at all). I remember seeing in *Life* magazine a marvel of incongruity: a tiny, beautiful Asian child in a lovely Sunday-go-to-meeting dress, sitting, bewildered, in the total desolation of the remains of her home that had been destroyed by enemy bombardment. As Fry (1963) has asserted, "The simply incongruous or surprising is not necessarily funny, even usually not so" (149).

Feinberg (1978) effectively renders the "incongruity theory" sterile:

> An obvious weakness of the incongruity theory is its failure to account for numerous instances of disharmony which do not cause laughter. It is only certain kinds of incongruity that result in humor; other kinds cause fear, shock, or disgust. (3)

Elliot Oring (1992) attempts to revive the "incongruity" explanation of all humor by digging it up out of the eighteenth century, dusting it off, and giving it his own new "modern" name, *appropriate incongruity*. He defines his concept: humor depends upon "the perception of an appropriate interrelationship of elements from domains that are generally regarded as incongruous" (2). It seems that incongruity alone *is not* sufficient to produce humor; but that incongruity *is* sufficient if it is perceived *suddenly* and is also *appropriate*. Oring never specifically defines *operationally* what he means by "appropriate." However, from the examples he uses, in terms of "my" theory, he must mean "incongruity which, when suddenly perceived, reveals a winner and a loser." For instance, his first example is a riddle, which, of course, is a *contest* to be won or lost:

Q: When is a door not a door?
A: When it is ajar.

If Person A poses the question, above, to Person B, and Person B cannot answer, Person A gives the answer and delights in his winning the little verbal contest. If, however, Person B either has heard the riddle before or is quick and bright enough to figure out the answer and replies, "When it is ajar," Person B "turns the tables," defeating Person A in the duel of wits. If this contest quality, this win/lose outcome is somehow *removed from the riddle*, it ceases to be humor! Oring provides other examples, and these will be taken up in my final chapter and shown to be without humor if the contest, win/lose quality is expunged from them.

Other various theories go under the name of "surprise" or "ambivalence." But anyone knows that a surprise can be deadly rather than funny; your doctor's diagnosis that you have terminal cancer might surprise you, but I doubt that you would get much of a laugh over such news. And psychotherapists wrestle daily with patients who suffer mightily from ambivalence, an inability to decide or act because of competing desires or forces (à la Hamlet). When's the last time *you* had a big guffaw over your inability to decide on what to do or think? Lew (1995) offered a number of jokes that depended for their humorous charge on "verbal ambiguity," such as

"Does your uncle still practice dentistry?"
"No, he finished practicing. He does it for a living now."

After Lew finished his presentation I pointed out to the assemblage that each "verbal ambiguity" joke Professor Lew had used as examples portrayed a person *making a mistake*, thus earning our ridicule; and that removal of the "mistake" removes both the verbal ambiguity and the humor.

So: keep this picture in your mind as we wander onto further plateaus of humor understanding: Man is a curious, aggressive and competitive creature who is constantly "thinking of Number One," forever asking "What's in it for me?"; a primate who will strive to "get what he wants," even (maybe especially) by beating someone else out of it. And a creature who can even get pleasure out of symbolically beating a fellow human being through enjoyment of that character's misfortune or flaw.

But, lest that last paragraph conjure up in your mind a brute a little too bloodthirsty, let us consider how Man has adapted his aggressive nature into socially acceptable behavior in order to live at least semipeacefully in this most unnatural of worlds which we now rule.

2

Conflict in Daily Life

Thou shalt not covet; but tradition
Approves all forms of competition.

—Arthur Hugh Clough

If happiness truly consisted in physical ease
and freedom from care, then the happiest
individual would not be either a man or a
woman; it would be, I think, an American cow.

—William Lyon Phelps

How interested would you be in reading a newspaper article topped by the following headline:

FARMER BROWN SPENDS DAY PLOWING, THEN PLAYS WITH CHILDREN AFTER DINNER; FALLS ASLEEP IN CHAIR LATER WHILE WATCHING TV?

Not very? How about this one:

LUCY SMITHERS, 11, ATTAINS B-AVERAGE; GETS PROMOTED TO SEVENTH GRADE?

Of course, you couldn't care less about little Miss Smithers and her academic skills. And who would blame you?

The plain fact is that newspapers don't print such stories. The publishers/editors know that the public wants something in which they can be *interested*. And in what is the public interested? Conflict, competition, success while striving against great odds, and just about any form of mayhem. As civilized creatures, we seldom get personally involved in the serious kinds of conflict and competition that make it into the newspapers, thank goodness, but that's the only kind of reading material we have the least bit of interest in reading.

27

I just happened to start this chapter on a Saturday; 1 August 1992, to be exact. Now browse with me through today's issue of one of the newspapers to which I subscribe, *The Atlanta Constitution/Atlanta Journal* (combined editions on weekends) and sample the conflict, violence, and competition which the editors have decided we would like to read about today. I realize that by using this particular newspaper I will "date" this chapter. But I invite you to browse through your own big-city newspaper to see if the stories there are not very similar in content to what I now place before you. When I saw David Lutken play "Will" in the road show (Atlanta, 23 August 1995) of "The Will Rogers Follies," one bit had Will scanning a 1925 newspaper. There was a story of a bank robbery, a gunshot homicide, a congressional scandal, and so on. He calls offstage for today's *Atlanta Constitution*, which Marla Maples Trump long-legs her way across the stage with said newspaper for Will. He then notes that the paper has stories of a bank robbery, a gunshot homicide, a congressional scandal, and so on. Will poses the rhetorical question of whether the newspapers are just printing the same issue each day but just changing the names and the fine details!

Because the Barcelona Olympics (1992) are presently underway, the lead article on page 1 blares the news that Georgia's own Gwen Torrence might *win* (beat others out of) the gold medal in the 100-meter dash today. Given almost equal billing is an article telling us that President Bush is sending 2,400 American troops to Kuwait as a physical threat as to just what might happen (again) to Iraq's Saddam Hussein if he does not knuckle under to the UN mandates he signed after getting whipped in Operation Desert Shield. Smaller columns trumpet America's coming in one-two in the Olympic shot put and the paper's hopes that Francis Larrieu Smith can *win* a medal in the marathon. We are also told that the Government Accounting Office (GAO) has "slammed" the Savannah River (nuclear) Plant for their delays and cost overruns at their waste facility.

Inside pages give us an interview with a female candidate for reelection (trying to beat someone else) to her congressional seat; and contains stories on the successful launch of our latest space shuttle (a *win* over gravity); the gamble by Mississippi gulf coast entrepreneurs to bolster the area's economy by instituting controversial floating gambling (win/lose) casinos; a decision by Louisiana law enforcement officials to ignore future *anonymous* tips on child abuse; a decision to not euthanize a group of monkeys in Florida that are infected with herpes; an attempt by environmental groups to *force* the Tennessee Valley Authority (TVA) to forbid the building of wood chip factories; a Marine helicopter crash in Alabama that killed two; ten Georgia schools whom the federal government is going to punish by disallowing federally-backed loans to their students; *castigation* of our EPA chief for his stance at a recent environmental summit; the death of Harrold G. Carswell, once *rejected* by the U. S. Senate for nomination to the Supreme Court; success of the K-reactor in tests of a nuclear plant; a South African pathologist trying to bring justice to a case involving the deaths of a number of black protestors; a Bosnian counterattack after the Serbs had killed eight people in a Sarajevo, Bosnia shelling; thirty-nine Americans perhaps held prisoner in what used to be the U.S.S.R.; alleged high governmental corruption in Brazil; a tough jail sentence urged in a French AIDS trial; eleven Americans feared dead in a plane crash in Nepal (which killed over a hundred in all); an intensification on the "war" on the Mafia in Italy.

The election campaign news tells us that President Bush is ready to "dish it" to the Democrats; that he seeks a "bounce" from Republican TV ads to come out soon; that Senator Gore has "lifted hopes" of a Democrat *victory*; that Ross Perot supporters ("Perotroopers?") are "fighting" amongst themselves, and cannot agree on much; that Republicans are wrangling over whether/when to allow former Bush primary foe Pat Buchanan to speak at their convention; that a lawsuit against Perot may be dropped; that "Clinton *Spars* Over Defense"; a report on the economy warning that voters will "go to the polls…with their wallets in mind"; BUSH, CONGRESS *DEADLOCK* ON U.S. ILLS states a bold headline.

The editorial page warns investors of falling interest rates and their *damaging* personal effects; applauds a court decision to keep President Bush from forcibly sending U.S.-bound Haitians back to their homeland without a hearing, and urges the Atlanta mayor to persist in his *fight* with an airport contractor. The "Letters to the Editor" section blares in headlines: IN A CRUEL WORLD, HATRED BEGETS MORE HATRED. Letters are about "an urban tragedy," "Gulf War, the sequel," a plea to end "the abortion war," a complaint about "no smoking" in the new Georgia Dome, a gripe about the papers' "left-leaning" editors, and an official's attempt to defuse an alleged "lie" about him which the paper had published.

The "Viewpoints" page urges the federal government not to *reject* a proposal to elect judges; bitches about no one ever bothering to find out that he, the writer, suffered from dyslexia; and complains that the GOP is going to run on a campaign *denigrating* homosexuals.

I won't bore you with the stories in the "Saturday Reader" or the "Local News" sections. Suffice it to say this material, also, is about struggle, wins, and losses ("Blue whales fight their own kind of Jonah"). I think you must get my point.

That leaves us with the sports pages (and, of course, the special Olympic Games section) which, being *all* about sports, are concerned with *nothing but* competition, winning and losing. And even the "society pages" are mostly concerned with "who won whom (marriages)." The comic pages we leave for later chapters.

Leaving aside "sports" and "games" for the time being, let us consider what *entertains* us. To be very candid, if it were not for competition, struggle, combat, contention, conflict, and discord, we would have practically *no* entertainment at all.

In America, probably more people are entertained most often by television. We can find multitudes of competitive sport, both amateur and professional on TV, of course. In some markets, entire channels are devoted to nothing but sports (and, of course, commercials). In my own cable system we have two. But, again, eschewing sports and games for the time being, what other kinds of entertainment do we find on TV? Why, the kind that thrives on competition and conflict by the long ton.

Take soap operas ("Please!"). I don't watch the things, but lots of folks do. Take out the conflict between and among the characters (they fight over what we all fight over-money, power, mating rights, etc.) and you would be left with pretty bland fare (and, no audiences). *TV Guide* provides a weekly update on the goings-on in those smarmy drammers. Last week's (for 5–11 August 1995) includes the following:

> After Taylor doctored the results of her pregnancy test, Noah promised that their child won't be fatherless. Brooke and Adam gave in to their passion and Adam proposed. A strung-out Erica insulted a guest on the air...

> Michael revealed that he has leukemia. Joe was wounded during a perilous incident. Jake searched for Bunny Everhardt. Carl posed as a mentally disturbed man to get admitted to the Swiss clinic...

> After Luke disappeared, Damian initiated a manhunt for Lily and Luke, and the Coast Guard searched the cargo ship where Lily and Mark were hiding. Orlena...took a serious fall...

> Ridge reached a decision and then paid Taylor a visit. Thorne joined Macy at Sally's bedside after being released from jail due to Anthony's confession. Maggie and Dylan were each devastated to learn of their relationship to Jessica...

Peter Reckell returned to the role of Bo, who was stunned that Gina opened the puzzle box. Meanwhile, Sami's sudden announcement that she's pregnant with Austin's baby stopped Austin and Carrie's wedding...

Things got hotter between Brenda and Miguel; while in Puerto Rico, Sonny met Lily's son. Mme. Maia successfully nudged Lucy in Damian's direction. Troubled with their own mates, Alan and Bobbie found themselves attracted to each other.

And so it goes, on and on. I bet you will never see on TV or see summarized in *TV Guide* soap opera goings-on like these:

As The Earth Rotates
Chuck and Ramona celebrated with chocolate-marshmallow sundaes their good luck in securing a 1964 Plymouth Duster for $450. Silvia, upon hearing that her mother-in-law was elected to the Building and Grounds Committee of the neighborhood swimming pool, scribbled and mailed to her a note of congratulation. Jasper came home after a hard day at the coal mines and began kibitzing over Jacqueline's shoulder as she played computer solitaire.

One Livelihood To Exist Through
Sheila and Don looked forward to their tenth anniversary and wondered out loud what in the world was wrong with them for being completely uninterested in a divorce. Ginny and Bill adopted a dog at the pound and were delighted to find that the mutt had had all his annual shots and was housebroken. Eustace tried to keep his $10 million gift to his alma mater anonymous, but is found out and urged to accept an honorary degree from the college. George watched seven hours of pro football on TV while his wife, Gloria, hand-fed him.

What is it about "sitcoms" that hold our attention so well? There's humor, of course, which I contend is all based on mock or play hostility, but what about the "sit" (situation) in "sitcom?" Same old story (the fight for love and glory). *I Love Lucy*, one of the most popular shows ever on TV, invariably involved the plot line of Lucy trying to accomplish some nearly impossible goal (like getting into show biz with Desi) and the comical difficulties entailed therein. *The Honeymooners* was one battle after another between Ralph Cramden and the world (and his spouse). Through *TV Guide*, let's look at some modern sitcom plot lines:

Waiting for God
Harvey schemes to have troublemaker Diana expelled from Bayview.

Mama's Family
Naomi is expecting a job promotion, but she finds her boss expects more from her than she's willing to give.

Living Single
Dating a princess (Vanessa Williams) is not all it's cracked up to be for Kyle; and flimflamming a couple of pool sharks could mean trouble for Khadijah.

Fresh Prince
Will goes overboard to make a good first impression on Lisa's visiting father and soon regrets it when the man decides to move to L. A.

Murphy Brown
FYI's thrown into turmoil when Murphy takes charge after Miles is tapped to revamp another news show.

Sitcoms without plots pitting characters against each other and against the environment would be coms without sits—and without laughs.

How about quiz shows, such as *Wheel of Fortune* or *Jeopardy*? Again, these shows are *nothing but* competition; competition among contestants and competition for the winning of the most money or the biggest prize. The audience (both "live" and at home) squeals with delight and laughter when *Wheel of Fortune*'s evening winner successfully cracks the "bonus puzzle." They groan in agony when our temporary hero(ine) cannot fill in the alphabetic gaps. Further screams of victory or defeat accompany the revelation of which rich prize the bonus contestant has won or lost. And these game shows even breed competition in the home-viewing audience. Viewers try to solve the puzzles before the on-screen contestants do.

My wife and I, avid fans of *Wheel of Fortune*, always compete with the studio contestants to solve each puzzle first, and, amicably, against each other! I cannot doubt that this kind of interfamilial competition occurs regularly in quiz show TV-land. With Marsha and me, success in first solving the problem brings great pleasure to him/her who does so, and, usually, praise (whether completely sincere or not) from the "defeated" spouse.

In each case, the "thrill of victory" (and, even the resultant compliment) varies with both the difficulty of the puzzle and the abruptness of its solution. I shall never forget the episode of 16 December 1992. We were watching "Wheel" at home. The category for the puzzle was given as "things." The squares were given as

☐☐☐☐

☐☐☐☐☐☐☐☐☐☐

☐&☐☐☐☐☐☐

The first contestant asked for an *S* and it was dutifully turned over by Vanna White, giving us:

☐☐☐☐
☐☐☐☐☐☐☐☐☐ S ☐
& ☐☐☐☐☐

I pondered the length of the words, the ampersand betweens words two and three; it occurred to me that we were within the "Christmas season." I had a gestalt, and loudly spoke the correct answer: "Gold, Frankincense, & Myrrh." I nearly burst with self-pleasure at so quickly arriving at this solution, and Marsha was oh-so-generous with flabbergasted congratulations!

Television airs lots of old movies. What goes on in *them*? *TV Guide* helpfully previews them for us. Samples:

> *Above the Law.* Violence, strong language. A Windy City cop suspects collusion when he's told to lay off a drug kingpin.

> *Blood Games.* Violence, strong language, sexual situations. Tale about malcontents stalking a women's softball team.

> *Crash and Burn.* Violence, strong language, sexual situations. In the year 2030, a murderous android stalks a remote TV station.

And so it goes. All our dramatic shows, including movies, rely on conflict and competition. It's cops against robbers, cowboys against Indians (or, more politically correctly, Native Americans, Out Of Asia), spy against spy, man against nature, human vs. alien, D.A. vs. defense lawyer, man against woman (involving both romance and divorce), or just general "good guy" vs. "bad guy."

One of my favorite TV shows is *Law and Order*. In the first half-hour the cops investigate and arrest; in the second half the D.A.'s prosecute and plea bargain. One episode I would *not* enjoy would carry forth the following plot line:

Detective Briscoe and his partner, Curtis, find the body of a murdered man. They place a classified ad appealing for the killer to come in and talk about it. The "perp" comes in the next morning and confesses. "I'm very sorry about it," he says. "I wish I had killed myself, instead. I feel just horrible." D.A. Jack McCoy and his assistant, Jamie Ross, bring the killer to trial, where he contritely pleads "guilty," then asks for the death penalty in order to assuage his conscience. The judge sentences the repentant killer to 200 hours of community service.

Aldous Huxley created a *Brave New World* (1932) in which all humans were scientifically programmed from conception in a test tube, through "birth," and throughout their entire lives to be free of all human negative emotions, such as aggression and jealousy. War and crime were thus eliminated from human behavior. Men and women were conditioned to completely avoid falling in love with any particular individual of the opposite sex, but were trained to "love everyone" and feel no compunction whatsoever in having recreational sex with any heterosexual partner, beginning with nude sexual play between little boys and girls. In fact, men and women were *expected* to have relatively *short* periods of sexual partnership; indeed, should a partnership lengthen to a point that even *suggested* permanence, the partners became suspect, and might be required to undergo counseling and reprogramming.

What kind of "entertainment" could keep such people occupied away from the job? After all, there had to be some sort of "entertainment industry" to provide employment, so there had to be customers of entertainment to keep the economy going.

Huxley gave his creations two major outlets (other than *soma*, a concoction that provided the best possible effects of alcohol, marijuana, cocaine, and morphine combined). One was a kind of "astral golf," that was not well explained. Suffice it to say that lots of people played, but there was little talk of working on one's game to improve it, or of side bets with foursome companions whom players contrived to "beat."

The other entertaining diversion was a sci-fi version of "the movies," called "feelies." Patrons not only heard, saw, and *smelled* what was going on up on the screen, but actually *felt* the ongoing action through electronic handles sticking from the backs of the seats in front of them. But did the "feelies" depict Cowboys vs. Indians, Cops vs. Robbers, Allies vs. the Axis? Certainly not. We have to suppose that plots had to be something like "Man vs. Nature" or "Man vs. Wild Animal," but the only "feelie" that Huxley lets his readers experience involves a normal, well-programmed guy who suffers a bump on the head, which causes him to revert to his "savage state" (normal humanness, to us) and run amok hurting people. When the poor, deranged amok-runner is finally overcome and apprehended, he gets, not prison, but a crash course in reprogramming to return him to his robotish, amiable self.

By the way: nowhere in *Brave New World* is there any mention of *comedy* or the telling of any *jokes*! Humor could hardly exist in this aggressionless, peaceful utopia.

One might make a case that music, especially instrumental and, maybe, classical, constitutes entertainment untainted by competition or conflict, but then I know little about music. It occurs to me that a lot of song *lyrics* smack of competing interests, especially "love songs." And "Ol' Man River" frustrates us with his indifference to human suffering, while most country-western music whines on about one human loss after another. The joke riddle about such music is, "What do you get when you play country-western music backwards? You get your job back, your 'baby' returns home to you, your pickup truck is restored to you, and your dog comes back to life." Psychotherapist Albert Ellis and his colleagues did a content analysis of popular music lyrics and concluded that the vast majority of them unhealthily encouraged humans to persist in negative emotions such as self-pity and general sorrow (instead of urging them to stiff-upper-lip it and "get a life").

And then there is sport and games.

William J. Baker has written an excellent history of *Sports in the Western World* (1982). In it he points out that the first human sports and games were children's imitations of their elders' hunting and warfare activities. Sports and games had periods of boom and bust during mankind's evolutionary climb to become masters of the modern world.

The three major influences on the amount and kind of gaming activity were (1) man's available leisure time (2) the kinds of sport activity encouraged and discouraged by political leaders (who usually wanted men to engage in sports preparing them for warfare and combat), and (3) the Church's changing attitude toward how much and what kind of sport should be allowed when.

But the competitive spirit inherent in Man most powerfully urged him to engage in contests.

When humans were relatively scarce in the world, sports *participation* was available to the many who wished to compete. As the population expanded exponentially, the less strong and swift had to more and more channel their competitive energy into *fanship*. And, as we know, spectator sport is big business. Why else would NBC spend a total of $705 million for rights to broadcast the Summer Olympics in Sydney, Australia?

In the modern Western world there are sports and games for anyone and everyone, of course. For instance, here in Athens, Ga. where I am writing this book, practically any school boy who can *walk* can make it onto a soccer team at some level or another. But we are also a world of sports *fans*, and as fans, we wish to support teams that *win*.

For years the Atlanta Braves baseball team dwelled near the cellar of the National League West Division. They were considered a league doormat. The very few people who watched them play, either scattered thinly around the stadium or viewing on TV, amused themselves by wondering what new way to lose the Braves would invent *this* time.

Then in 1991 the Braves, last in the league the previous year, won their division. In the drive for the crown they began to draw standing-room-only crowds at Atlanta-Fulton County Stadium. Fans denied tickets glued themselves to the TBS superstation screen. When the Braves beat the Pirates for the National League pennant the fans' enthusiasm lit up the skies. The Braves lost the World Series "by one run." But they were hosted in a ticker tape parade through Atlanta which nearly became a dangerous, out-of-control victory *riot*.

In 1992 they duplicated their championship ways of winning (but, losing the first World Series to a non-American team)! And the home stadium is setting records for consecutive sold-out houses. Total attendance for 1992 exceeded three million paying fans for the first time in history. In August 1993, attendance of three million was a reality in August! The 1994 strike wiped out league championships and the World Series, but in 1995 the Braves' winning ways drew the strike-disgruntled fans back to cheer the team to its first modern-day World Series triumph. Victory is sweet, and sweeter still when long-denied.

If victory seems too easy, fans and players often try to adopt new ploys to "make it interesting." Baseball teams (and their fans) who find themselves ahead, say 7–0, going into the seventh inning, usually escalate their "victory hopes" into wishing/hoping for a *shutout*. In fact, should a winning pitcher "lose" his shutout in late innings, he often is replaced by someone from the bullpen; a pitcher who continues to get the batters out is allowed to stay in to "get his shutout," considered a real "notch in the belt" (or, feather in the cap) of a pitcher.

Football teams (and their fans) leading big-score-to-nothing late in the game also adopt the "let's-get-a-shutout" attitude. Just plain old winning is no longer satisfying enough.

Shutouts are impossible in some sports.

A basketball team leading 93–56 in the waning minutes are often urged by their fans to "break 100!" At the 1992 Barcelona Olympic Games, the American basketball team was dubbed "The Dream Team." For the first time in history, America had sent out *their* professional players to compete against the professional players from the other countries.

The "Dream Team" was expected to win all games by large margins, and they did; sports writers and letters-to-the-editors expressed hopes that the Americans would score "at least 100 points" *in each and every game*, which they did. Many would probably have been gravely disappointed with "mere wins" of a few points.

Golfers who play in regular foursomes often know each other's strengths and weaknesses, and so may bet a few bucks on the round or each hole "to make it interesting." (There's the old joke about the guy who made a bet with a rival, putting his *wife* up as the prize to the winner, but who also wanted "a side bet of fifty bucks *to make it interesting*.")

I have spent a lot of time in the company of young boys, through Little Chief and Little League baseball, Cub Scouts, and Boy Scouts. It has been my experience that these fiercely competitive guys will and can make a game, a *contest*, out of just about anything. Simple batting practice becomes a contest to see who can hit the most often, or the furthest; who can get to first base fastest, and so forth. Cub Scouts compete with their den buddies to make the best ash tray for Daddy, or the best basket for Mommy; Scouts vie to build the best and most efficient cooking fire, or to find and harvest the most treasured "fat wood."

Once, upon the completion of a grueling backpacking trip, our troop flopped down on a grassy spot near the highway to await our bus pickup. Within five minutes the boys had invented a game of tag and were chasing one another around with a sock filled with dirt as the tagging instrument.

The human competitive spirit need not rely on physical exertion and vigorous activity. Humans enjoy a cornucopia of games and puzzles for competition with others or self. We have word games, board games, computer games, card games, puzzles (jigsaw, crossword, etc). A current television commercial involves an airline customer who is told there will be a lengthy delay before his flight leaves; instead of expressing disappointment, he happily replies "Cool," since he has his handheld "gameboy" device to while away the hours competing with himself and the electronic antagonists programmed into his toy. I, myself, when temporarily overcome by a mild case of "writer's block," tap a few keys on my computer and get in a few rounds of computer solitaire.

And, in all these competitive endeavors, when the victory is hard-won and is achieved suddenly, the basic human reaction is to laugh victoriously. We can even think of it as the "Eureka" response.

And, of course, we also revel in our sudden hard-won victories in the "games of life." Sudden news of a promotion, a breakthrough in the logjam down at work, or the solution to a long-puzzling personal problem revives our spirits, quickens our pulse, and brings on exuberant behavior, including smiles and laughter.

In the fall of 1974 my own career was still developing and littered with the details of the upward climb. I was under consideration for promotion to full professor; I was engaged in the often frustrating task of finding a publisher for my book-length manuscript, *Understanding Laughter*; but otherwise the teaching and research was going well.

My wife, Marsha, and I went to Sanford Stadium for the Georgia-Auburn football game one Saturday that Fall with solemn trepidation. Auburn was greatly favored over our beloved Bulldogs. But, loyal fans that we are, we donned our Red-and-Black and prepared for the worst.

The awesome Auburn Tigers were rendered tame as tabby cats by the triumphant Bulldogs of Coach Dooley. Great upset! Marsha and I drove home in exultant glee, our victory pennants waving from our cars' rain gutters. Then, upon arriving home, we found in our mailbox a signed contract to publish *Understanding Laughter*. A trade book contract would punctuate my promotion dossier as the atomic bomb did the ending of World War II. The remainder of the weekend was just about the merriest on record for the Gruners!

Talk about feelings of "sudden glory!"

Quite often a "scholar" wishes to appear erudite or original, by making some old, shopworn idea look novel (perhaps even "creative") in order to get his work noticed (or, even *published*). One tactic for accomplishing this goal is to create a scholarly-looking chart or *diagram* elucidating (and/or obfuscating) the scholar's blinding brilliance. The practice has gained acceptance through long practice, and I refuse to go against the tradition; therefore I unabashedly present my "laughing is winning" theory in diagram form.

Stage 1 represents Man as I have described his basic nature, above, as it has evolved: acquisitive, competitive, exploratory-seeking physical comfort and safety, peace of mind, self-reproduction (sex), the enter-

1. Man's Evolved Nature: Acquisitive, Competitive, Explorative

↓

2. Conflict Situations		
Conflict with others	Conflict with Self	Conflict with Environment

Resolution of Conflict

3. Ambiguous Resolution	4. Unsatisfactory Resolution	5. Satisfactory Resolution
↙	"Losing"*	"Winning"**
Ambiguity, Frustration, Ambivalance, etc.		

↓   ↙

Perception of:

↙   ↘

Losing		Winning	
4a. Gradual	4b. Sudden	5a. Gradual	5b. Sudden
Disappointment	Anger	Feelings of:	Smile
Sorrow	Yell	well-being	Squeal
Determine to	Curse	satisfaction	Laugh
do better	Vow revenge	pleasantry	"Eureka!"
Become	Weep	relaxation	Shout
philosopher	Gnash teeth	smugness	Jump for
Rationalize:	Smash things	mastery	joy
"sour grapes"	Blame others, etc.	worth, etc.	Sing, etc.

tainment of novelty and adventure, success and mastery (of others *and* self), and self-actualization.

In seeking what he wants, Man (Stage 2) does not get everything handed to him on a golden platter. He must compete against (a) other people, (b) his own weaknesses, appetites, selfishness, and excesses, and (c) the natural impediments that physical nature places before him (weather, geography, pestilence, illness, death, etc.). These conflicts must be resolved (one cannot live in a constant state of discord). Resolutions of conflict can be ambiguous (3), relatively unsatisfactory (4) or satisfactory (5). If (4), you lose; if (5), you "win."

If you perceive that you are "losing" gradually (4a) you are likely to feel sorrow, disappointment, ambiguity. You may decide to "give up" the particular struggle; you might decide to renew your efforts and "do better;" you might rationalize ("Those grapes were probably sour, anyway!"). But you don't wind up very happy.

If you perceive your loss suddenly (4b), then stronger emotions might grip you. You get angry, "hot under the collar," perhaps shocked into total inaction. You might scream away your emotion, weep prodigiously, tear up or break something, strike out at someone nearby, or swear revenge upon whatever or whomever has blocked your path to success.

If, on the other hand, you satisfactorily resolve your conflict (5), you "win." Gradual perception of your improved status (5a) might give you a warm feeling of well-being, relaxation, security, and self-congratulation. You are pleased with now getting what you wanted. You probably smile, outwardly or inwardly. You are contented.

If your "victory" comes suddenly, though, (5b) you feel an abrupt and impetuous rush of pleasure that may produce a burst of physical activity. You might squeal with delight, briskly sit up in your chair or jump to your feet, wave a fist in the air, shout "Eureka" (or some such exclamation of discovery/victory), and so forth. Or you might laugh, or merely smile.

Laughter is mentioned here as only a *possible* response to a sudden perception of satisfactory conflict resolution ("winning") as the result of a joke, wisecrack, puzzle-solution, etc. because, obviously, not every joke, wisecrack, pun, etc. elicits overt laughter. After all, laughter is more social than solitary; and it is not only a *response*, but can be a *stimulus*. We can laugh at things that we find unfunny merely to please others. We know that it is impolitic *not* to laugh at the boss's jokes!

Various writers analyzing wit and humor refuse to accept the idea that *all* humor can be explained by such a superiority-disparagement-aggressive theory as the above. This, they insist, is true because there exists "innocent," nonaggressive, nondisparaging humor. But in making this argument, they unfortunately attempt to provide examples of "innocent" humor. In the rest of this book we take a close look at these examples, particularly in the final chapter, and see if we can find any superiority, disparagement, hostility, aggression—in short, "winners and losers" in them.

3

Drollery in Death, Destruction, and Disaster

My uncle is a Southern planter. He's an
undertaker in Alabama.

—Fred Allen

I never wanted to see anybody die, but
there are a few obituary notices I have
read with pleasure.

—Clarence Darrow

Human death, which we all fear and dread, remains the bread and butter content of much of our humor. By telling jokes about death and making fun of those in the life-and-death industries of medicine, grave-digging and undertaking, we enable ourselves to momentarily, at least, feel superior to that final process which will take away from us all that we own and all that we have known. We also allow ourselves to express and justify, in the socially acceptable play-frame of humor, our natural animosity and wish for death of those we would like to see as direct customers of Fred Allen's uncle.

There is the story of a lady who had reached her 100th birthday, on which she was being interviewed by the local media folk. To the question, "What is the *worst* and *best* aspect of living to be 100?" she replied, "Well, it is very sad in that you have to see so many of your friends die." Then, perking up with a twinkle in her eye, she continued: "But then, you also get to see your *enemies* die, too!"

And we greatly enjoy a joke in which a person dies somewhat "deservedly." Consider the Old Zeke/Minister joke of chapter 1. Why laugh, smirk, or smile at the sudden demise of the minister? Because he is out to use his verbal wiles (which we may resent) to prevent something that actually happens, in a "turn of the table," to *him!* We also tend to harbor mostly subconscious resentment toward men of the cloth for a couple reasons. One, they are "holier than us" and therefore morally superior, which we tend to resent (also mostly unconsciously). Two, we perceive them as constantly wanting from us more *money*. The minister's sudden perception of forthcoming churchly riches is too much for his heart. Consider the story of the cruise ship badly listing and presumably on its way to sinking. A frightened passenger screams for someone to "Do something religious!" whereupon another passenger passes the hat.

There are some among our species who enjoy *actual* death and suffering of fellow humans. For instance, Harlow (1969) has reminded us that:

> The most primitive form of humour is that of sheer brutality in which degradation of the recipient is achieved by his anxiety, anguish or agony. This is the kind of humour reputedly enjoyed by the Nazi *Gauleiter* who ran the concentration camps in Second World War Germany, but it is a kind of humour enjoyed by all those who perpetrate terror and torture.... After all, there is a narrow boundary between sarcasm and sadism, between bantering and bestiality. (229–30)

I recently toured Warwick Castle in England. One room contained an assortment of instruments of torture, either refurbished relics or authentically reconstructed from old woodcuts, used during medieval times. I could hardly imagine men being able to use these terrible machines on other human beings without deriving some pleasure from their use. Such activity would gravely sicken normally civilized beings.

One cannot read reports by survivors of the Holocaust without realizing that many Nazi concentration camp supervisors took great sport in making life-and-death decisions for their captives. For instance, Garbarz and Garbarz (1992) tell us:

> I saw a man running toward the barbed wire as the SS shot at him. The guy fell and got back up. All his insides were hanging out; he grabbed them in his hands and started running again. The SS shot once more, this time aiming for his head. The victim finally dropped....
>
> The *kapos* rushed to pick him up. He was nothing but a mass of flesh; it was as if a big truck had squashed his stomach. From the watchtower, the SS stopped them:
>
> "Leave him; I want to take a closer look." It was time for the change of shift. He came down to confirm that the bullet had indeed pierced the skull and *the broad smile* on his face indicated that he was quite satisfied with his accuracy.
>
> I thought the SS had wanted to put the man out of his misery, since the first bullet hadn't done the job.
>
> Not at all. Both shots were on target: the first was fired *for fun* and the second to protect the electrified barbed wire. (87)

After being forced to stack bodies of men who had been clubbed to death, Moshe Garbarz reported that

> When our task was finished we went back to the barracks. Laybich [the supervisor] was laughing: "What the hell have you been wallowing in? You must have been killing pigs, right?"....He rejoiced to see us in such a deplorable state. (122)

The *wish* for death of others can be made socially acceptable by the joke format. A man asked his boss if he could have the next day off because he "wanted to attend the funeral of his mother-in-law." The day off was granted, but several days later the boss confronted the man in question with: "You wanted the day off last week for your mother-in-law's funeral, but I saw her on the street yesterday with her husband."

"Oh," replied the man, "I didn't say she had died. I only said that I would *like to attend* her funeral that day."

Death can be funny in the most far-fetched situations. Many years ago a movie animated cartoon took the form of the so-called nature film. In one scene the screen was a pond full of lily pads; the announcer proclaimed that "We will now see a frog *croak*." The camera zoomed in on a lily pad onto which a frog climbed. Suddenly the frog pulls from behind himself a large revolver, points it at his temple and pulls the trigger with a resounding report, after which he plunges backward to a watery grave.

And we make ironic quips about the dead and dying, especially "nontragic" deaths. Recently the newspaper from our old home town arrived by mail with the news that Eleanor Wilks, age 102, had died. I read the obituary first, and remarked to my wife, "My word! Eleanor Wilks died. And she was only 102." My wife's quip: "I suppose she went quite *suddenly*." "Yes," I replied. "Probably altogether *unexpectedly*." To which she came back with, "And I'll bet that her parents predeceased her!" And so we trivialize, thus temporarily and symbolically winning out over, the Grim Reaper.

We humans also get much entertainment out of *destruction*, and, usually, the more *disastrous* is the destruction, the more we enjoy it. Modern action-adventure motion pictures are much criticized for their great amounts of violence against people, but also for the many raging infernos, spectacular automobile crashes, train derailments, building explosions, airplane "other than routine" landings, volcanic eruptions, and ship sinkings.

I had always considered *vandalism* as mindless, motiveless, and "sense-less" until I read up on the modern research on the phenomenon. "Why would any juvenile above the level of low-grade moron get a kick out of demolishing my curbside mailbox," I have had to ask myself more than once. Well, it appears that the juvenile practice of vandalism has much to do with why we laugh. There is apparently a large hedonic component to vandalism. As reported by Allen (1984):

> A perusal of data from case reports reveals many instances in which youngsters who discuss their own acts of vandalism make unsolicited comments indicating that the episode was simply enjoyable in itself—or to use their own words, "It was fun." For example, a member of a boys' gang studied by Thrasher (1936) stated, "We would always tear things down. That would make us laugh and feel good (95). And a boy explaining the reason for an incident of school vandalism said: "To have fun. They thought it was a big joke breakin' things. Somebody said, "Let's break the winders." (Martin 1961)

Interestingly, the hedonic or "aesthetic" theory of vandalism has led researchers to investigate the apparently normal urge to break things. Allen and Greenberger (1978) had subjects look at various panes of glass breaking in standard ways and asked them which they would most enjoy breaking themselves. Results showed that subjects would prefer to break the panes that shattered in the more complex ways.

Allen and Spencer (1977) did a comparable experiment in which the complexity of the to-be-destroyed object was varied. The subjects preferred breaking the more complex forms exhibited. And Allen and Greenberger (1979) performed an experiment in which subjects preferred to break things that fell apart in the more *unexpected* patterns (an analogy to the "surprise" of the punch line?).

The impetus to destroy may be a small boy trait, noticeable in almost any three-year-old lad, which men never quite outgrow, given the right circumstances. A sure moneymaker in any carnival or street fair is to place an intact older (cheap or free) automobile in a spot and sell three blows upon it with a sledgehammer for a buck. Men will line up, pay their buck, and thrash away at the jalopy until it is unrecognizable as a car.

The humor of death, destruction and disaster ought also to include an explanation of that humor which is generally regarded as "sick." Dundes and Hauschild (1938: 249) have pointed out that "Nothing is so sacred, so taboo, or so disgusting that it cannot be the subject of humor." They might well have had in mind that form of humor that we today call "sick" humor. And "sick" humor embodies the aggression, the "contest element" that fits so neatly the theory that constitutes the major thesis of this book. For the content of sick humor includes the taking lightly of such horrors as infanticide, matricide, mutilation, infirmity, disability, debilitating illness, dismemberment, amputation, monsterism, vampirism and, I would include, incest:

> A young man takes a seat in a very dark movie theatre. After some minutes he realizes a woman sits beside him. She smells good. He touches her arm, and she does not pull away. Soon they are holding hands warmly. He pecks her on the cheek; one thing leads to another quickly, and within minutes they are off into heavy, panting petting. Suddenly the lights go on and they look at each other. "John!" shouts the woman.
>
> "Mother!" he cries.

Or:

> How do you define "hillbilly virgin?" A thirteen-year-old girl who can outrun her brothers.

And:

> The sixteen-year-old mountain boy was having sexual intercourse with his fourteen-year-old sister. "Sis," he wheezes, "you're dang near as good as Maw."
>
> "Yeh," she answers, "that's what Paw says."

There has been some controversy over the history and origins of sick humor. When a "new" form of sick humor called the "Bloody Mary's" erupted into popularity in the mid-1950s, Gerald Walker claimed in an *Esquire* article (1957) that only in the particular social/psychological climate of 1950s American society could such monstrosities have been born. Mr. Walker did not know his humor history very well—nor did he show great understanding of the human animal as I have tried to explain him in the early part of this book.

Dundes (1987: 15) argues that the genre goes back to antiquity. As evidence he cites the case of Theristes, in the second book of the *Iliad*. Theristes was "the ugliest man who came beneath Ilion. He was bandy-legged and went lame of one foot, with shoulders stooped and drawn together over his chest." He cites the instance where Odysseus "dashed the scepter against his (Theristes') shoulders, and he doubled over, and a round tear dropped from him, and a bloody welt stood up between his shoulders." This cruel whipping of the hunchback drew an interesting response from those around him: "Sorry though the men were they laughed over him happily."

Dundes also suggests that human interest in and curiosity about monsters, freaks, and the deformed is easily documented. He points to the long history of circus sideshows with their human beanpoles, fat ladies, hermaphrodites, "dog-faced boys," midgets, human pincushions, fire-eaters, bearded ladies, Siamese twins, and two-headed calves. He might also have mentioned the gore and horror that can be seen dripping from the movie screens around our nation and which draw hordes of paying customers. One need only a modicum of experience in driving our interstate highways to notice the fascination which Americans demonstrate when coming upon a multi-vehicle accident on the road. Even if the accident has occurred a hundred yards away in the opposite-direction lanes, and causes no obstruction to their own lanes, drivers slow down to a walk in order to get a better look at the destruction and, hopefully, the highway carnage. The result is a huge traffic jam, with two or three lanes of traffic turning into an instant parking lot. Auto racing fans throng to tracks around the nation so as not to miss any of the grinding, high-speed crashes that might occur. But why *joke* about human disaster?

Etiquette and social custom requires that we remain respectful and deferential toward death and disability, that we remain solemn and express sympathy. This thin veneer of civilization conceals an aggressive, competitive, combative streak in humans that accounts for their zeal for bloodsports like bullfighting, hunting, fishing, cockfighting and war (and, in an earlier time, bear-baiting)—and their thirst for violent sports such as football, hockey, boxing—their hunger for action and violence in TV and films.

We cannot speak frankly about human disability, death, and so forth without euphemisms. If we harbor resentment for all the extra taxes that must be spent to make buildings, curbs, and public transportation accessible to the handicapped, we can't complain openly. We can't mutter angry oaths as we drive past the many special (mostly vacant) parking spaces provided for the physically disadvantaged, or argue openly against the government's spending extra money on training for the physically challenged. We can't complain about the extra time clerks may have to take to service the blind or deaf or stuttering ahead of us in line. Only within the "play frame" of the joke or riddle can we "let it all hang out" and laugh at the "unfunny" and the unspeakable.

Folklorists point out that material, such as joking, that is likely to be censored as obscene, scatological, offensive, or insulting usually does not find its way into print. Even if governmental censors might allow it, publishers of print media and producers of electronic media would fear audience reprisal. As a result, such censorable material finds its way around through word of mouth, through *folklore*, which today can be quite rapid. Through the medium of long-distance telephone lines and the use of computer bulletin boards, an offensive joke born on the east coast of the United States can spread to the west coast within minutes.

One reason why the "history" of sick humor is not well-documented is that the study and collection of folklore is a relatively recent phenomenon. The several U.S. journals devoted to folklore are products of the twentieth century.

But there are some landmarks on the sketchy history of sick humor. The earliest known "joke book" in English was produced in 1739 by an unsuccessful poet named John Mottley. He called his book *Joe Miller's Jests*. The book had nothing to do with Joe Miller, a deceased but famous actor of the time, but Mottley felt that use of the well-known name might help sell his book. Along with some "gallows humor" (in which condemned men make light of their impending fate) Mottley included three jokes that could be considered as belonging to the "sick" genre.

> *Sir William Davenant*, the Poet, had no nose [lost to syphilis], who going along the Meuse one Day, a Beggar-Woman followed him, crying ah! God preserve your *Eye-Sight*; God preserve your *Eye-Sight*; Why, good Woman, said he, do you pray so much for my *Eye-Sight*? Ah! dear Sir, answered the Woman, if it should please God that you grow dim-sighted, you have no Place to hang your *Spectacles* on.

Ok, bad joke. But *old*, remember. And *sick*.

An eighteenth-century English euphemism for "cripple" was "crooked." Joe Miller jest number 222 took a swipe at this kind of physically challenged:

> One observing a crooked Fellow in close Argument with another, who would have dissuaded him from some inconsiderable Resolution; said to his Friend, *Prithee, let him alone, and say no more to him, you see he's bent upon it.*

And number 226 sees a "faithful servant" reveal his true feelings toward his master, who lies on his deathbed:

> A Gentleman lying on his Death-Bed, called to his Coachman, who had been an old Servant, and said, *Ah! Tom, I'm going a long and rugged Journey, worse than ever you drove me; Oh dear Sir*, replied the Fellow (he having

been but an indifferent Master to him,) *ne'er let that discourage you, for it is all down Hill.*

Again, not very funny. That's why they call old jokes "Joe Millers" (sometimes "joemillers"). And the servant's indifferent consignment of dying old Master to hellfire can easily qualify for the label of "sick."

The year 1899 was a red-letter date in the history of sick humor. This was the year that saw publication by Harry Graham, a member of the English Coldstream Guards, of a book of ditties called *Ruthless Rhymes for Heartless Homes.* These flippant poems, mostly quatrains, combined the lightest and airiest of language with content of the most catastrophic bent. One of his most famous was entitled "Billy."

> Billy, in one of his nice new sashes,
> Fell in the fire and was burnt to ashes.
> Now, although the room grows chilly,
> I haven't the heart to poke up Billy.

Another, "Aunt Eliza," showed concern, but not for the old girl:

> In the drinking well
>   Which the plumber built her,
> Aunt Eliza fell.
>   We must buy a filter.

In an allusion to the Marquis de Sade, Graham speculated on the fate of a young woman in "Compensation:"

> Weep not for little Leonie,
> Abducted by a French *marquis.*
> Though loss of honor was a wrench,
> Just think how it improved her French.

Graham's book was extremely popular. He published *More Ruthless Rhymes for Heartless Homes* in 1930, and in 1984, through the efforts of his daughter Virginia Graham Thesiger, *Ruthless Rhymes* was published in 1986, combining the two books.

Graham wrote more than a score of books of light verse. Some of the best of these were combined with his "ruthless rhymes" in a 1986 effort, *When Grandmama Fell Off the Boat: The Best of Harry Graham*. The title of the book came from one of Harry's originals, "Indifference:"

> When Grandmama fell off the boat
> And couldn't swim and wouldn't float,
> Matilda just stood by and smiled.
> I very nearly slapped the child.

Graham's 1899 book's popularity sparked an explosion of similar efforts in the English-speaking world. Readers composed their own quatrains and sent them in to their newspapers. According to Untermeyer (1946), "Every paper began to print 'ruthless rhymes,' and every contributor tried to invent a catastrophe more gory in event and more nonchalant in effect than its predecessor" (301). Probably because of the popular Graham quatrain "Billy," the most popular hero of the later efforts became "Willie," and these verses came to be known as "Little Willies." Some examples:

> Willie poisoned his father's tea;
> Father died in agony.
> Mother came, and looked quite vexed:
> 'Really, Will,' she said, 'what next?'

> Willie in the cauldron fell;
> See the grief on Mother's brow;
> Mother loved her darling well—
> Willie's quite hard-boiled by now.

> Willie fell down the elevator—
> Wasn't found till six days later.
> Then the neighbors sniffed, 'Gee whizz!
> What a spoiled child Willie is.'

> Willie saw some dynamite,
> Couldn't understand it quite.
> Curiosity never pays;
> It rained Willie seven days.

And one eight-liner:

Little Willie from the mirror
  Sucked the mercury all off,
Thinking, in his childish error,
  It would cure his whooping cough.
At the funeral his mother,
  Weeping, said to Mrs. Brown:
'Twas a chilly day for Willie
  When the mercury went down.'

According to Evan Esar (1952), the Little Willie rhymes got further and further away from the spirit of what came to be known as "*truthful* rhymes for heartless homes" and became passé. At the time, Esar, of course, did not know that Graham's work would be later reproduced for more modern consumers. He was also apparently unaware of a brief renaissance of "ruthless rhymes" that occurred during World War II.

London's *New Statesman and Nation*, a news and literary weekly, for years ran a literary-type contest in its pages. The rules for each upcoming contest would be detailed in the publication, and three weeks later the results would be announced and the winning (and other) entries would be printed. Their publication of 25 October 1941 presented the results of the "ruthless rhymes" competition, number 609, defined as:

The usual prizes are offered for a set of three Ruthless Rhymes on the model of those by Harry Graham, for example:

Phillip, foozling with his cleek,
Drove his ball through Helen's cheek,
Sad they bare her corpse away,
Seven up and six to play.

Many of the entries deal with fictitious events of The War. For instance, Allan M. Laing's entry went like this:

By U-boat sunk, in mid-Atlantic,
Eliza's howls for help were frantic;
But twelve men in the rescue boat
Left her to drown, or swim or float:
Their conduct may sound rather mean,
But after all, you know—thirteen!

The Battle of Britain played a role in some of the verses. "W.R." offered:

> When German bombers, circling o'er,
> Smote Wren churches by the score,
> Young Reggy cried, 'They're men of taste!
> Regent street is not defaced.'

A second verse by Mr. Laing goes:

> Playing hookey, little Tom
> Teased an unexploded bomb.
> At the Pig and Whistle bar
> They'd always said he would go far.

"H.P.B." chimed in with:

> Landing from their parachutes
> Huns raped Cousin Flo, the brutes!
> 'Cheer up, Flo!' exclaimed her mother,
> 'One man's very like another.'

An armed service accident was submitted by Stanley J. Sharpless:

> Straying near the prop, a Waaf
> Managed to get cut in half;
> 'See, the wood's not even frayed,'
> Jim said, as he wiped the blade.

One reader, instead of sending in an entry, protested that this was not the time for such tomfoolery: "Do not woes of total war this week's competition bar? Who but in his own last breath Should be pardoned jokes on death?"

The editor's response:

> Ruthless rhymes are essentially satires upon Man's indifference to the fate of others except in so far as this affects his personal convenience. Evidently jokes about death can all be thought in bad taste, but the fact that most of us have, during the last year, been in danger does not, as far as I can see, aggravate the offence; it merely increases the desire to make such jokes. I note that a rhyme about an undisposed bomb exploding comes from a member of a bomb-disposal unit, and one about a propeller killing somebody comes from an aerodrome. The number of competitors, moreover constitutes, I am told, a record. I became a little

tired after reading the sixtieth rhyme about using a body to manure the vegetable-plot, and the seventieth rhyme about cannibalism.

You probably have an interest in the winners of this little competition. Here are the three entries from Nancy Gunter, which won for her Second Prize:

Herbert, following a tiff,
Pushed his sweetheart o'er a cliff,
Now his action he regrets,
She had got their cigarettes.
    [Cigarettes, like most luxuries, were in short supply.]

Careless Cuthbert threw a dart
Straight into a woman's heart;
Said her brother, 'Now then, Stupid,
Who do you think *you* are—Cupid?'

'One of ours!' said know-all Ted,
Bombs came down and killed him dead;
Cried his wife, with laughter merry
'There, I *said* it was a Jerry!'
    [Jerry: slang for German.]

And the winner! Three from E. W. Fordham:

Our bulldog ate the larger half
Of Aunt Matilda's ample calf:
I should, I trust, have been upset
Were dog food not so hard to get.
    [Wartime shortages, you know]

I was, I knew, the certain heir
    Of father's wealthy sister;
I saw her strolling near my car,
    I swerved and nearly missed her.

James, reposing on a bank,
Was rudely wakened by a tank;
The ground was soft, the tank was large,
So James was buried free of charge.

This wartime "revival" of ruthless rhymes notwithstanding, the Little Willies (which some say gave rise to the slang expression "—gives me the willies") apparently gave rise to another form of sick humor, the Little Audrey stories. Young people of the 1930's carried around several of these stories, the heroine of most of which was "Little Audrey." Although, as Cornelia Chambers (1937) reported, "Sometimes Little Audrey parades as Little Emma or Little Gertrude, but she usually is recognizable by a catch phrase—'she just laughed and laughed and laughed.' The amusing incident is typically a catastrophe. Little Audrey sees the humor in any situation." Some examples of this form of sick humor will acquaint you with the technique:

> Once upon a time Little Audrey got lost on a desert island. Along came a big bunch of black cannibals and kidnapped her. They tied her up to a tree and started their pot to boiling. Little Audrey knew they were going to make stew of her; so she looked around at those lean, hungry cannibals and counted them. There were nineteen. Little Audrey just laughed and laughed, 'cause she knew she was not big enough to make enough stew to go around. (Botkin 1944: 373)

As above, in some stories Little Audrey is the victim (but she laughs and laughs anyway). In other stories she laughs at other victims:

> One day Little Audrey and her mother were driving along when all of a sudden the car door flew open and Little Audrey's mother fell out. Little Audrey just laughed and laughed, 'cause she knew all the time that her mother had on her light fall suit. (Botkin 1944: 374)

Little Audrey could even get a laugh out of *sexual* situations:

> [One] night Little Audrey and her date were sitting on the sofa when all of a sudden the lights went out. "Oh," said Little Audrey's boyfriend, "it sure is dark in here. I can't even see my hand in front of me." Little Audrey just laughed and laughed, 'cause she knew all the time that his hand wasn't in front of him. (Botkin 1944: 375)

The predominant replacement for the Little Audrey stories was the Little Moron variety. According to Esar (1952):

> A few years after the demise of *Little Audrey* a new comic character arose, the *little moron*. He was even more popular than his laughing predecessor had been in the 1930s, for he bloomed not only on college campuses but also in huge war plants. He was both a war baby and a war casualty. Born with the advent of the Second World War, he died, at least as an adult type, before V-J day. (111)

The little moron bits were in the form of the rhetorical question, beginning, "Did you hear about the little moron who...?" a kind of emended
riddle form. And many of them would be considered fairly "harmless,"
although they earned their merriment with the one comic feature of the
moron himself: his utter and whacky *stupidity*. Examples:

> Did you hear about the little moron who
>> stayed up all night studying for his blood test?
>> took a bale of hay to bed with him to feed his night*mare*?
>> took a bike to bed with him so he would not sleepwalk?

But other little moron jokes dealt with the kind of content we would
consider "sick":

> Did you hear about the little moron who
>> cut off his fingers so he could learn shorthand?
>> jumped off the Empire State building because he wanted to be a smash hit on
>> Broadway?
>> cut off his arms so he could wear sleeveless sweaters?
>> cut off his hands so he could learn piano by ear?
>> killed his parents and pleaded for mercy on the grounds he was an orphan?

The 1940s also saw popularized the plain "moron jokes" (Davidson 1942)
which were not "formulized" as was the rhetorical-question *little* moron
joke-form. The jokes were funny to the extent that you appreciated the
stupidity of one or the other of the two (at least) morons in the story, such
as a moron who asks another moron what letter comes alphabetically
after the *A*. His response: "All the rest of 'em." But I have not found any
examples of these "moron jokes" that I would classify as "sick."

The next new form of sick humor appears to be the "cruel jokes" of
the 1950s, already mentioned. Between September and December of 1958
Sutton-Smith (1960) collected 155 specimens. He listed the various names
given to this genre as "Cruel Jokes, Bloody Marys, Hate Jokes, Ivy League
Jokes, Sadist Jokes, Gruesomes, Grimsels, Sick Jokes, Freddie Jokes,
Depression Jokes, Meanie Jokes, and the Comedy of Horror." Sutton-
Smith divided his specimens into twelve categories, based on content.
These categories, with examples, follow:

> 1. Murder of friends and relatives:
>   "Mama, why are we pushing the car over the cliff?"
>   "Shut up or you'll wake up your father."

2. Mutilation:
"Mommy, why do I keep walking in circles?"
"Shut up, or I'll nail your other foot to the floor."

3. Cannibalism:
"Mommy, can we have grandma for dinner?"
"Shut up. We still have half of Aunt Mary in the ice box."

4. Corpses:
"Johnny, if you don't stop playing with your little sister,
I'll have to close the casket."

5. Beasts:
"Mama, what is a werewolf?"
"Shut up and comb your face."

6. Excrement:
"Mommy, can I lick the bowl?"
"Shut up and flush like anyone else."

7. Indifference to the Young:
"Mommy, why can't we get a garbage disposal?"
"Shut up and start chewing."

8. Degenerate parents:
"Mommy, can I go out and play?"
"Shut up and deal."

9. Afflictions, Disease, and Mutilation:
"No, Billy can't come out to play. He has leprosy."
"Then can we come in and watch him rot?"

10. Religion:
"I'm going to take you out of the parade, if you don't stop dragging your cross."

11. Famous People:
"Happy Father's Day, Mr. Lindberg";
(The most famous: "Other than that, Mrs. Lincoln, how did you like the play?").

12. Miscellaneous:
Humpty Dumpty sat on the wall.
Humpty Dumpty had a great fall.
All the King's horses and all the King's Men, Ate egg.

So far we have seen that sick humor may well have been around in antiquity, that it showed up in a joke book in the eighteenth century, was wildly popular in verse from the turn of the present century up to about 1930, lived on in Little Audrey through the 1930s and the Little Moron through World War II, then erupted in the 1950s as "cruel jokes" or "Bloody Marys." It seems safe to assume that this rather childish form of humor has been with the human race steadily from a long way back in our history. Reports from the folklore journals most often record that the sickies are gathered mostly from *children* (though adults certainly enjoy and circulate them widely and quickly).

It seems to me that sick humor fits the younger and less civilized members of our race. Children can usually tell the most outlandish sick jokes with the least qualms and squeamishness than the adults. Children revel in violence, amputation, horror, lousy manners, bestiality, and the like without the pangs of consciousness that we adults have had laid on us by our longer individual histories and more stringent socialization. In 1956, while teaching a course in speech to seventh-graders, one of my little charges told me the following:

> A man died and was taken to the mortuary. The undertaker called the widow and told her that her husband would be ready for her inspection the following after-noon. When she went in she remarked that her husband looked just fine for the "visitation" and the later funeral. However, she objected to the brown suit in which they had dressed her husband. "He always liked blue, he wore blue a lot; could you have him in a blue suit for the events tomorrow?" The funeral director said it could be easily arranged. The next day the dearly departed was neatly dressed in a blue suit.
>
> When the widow got the funeral bill in the mail, it was itemized, and one item said "Blue suit: $10.00."
>
> When she dropped in to pay the bill she asked how the blue suit was arranged for so economically.
>
> "Oh, that worked out very well, Ma'am. You see, while we had *your* husband downstairs here, we had another gentlemen in the *upstairs* parlor; he was dressed in *blue*; *his* widow wanted *him* buried in a *brown* suit so we just-switched heads."

The Atlanta newspapers recently ran a poll to find out the favorite comic strips of those they run. Coming in first place for adults and second place for kids was *Calvin and Hobbes*, featuring the "all-boy" Calvin, who relishes loud burping, refuses to eat most of what his long-suffering mother places before him, and fantasizes his parents, teachers, and other adults into horrid space-monsters which he blasts to bits with his ray gun as Spaceman Spiff. Coming in fourteenth for kids was *Big Nate*. In his strip of 16 October 1993 Nate tells his little friend Frances that he is working on his entry for the young playwright's competition. His work is entitled "Doctor Cesspool: The Musical." In the very first scene Dr. Cess-pool amputates the legs of a dozen different patients. Then, he tells Frances, he has to figure out what comes next. Frances suggests "How about the closing curtain?" Nate replies: "Obviously a dance number is out of the question."

In the *Walnut Cove* strip of 15 October 1993 (a new strip, but coming up with the kids, now twenty-fourth) Joey has finished his English project for Mrs. Crubbley. He adapted *King Lear* to modern times by first killing off all the "original characters," a "bunch of dweebs," in a train wreck.

Because of children's proclivity for the macabre, then, it is little wonder that it was mostly from public school students in Pennsylvania that Barrick (1980) collected so many "Helen Keller" jokes. Ms. Keller, blind and deaf nearly from birth, offers comic scripts pregnant with promise for the sick joke genre. Some examples he came up with:

Helen Keller's new book, *Around the Block in 80 Days.*

How did Helen Keller fall out of the tree? She was yelling for help.

Helen Keller was mugged, and broke three fingers screaming for help.

"Hi, Helen. Taken in any good movies lately?"

Barrick suggests that the movie *The Miracle Worker*, featuring Helen Keller as a young girl first learning to grope her way out of her darkness, was responsible for the popularity of the joke cycle about her afflictions.

Other current events produce sick (and not-so-sick) jokes with content peculiar to those events. Usually a joke cycle is fairly brief, or sometimes it changes because of changes in the news. For instance Christopher (1984–85) has pointed out that "No serious student of American folk humor can fail to observe that the genre of 'current event jokes' has become embedded with increasing depth and tenacity in the annals of verbal aggression."

Although his article mainly concerned "Ethiopian Jokes," Christopher reminds us that big stories breaking in the news give birth to a new litter of aggressive joking. He lists such stories as those involving "Billie Jean King, Karen Ann Quinlan, Renee Richards, Rosie Ruiz, Richard Pryor, Michael Jackson, Grace Kelly, Gerry Studds [homosexual politician], Geraldine Ferraro, Jesse Jackson, Karen Carpenter, Natalie Wood, and Baby Fae, or the incidents at Dan's Pool Hall [multiple rape] and the San Ysidro McDonald's [a gunman's massacre of the innocent]."

The jokes *he* gathered were prompted by the media's wide pictorial coverage of the starvation in Ethiopia:

How many Ethiopians can you fit into a shopping cart?
    None. They fall through the holes.
What's the lowest-selling product in Ethiopia?
    After-dinner mints.
How many Ethiopians can you stuff into a phone booth?
    All of them.
What do you call an Ethiopian walking a dog?
    A vegetarian.
What do you call an Ethiopian walking two dogs?
    A caterer.
What do you call an Ethiopian walking ten dogs?
    A rancher.
What do you call a forty-pound Ethiopian?
    Bubba, or "Fatty."
Who's the patron saint of Ethiopia?
    Karen Carpenter.
How can you tell the sex of an unborn Ethiopian baby?
    Hold the pregnant woman up to the light.

These "Ethiopian Jokes," since the heavy TV coverage of the starvation in Somalia, have been recycled as "Somalian Jokes," just as "Polish Jokes" can be converted to Georgia Techie Jokes or (Dumb) Blonde Jokes. That is, any workable comic script (starvation, stupidity, promiscuity, canniness, etc.) can be used on any group on which it fits in the folk culture.

With the advent and shockingly growing problem of Acquired Immune Deficiency Syndrome (AIDS) in the world we have a concomitant upsurge in "AIDS jokes." Tannen and Morris (1989) indicate that

> Many AIDS jokes are overtly anti-homosexual. Telling AIDS jokes can be a way for heterosexual men to defend themselves both from their fear of the disease and from the stigma of homosexuality. Alan Dundes views AIDS jokes as yet another cycle of "sick" jokes that "constitute a...collective mental hygienic defense mechanism that allow people to cope with...disasters." (1987: 73)

AIDS jokes also allow people to speak openly about a taboo topic, their actual fear of contracting the dread disease. These jokes also often reflect the widespread antagonism of heterosexual men toward homosexual males.

What does GAY stand for? Got AIDS Yet?

A gay man is hospitalized with AIDS. His doctor assures him that he will be well
cared for and fed plenty of pancakes and flounder.
"Does that diet cure AIDS?" asks the patient.
"No," says the doctor, "but that's all we can slip under your door."

Schmidt collected a number of AIDS jokes while collecting other
material on the illness. He quotes Legman (1968: 13–14) that the purpose of these jokes, like all humor, is "to absorb and control, even slough
off, by means of jocular presentation and laughter, the great anxiety that
both teller and listener feel in connection with certain culturally determined themes." Schmidt's thesis seems to be embodied in the definition I
have heard, that AIDS is "Jerry Falwell's Revenge." The article ends, in
fact, in a cartoon: depicted is Jerry Falwell in pajamas, kneeling at his
bedside, eyes closed, praying: "We thank Thee for the gift of Thy bountiful herpes and Thine blessed AIDS, O Lord…Now send us something
for all the other weirdos."

The first AIDS joke Schmidt ever heard involved probably America's
best-known female homophobe:

How does Anita Bryant spell "relief?" A-I-D-S. (A pun on the Rolaids commercial.)

Schmidt says that further anti-gay jokes came later:

What do you call homosexuals camping out at the North Pole? Koolaids.

What do you call homosexuals on roller skates? Rollaids.

A medical student in the Bronx provided him with

What's the most difficult thing about getting AIDS?
    Convincing your mother that you're Haitian.

Schmidt implies but does not specify another popular item:

What turns fruits into vegetables? AIDS.

"The nuclear disaster at Chernobyl of early morning, 26 April 1986
was one of the most serious man-made disasters in Eastern Europe since
World War II" (Kurti 1988: 324). This recent event became the subject
of a great deal of sick humor.

What's the new greeting among comrades?

"How are you?"

"Glowing."

Why are Chernobyl girls the prettiest?

They glow.

What's the new name of the Peace Bicycle Race? [run shortly after the accident, near Chernobyl, to distract public attention from the danger]

"The Tour de Madame Curie."

What's first prize in the bicycle race?

A free bone marrow transplant.

What will they call Gorbachev in the history books after Chernobyl?

First Isotope.

The famed and dreaded Berlin Wall, now dismantled, was the cause of a little "sick humor." One item collected by Stein (1989) ridiculed the East German so-called policy that "shoot-to-kill" orders had been replaced by more humane measures regarding potential escapees:

When does a good border guard fire the warning shot?

At the end of the second clip of ammunition.

Politicians serve as the butts of jokes frequently in our society, but not very often is the humor grim enough to be labeled "sick." Some U.S. politicians in recent years have inspired a number of jokes which come close to falling into this category.

In 1987 the hottest new challenger for the presidency occupied by George Bush was Gary Hart. Then Hart, a married man, was caught by the press on a lark, afloat with a twenty-nine-year-old blonde, sometime actress-model named Donna Rice on a boat aptly named *Monkey Business*. There were no eyewitness accounts of sexual activity between Hart and Rice, but the jokes which quickly followed filled in where the imagination alone could suffice:

What's Gary Hart's favorite dish? Rice Pilaf (peel off).

First we had Watergate, then Irangate, now we've got Tailgate.

Hart's aides had told him: "We said Bush was the opposition, not the goal."

When Donna Rice was asked who was her favorite candidate, she replied, "My Heart belongs to Bush, but my bush belongs to Hart."

These jokes come from Dundes (1989). He points out further that, at about the same time, another sex scandal broke upon the scene.

Televangelist Jim Bakker (now just out of jail) was reportedly involved with a sexy secretary, Jessica Hahn, whom he had to "pay off" for silence. An acronymic joke became popular regarding Bakker's Praise The Lord (PTL) TV network:

What does PTL stand for? Pass the Loot (or, Pay The Lady).

Dundes shows how Hart and Bakker could be combined in the same joke cycle:

Did you hear that Jim Bakker and Gary Hart are founding a new university in Utah? They're calling it "Frig-em Young."

Senator Ted Kennedy, who drove off the famous Chappaquiddick bridge, resulting in the drowning death of Mary Jo Kopechne, even got caught up in the Gary Hart joke cycle. Earlier it had been said of Kennedy:

What law firm represented Ted Kennedy in the Chappaquiddick case? Weiner, Diner, Dicker and Dunker.

Mixed in with Hart we get:

What was Gary Hart's greatest regret? He didn't ask Ted Kennedy to drive Donna Rice to the airport.

Did you hear about the new law firm: Richard Nixon, Gary Hart, and Ted Kennedy. It's called "Trick-'em, Dick'em, and Dunk'em."

One popular Hart joke helped Dundes to a title for his article:

What's the title of Gary Hart's new book? *Six Inches From The Presidency.*

Toward the end of his piece, Dundes (49) agrees with the thesis of this chapter regarding the nature of the Gary Hart jokes. He opines:

Some readers may feel that the folk were too unremittingly *cruel* in their treatment of Gary Hart in the joke cycle; others may consider that he got just what he deserved. In either case, there can be no question that Gary Hart's political future was not helped by the spate of Gary Hart jokes that seemed to appear almost instantaneously after his alleged sexual peccadilloes were revealed in the press.

News items, especially of celebrities or mass murderers, seem to spawn instant "sick jokes" with the celebrities or the killers (and their victims) as the subject matter. After Natalie Wood, movie actress and wife of

Robert Wagner, drowned one night beside the family boat, sick jokes erupted, some of which punned on her name:

What kind of wood does not float? Natalie.

What is her middle name? Drift.

What were Robert Wagner's last words to his wife?
You can have a few drinks, but don't go overboard.

Why didn't Natalie Wood take a shower on her boat?
Because she figured she'd wash ashore.

This latter joke was later recycled for the *Challenger* tragedy. The Natalie jokes came from Aman (1983).

Aman also reported that, in 1984, when Robert Hansen, an Alaskan baker, admitted having raped thirty women and killed at least seventeen, jokes about his activities appeared soon after. One such was "How do you stop a baker from raping?"—"You twist his penis into a pretzel."

When actor Vic Morrow was accidentally decapitated by a helicopter while making a film in Hollywood, a joke circulated soon after: We know now that Vic Morrow had dandruff; they found his head and shoulders in the bushes. (This bon mot was also resuscitated later for the cycle of *Challenger* jokes.)

Aman reports also on "the biggest crop of macabre, black humor" that he knows of came "after Edward Gein was arrested for multiple murders and other atrocities, recorded in the nightmare-inducing book *Edward Gein: America's Most Bizarre Murderer*" (Delavan, WI: Chas. Hallberg & Co, 1981).

The following examples make sense only if one knows the details: in 1957, Ed Gein, a fifty-one-year-old hermit and bachelor, murdered several women, made a belt, wastepaper basket, lamp shades, chairs, bowls, and face masks of the victims' nipples, skulls, bones and skin. He hung the corpses on meat hooks and eviscerated them like deer, cut off their heads, cut out their hearts, cut out their genitals and rectums (and wore them), ate and served to others their flesh, robbed graves, and was a necrophiliac. These revolting deeds shocked his Plainfield, Wisconsin (population 642) neighbors who tried to control their horror and reduce their fear by a wave of grim "Gein Humor" centering on cannibalism and sexual perversions. I have here recast in riddle form some of the clumsily-told examples, from pages 211–12:

What did Ed Gein say to his late-arriving guests?
Sorry you weren't a little earlier. Everybody's eaten.

What did Ed Gein say when asked how his folks were?
Delicious.

Why couldn't Ed Gein operate his farm?
Because all he had left was a skeleton crew.

What did Ed Gein say to the Sheriff who arrested him?
Have a heart.

What was the favorite beer in Plainfield?
Gein Beer. Lots of body but no head.

Why did they have to keep the heat up in Ed Gein's house?
Because otherwise the furniture would get goose bumps.

Both Richard Pryor and Michael Jackson were victims in "fire" accidents. Michael Jackson's hair caught fire while he was rehearsing for a movie, and Richard Pryor caught fire while trying to freebase cocaine. This made them apt material for sick humor, as "What new charitable foundation did Michael Jackson and Richard Pryor start?"—"The Ignited Negro College Fund."

After the horror of murder and cannibalism in the Milwaukee apartment of Jeffrey Dahmer was uncovered, one resulting entrepreneuring project was the publication there in Milwaukee of a *comic book* of Dahmer's ghoulish adventures, which greatly agitated the families of both Dahmer and his victims. An editorial entitled "Sick Jokes" published in the *New York Times*, 6 August 1991, railed against the murder-cum-cannibal jokes which sprang up around the event; the editorial also lambasted the sickie sex jokes regarding the arrest of Paul Reubens ("Pee-wee Herman") for indecent exposure. One Dahmer joke provided by my good friend Bill Lampton:

Dahmer wanted out on bail, but it would have cost him an arm and a leg.

In early 1993 a religious cult called the "Branch Davidians" and led by a self-proclaimed messiah calling himself "David Koresh" barricaded themselves in a fortress-like compound near Waco, Texas. They were armed to the teeth. When officers of the Alcohol, Tobacco and Firearms (ATF) agency attempted to arrest them, a gun battle broke out, killing four ATF members and wounding a number of others. After a quiet siege of more than a month, another invasion, this time with tear gas and tanks, was attempted. The Davidians set fire to the complex and all burned to death. This prompted a good many sick jokes among the folk, such as

> They found David Koresh dressed fashionably; charcoal trousers and smoking jacket.
> What does WACO stand for? What A Cook Out.
> or We Ain't Coming Out.

The Branch Davidian conclusion even prompted at least one more Jeffrey Dahmer joke:

> After the event in Waco, Jeffrey Dahmer escaped. He was recaptured as he headed toward Waco with fifty pounds of barbecue sauce.

Some jokes compared the Branch Davidian self-massacre with that of the "Jonestown" mass suicide fourteen years earlier. Then, 914 people, leader Jim Jones and his followers, died, mostly poisoned with cyanide-laced Kool-Aid punch which they drank voluntarily and/or fed their children. One joke went,

> Why are Branch Davidian jokes funnier than "Jonestown" jokes?
> Because with the Jonestown jokes the punch lines are too long.

A number of "sick jokes" exist with reference to the Holocaust, the attempt by Nazi Germany to rid Eastern Europe of Jews by extermination. Dundes (1983) calls such jokes definitely anti-Semitic, based on this logic: Jews, themselves, *will* tell such Jewish jokes as:

> How do you cure a Jewish nymphomaniac? Marry her.
> What is Jewish foreplay? Twenty minutes of begging.

On the other hand, Jews will *not* tell "Auschwitz jokes" like:

> How many Jews will fit into a Volkswagen?
> 506. Six in the seats, 500 in the ashtray.

> What is the difference between a ton of coal and a thousand Jews?
> Jews burn longer.

> A child plays with a bar of soap. Granny says, "Keep your fingers off Anne Frank."

Dundes collected most of his examples in West Germany, further "proof" that anti-Semitism is alive and well.

I can't agree completely with this logic. Unless one is automatically guilty of anti-Semitism *because* one tells and enjoys such jokes, I cannot in the least consider myself anti-Semitic (or anti-very much at all!). But I *do* tell such jokes, and I enjoy them (not, of course, when knowingly in the company of Jews, who might very well be offended!) But I feel that these Auschwitz jokes, in fact *all* truly "sick" (and ethnic) jokes, are so outlandish in the degree to which they hyperbolize their comic scripts (or, stereotypes), that any sensible, logical person would be *compelled* to recognize that this material *cannot be taken seriously*! Any citizen who made such outlandish remarks in public, and expecting to be taken seriously, would quickly attain the status of social pariah, at the very least. And, if I were a true anti-Semite I think I could figure out things to say and *do* to show my feelings about Jews that would be *much* more serious than telling incredibly ghoulish jokes.

Schmaier (1963–64) identified a *pattern* of joke-telling that appeared to him to be of recent origin, the "doll joke." He explains it as "oral humor in which an imaginary windup doll is given the identity as well as a distinctive actual or imagined characteristic of a well-known historical person" (205). The joke involves winding up the doll, after which it performs the distinctive action which makes up the doll persona's characteristic comic script. Some of these "doll jokes," like some "little moron jokes," are relatively "harmless" (not "sick") such as:

> The Eisenhower doll: wind it up, and it does nothing for eight years.
> The Elizabeth Taylor doll: wind it up, and it wrecks two marriages.
> The Dean Martin doll: wind it up, and it gets drunk.
> The Brigitte Bardot doll: wind it up, and it drops its towel.

Others have a determinedly "sick" cast:

> The Marilyn Monroe doll: wind it up and it commits suicide.
> The Roy Campanella doll: wind it up and it sits.
> The Helen Keller doll: wind it up and it walks into walls.
> The Lenny Bruce doll: wind it up and it laughs at the Helen Keller doll.
> The Eichmann doll: wind it up and it makes lampshades.
> The Leprosy doll: wind it up and it rots.
> The Hanukkah doll: wind it up and it walks into a gas chamber.

The Cerebral Palsy doll: wind it up and it sings, "I'll Never Walk Alone."
The Muscular Dystrophy doll: wind it up and it falls down.

The history of the sick joke cycle regarding "dead babies" was traced by Dundes (1979) as going back at least as far as the "Ruthless Rhymes" of 1899. He traces it from there, as I do, through the "Little Audrey" stories of the 1930s, the Bloody Marys of the 1950s and two other forms of sick humor popular in the 1970s "sick Jesus jokes" and the "good news/bad news" format. The former includes items such as:

Why doesn't Jesus eat M&M's? They keep falling through the holes in his hands.
What were Jesus's last words? "What a helluva way to spend Easter vacation!"

The latter can be represented by a joke I heard after moving to Georgia in 1969. The state's governor at the time was fiery Lester Maddox; "Axehandle Lester" they called him, for his headline-grabbing habit in his fried chicken days of running blacks out of his restaurant by wielding an axe handle against them, in violation of federal civil rights laws.

Doctor: Gov. Maddox, I have good news and bad news for you.
Maddox: What's the good news?
Doctor: You have six months to live.
Maddox: That's *good* news? What's the *bad* news?
Doctor: You have sickle cell anemia. [A disease unique to black Americans.]

The "dead baby" joke cycle included the following:

What's red and swings? A baby on a meathook.
What is blue and sits in a corner? A baby in a baggie.
What is blue and stiff? Same baby three days later.
What's red and green, red and green? A baby going through a lawnmower.
How do you make a dead baby float? Two scoops dead baby and one pint root beer.

Dundes claims that the dead baby joke, like all folklore, reflect what is going on in the culture, and that "If we do not like the image, we should not blame the mirror." What is wrong with the culture, he further claims, is our more modern attitude toward babies and sex.

Having sexual relations without wishing to have babies or even the very knowledge of the fact that abortion clinics are a part of modern society has provided a

source of anxiety which I believe is clearly a factor in the generation and transmission of dead baby jokes. (157)

Dundes also reports evidence that "dead baby jokes" are spreading to Europe.

The next group of *topical* sick jokes to be discussed is the last of this section. These are the cycle of jokes which grew up around the tragedy of the *Challenger Seven* space shuttle which blew up seventy-three seconds after liftoff on 28 January 1986. One day after the explosion, according to Simons (1986), California school kids were enjoying:

What does NASA stand for? Need Another Seven Astronauts.

Later answers to the question above became:

No Aging Survivors Agency
National Aquatic Sports Agency
Not A Seal Anywhere [A defective seal was diagnosed as the cause of the accident.]
Now Accepting Seven Applications

Some "classic sick jokes" hit on the dead astronauts:

What is the official NASA cereal? Space Crispies.
What do the sharks eat at Cape Canaveral? Launch meat.

Even racism got into the act:

Why did *Challenger Seven* have only one black astronaut?
No one knew it would blow up.

The only well-known name among the seven dead astronauts was the civilian teacher, Christa McAuliffe, who was to "teach a lesson from space." Being the "name" astronaut, many of the sick jokes concerned her:

How do we know Christa McAuliffe had dandruff? They found her head and shoulders [mentioned earlier as a "Vic Morrow" sick joke].
Why did Christa McAuliffe skip her shower before launch?
She expected to wash up on shore [used earlier here in relation to Natalie Wood].
What were Christa McAullife's last words? What's this red button for?
What were the *Challenger* commander's last words? Don't touch that button, bitch.

What were Christa McAuliffe's last words to her husband?
You feed the dog; I'll feed the fish.

There has to be very good reason for the proliferation of sick humor such as has been chronicled in this chapter. Sick jokes are circulated mostly by word-of-mouth, as *folklore*. The mass media had real trouble handling it in public discourse. Self-censoring and fear of reprisal from all directions keeps newspapers and electronic media, especially, from repeating much of this. In fact, Smyth (1986) reports that "a Los Angeles radio broadcaster was reputed to have been fired for repeating two *Challenger* jokes over the air." Smyth quotes a von Hoffman (1986) magazine article as his source.

According to Smyth (1986), "Sick jokes offend in two respects: their targets [butts] are aspects of the culture usually considered immune from joking, and the jokes are often disgusting (gross) and/or violent." According to the laughter = winning concept, the loser is always quite evident, and "loses" in a substantial (gross) manner; the winner is the audience of the joke on whom *no* catastrophe has descended. By adopting the "play frame" of joking behavior, we allow ourselves to enjoy our primitive appreciation of violence, gore, and destruction in safety, both physical and social. This may represent a descent into a more childish mode of behavior; if so, so be it. Most play, after all, is a kind of return to childhood, a way of forgetting the stresses and strains of adult reality. Play is a socially-accepted way to regress from the laws of decency and morality imposed upon us by the necessity of living in large groups of faceless strangers. Play is much akin to folklore.

As Dundes explains:

> Folklore provides a socially sanctioned outlet for the discussion of the forbidden and tabooed. American idealism proclaims the Christian principle of "love thy neighbor" and celebrates such political rhetoric as "all men are created equal." Yet not all Americans really love their neighbors or believe in equality. Accordingly, American ethnic humor permits the expression of hate and the indulgence in the articulation of inequality. In similar fashion, we can see that if Americans worship health and refuse to deal with disease—even after being struck by it— then it might reasonably be expected that American folklore would in this as in so many analogous instances treat in fantasy what is avoided in reality. (146)

As I write this page (20 October 1993) I read in the newspapers that controversy is arising over a new video game for the kiddies called "Mortal Kombat" in which the on-screen combatant can be directed to decapitate or "rip out the spine of" his enemy, producing plenty of bloody gore on the interactive screen. Parents may rise up in arms at this straw breaking some camel's back, but I would rather have my children exercising their natural-but-culturally-suppressed aggression in video games and sick humor than in the real-life hardware-assisted combat that is presently decimating and terrorizing our school-age population.

Before leaving the realm of humor in death, destruction and disaster, we must take up it's most popular nonverbal form—*slapstick*, which fits the "win/lose" theory to a "t." As Fry (1963: 11) puts it: "Whatever the specific form, the general theme of slapstick is contest."

Slapstick is that form of humor that is physical, visual, nonverbal, and playfully violent. It would be difficult, indeed, to argue that this physical kind of humor does not compare directly to "winning," with both a loser and a winner for each occasion.

The "slapstick" was originally a device consisting of two thin boards so connected that when one comedian or clown hit another with it, a very loud *slap* was heard, no matter how light and harmless the blow. Eventually the name of the device came to mean any comedy based on roughhouse, horseplay, or mock physical assault. Clowns, mostly mute throughout history, have specialized in this form of entertainment.

Writing about slapstick is difficult because it is nonverbal and visual. But I will try, anyway, and hope that I can turn the words of this section into pictures in your mind.

Slapstick consists, of virtually *nothing but* mock aggression. It includes the pratfall, the kick in the seat of the pants, the whacking of the head or body with a stick or mallet, the pie in the face, the sudden departure by trapdoor, the quick drenching from a sea of various liquids, a two-fingered poke in the eyes, the accidental spill of food or drink, touching of or sitting on "wet paint," the uneven, lurching gait of the funny drunk, the tumbling, rolling fall down the stairs, teetering scarily on an unstable ladder, mightily striving to maintain one's security while hanging from high buildings or mountains, two human heads knocked together, calamitous destruction of property, and so on.

Circus clowns predominate as the archetypical purveyors of slapstick. But clowns need not be in whiteface.

Comedian Chevy Chase has nearly made an entire career of pratfalling his way through TV's *Saturday Night Live* and, since then, a number of movies. He lately claims to be getting too old to take his normal number of pratfalls, but that is what he is most remembered for. Also in his younger days, Red Skelton was the supreme clown, with his wacky characters, rubbery face, and ungraceful full-body collapses to the stage floor. The Three Stooges made two careers, one in the movies of the forties, and another in TV of the fifties and sixties, with their crude slaps and head-knockings (greatly augmented by sound effects).

Many animated cartoons rely almost exclusively for their humorous impact on slapstick. Two of the most popular such cartoons, first at the movies, then on Saturday morning TV, are *Tom and Jerry* and *The Roadrunner*.

Tom (the cat) and Jerry (the mouse) are animals; thus they do not talk (even though they sometimes sing, and they also, apparently, can read); their humor, therefore, must be nonverbal. It must be slapstick.

The usual scenario has Tom pursuing Jerry with some sort of mayhem in mind to commit on the little mouse. Tom is often stymied in his murderous pursuit of Jerry by the family mastiff. Both Tom and the dog wind up being slammed by clubs, fry pans, boards, trees, hammers, and so forth; Tom will seek sure haven in a closet, only to find the dreaded dog hiding there. The offscreen trashing of Tom by the canine sounds like the total destruction of a sizeable housing project.

Equipment is brought to bear on the counterfeit demolition derby: Tom is set to fleeing with a string of bursting firecrackers tied to his tail; he is blown sky-high by dynamite; shot from a cannon into whose muzzle he has crawled in search of Jerry; he gets frozen stiff and shot as an arrow from a bow into a target bullseye, and so on.

Wiley Coyote's frenzied attempts to catch the Roadrunner for his dinner constantly backfire. Tying rockets to his body to make his foot-speed equal to that of the bird, Wiley shoots past our hero to flatten himself against a boulder. Setting up a cannon to blast his prey, Wiley is stymied when the cannon refuses to fire; poking his head inside the barrel to investigate, Wiley—well, you know what happens. You saw the cartoon too.

Mr. Magoo can talk (voice by the late Jim Backus), but his comedy stems from the fact that he can not *see*. He is *blind*. As a result, he gets into all kinds of trouble, much of which could result in his demise.

Bugs Bunny and Elmer Fudd can talk, also, but their resultant comedy is all too seldom verbal; it is sheer slapstick.

The first motion pictures were silent, of course. For comedy, then, they had to rely strictly on visual humor—slapstick. They specialized in mock mayhem on the flickering characters from as harmless (yet deflating) as a pie in the face to potentially dangerous (but quite survivable) exploding rooms.

A scene from Laurel and Hardy's *Two Tars* does for the trashing of automobiles what other silent movie scenes got from pies in the face and exploding rooms. "The Boys" play two U.S. sailors on shore leave. They have picked up two bimbos in their rental open-top Model T and have come to a stop at a road construction site at the head of a double-line of vintage jalopies.

While stuck there they are bumped from the rear by a sedan driven by the great Edgar Kennedy. Hardy retaliates; he pulls up, then reverses back into Kennedy's car, puncturing the other car's radiator. Kennedy backs up, slams forward into the boys' car again; they move up, slam back into Kennedy's car again.

Kennedy exits his vehicle, walks up to the boys' auto, and kicks it in the side, soundly. Twice. Stan marches back to Kennedy's car, wrestles off one of his headlights, and slams it to the pavement. He then gives it a mighty placekick, propelling it back through the windshield of the car behind Kennedy's. The miffed driver of this car walks up and argues with Laurel and Hardy, but gets no satisfaction. He then deliberately pops a big, gay balloon on the hood of our heroes' machine, which piques the girls. Laurel and Hardy stride back to the offender's car and, each taking hold of a front wheel, jerk both off their axles.

Now a pushing match erupts among the drivers, and Kennedy is shoved back across the road where a second line of cars sits. Kennedy crashes against a car heavily laden with bundles, a rolled carpet, suitcases, and so forth—all of which now spill off onto the roadway.

As the driver of the accidentally-unloaded auto complains and tries to make repairs, Stan starts hand-cranking their gas buggy so they can leave. But Kennedy jumps in his car and rams our foursome's vehicle from the rear, pushing it into and over the hapless Stan Laurel, who climbs out from under, covered with dirt and grease, fighting mad again. He and Ollie now go back to Kennedy's car and rip its radiator off. When Kennedy loudly protests, they tear off one of his front doors.

Some truck drivers behind Kennedy begin yelling at "the boys," just as another driver arrives with a basket of fruit. There is some fruit-throwing-into-faces, which draws more potential contestants into what is developing into a chaotic riot. One combatant is thrown across the road into a Model T coupe, which falls over on its side.

Kennedy's girlfriend goes up to the boys' car and messes up the blond hair of one of the bimbos, who retaliates with a grease-gun shot to the face of her tormenter. After a verbal taunt from a guy in another coupe, the boys go over and peel his front fenders/headlights back even with the coupe's doors.

As things degenerate into a general melee, a motorcycle cop arrives and attempts to take charge. As a result, the vehicles move out, most in various stages of destruction; the cop's cycle is run over and flattened, and the girls desert the boys, who end up being chased by all the other cars into a railway tunnel. Of course, a train comes through while they are inside, and they come out the other end squeezed and flattened to half the original width of the car. *Two Tars* is a comedy classic.

What has been said of slapstick can readily be applied to another of the "lowest form" of humor: the practical joke.

The practical joke, like slapstick, can be totally nonverbal, as in the case of the "lost purse." Here the prankster places a rich-looking purse on the sidewalk or some other place where it is likely to be seen by his friend. As the friend, spying the purse, reaches down for it, anticipating a rich prize, the concealed joker pulls the purse away with a hidden string. The victim feels disappointment (and the joker and observers feel the delight of superiority); once the victim recognizes that his "loss" was *play* and not *real*, he too can laugh.

But the practical joke can involve verbalization, sometimes to quite an elaborate extent. A popular movie, *The Sting*, was one great, monumental practical joke on a gambler. TV shows such as *Bloopers and Practical Jokes* portray quite intricate and detailed stunts pulled upon unwary celebrities. In one of these a large truck full of pigs arrived at the smallish home of an actress and her husband with "official" written orders to deliver the swine to her home. The actress was genuinely discomfited at this prospect, and her husband (in on the gag) *appeared* equally unhappy with the truckload of live pork. After several agonizing minutes of effort to be rid of this shipment, the actress, once told of the joke, collapsed in a paroxysm of relief and laughter. The long-running *Candid Camera* (formerly, *Candid Microphone* on radio) employs the practical joke as its raison d'être. In one famous episode a woman coasted into a service station in her car and complained that it "quit running." The perplexed attendants, upon opening the hood, found the engine missing! They were baffled! We so enjoy the feeling of superiority over the discomfiture of the victims of these episodes! Today's *America's Funniest Home Videos* and *Rogan's Heroes* continue the hilarity of physical falls, spills, embarrassments, denudings, and plans-went-wrong.

Beginning in the next chapter we now take up and analyze verbal humor. "Different types" of verbal humor, but this is no claim that these "types" represent valid *categories* that make up all-inclusive and mutually exclusive groupings of humorous material. For no valid argument for such a taxonomy has yet to be made. The kinds of humor chosen for analysis in the following chapters only represent *types* in that they have been useful categorizations.

4

Comic Scripts:
Laughing at People, Groups, and Concepts

Is there any group I haven't offended yet?
—Frequent quip of standup comic Mort Sahl

Laughing at jokes is a very pleasant activity for most folks most of the time. During the telling and hearing of jokes, the people involved usually are in a pleasant and convivial mood, bonded together in the pleasant fellowship that comes from shared laughter at humorous situations. Occasionally a joke-teller is surprised, perhaps even dumbfounded, by a negative reaction from a listener who bristles in indignation at the "insult" imbedded in a joke.

I was once a member in a social group that evolved into joke-telling. Considered something of an "expert" on humor, I was queried and encouraged to expound on the subject, and to give examples of various "kinds" of humor. The subject turned to "Little Moron" jokes (see previous chapter), very popular during the 1930s and 1940s, and I gave some examples. For instance, I pointed out that many such one-liners merely poked fun at the low intelligence of "little morons" by exaggerating their moronity beyond reasonable limits:

> Did you hear about the little moron who stayed up all night studying for his blood test?

> Did you hear about the little moron who took a ruler to bed so he could tell how long he had slept?

During this joke-telling session everyone laughed except one lady, who, her facial expressions told me, was growing more and more irritated. She finally broke up the session by confessing that she was not amused.

75

She was a teacher of the Educable Mentally Retarded (EMRs), and did not enjoy hearing her "little morons" ridiculed. She empathized with the *losers* of these jokes.

Ordinarily we enjoy jokes based upon stupidity (because we win!), no matter who is the butt of the joke. But when the stupidity (or any other shortcoming) is assigned, for the purpose of the joke, to a person, a group, or an institution dear to some listeners, they can respond with negative, not positive affect. This result is unfortunate, since "Whatever the esthetic and moral judgment of them, ethnic jokes, comic insults, and dirty jokes are the popular humor of America" (Schutz 1989: 167).

Most jokes usually involve "anonymous" people and so are rarely offensive. Stories that open with introductions such as "This guy was driving down Interstate 81 when..." or "A man walked into the post office to..." or "A lady pushing her cart down a supermarket aisle..." or "Two fellows in a bar are arguing over..." rarely produce a noticeable sting in the audience unless someone therein happens to make a psychological or social connection to the butt of the joke.

In jokes involving such anonymous people (or, animals representing humans through *analogy*) the "comic script," the important event or characteristic of human nature or human failing that makes the joke funny is *universal*. For instance, in slapstick comedy the comic scripts of persons being (nonseriously) injured by falls, explosions, blows, or property getting demolished almost always evoke our laughter under the "play frame" conditions.

In jokes ridiculing faceless men and women we laugh at the comic scripts involving humans' failures to be perfect. As William Hazlitt (in Wells, 1923) put it:

> We laugh at [human] absurdity; we laugh at deformity. We laugh at a bottle-nose in a caricature; at a stuffed figure of an alderman in a pantomime,... A dwarf standing by a giant makes a contemptible figure enough.... We laugh at the dress of foreigners, and they at ours. Three chimney sweeps meeting three Chinese...laughed at one another till they were ready to drop down. Country people laugh at a person because they never saw him before. Any one dressed in the height of the fashion, or quite out of it, is equally an object of ridicule. One rich source of the ludicrous is distress with which we cannot sympathize from its absurdity or insignificance. It is hard to hinder children from laughing at a stammerer, at a negro, at a drunken man, or even at a madman. We laugh at mischief. We laugh at what we do not believe. We say that an argument or an assertion that is very absurd, is quite ludicrous. We laugh to show our satisfaction with ourselves, or our contempt for those about us, or to conceal our envy or our ignorance.

We laugh at fools, and at those who pretend to be wise—at extreme simplicity, awkwardness, and affectation.

People who question me about "my" superiority theory often ask, "How can I feel superior to *myself*?" Of course it is easy, in fact quite natural and normal, for us to laugh at the mistakes, misfortunes, and sins of *others*—but our *own*? Recently I sang a little song to my wife at home. She retorted with an old saw, "I used to wish that I could sing; now I wish *you* could." She then chuckled at her little put-down.

But why could I also laugh? Because I know I can't sing worth a hoot, and this shortcoming just brought to my attention is one that I hardly take seriously. I can feel superior to poor singing ability, just as I can feel superior to and disregard (not take seriously) most of my mistakes and shortcomings. Being able to do so makes one a "good sport," and indicates to others that you have "a good sense of humor."

One of the techniques which Dr. Albert Ellis uses in his Rational Emotive (psycho)Therapy is to get patients to see the absurdity of their ridiculous attitudes and feelings, and, by ridiculing them, overcome them (see Ellis and Harper 1975). In a similar vein, Mensa member Marilyn Vos Savant (*Parade*, 4 December 1994) advises in her column, "Ask Marilyn": "I believe that one becomes stronger emotionally by having more experience and *by taking life less personally.*"

Although we laugh at *universal* comic scripts common to all anonymous individuals, we laugh at some comic script supposedly common to all or most members of a group when the butt of the joke is that group. If there is any feeling of offense from ethnic or other jokes it usually arises from the assumption that the joke-teller enjoys the ridiculing of the joke's butt because of his/her ill-will, even hate for, the ridiculed group. Such an assumption is more than likely a grievous error. People tell, listen to, and laugh at jokes and humorous stories about Jews, Poles, blacks, Asians; the Irish, British, French; Baptists, Catholics, politicians, professors, students, judges, Masons, Newfoundlanders, Kerrymen, Belgians, women (especially feminists and "women drivers"), men (especially "male chauvinist pigs"), Egyptians, Italians, Greeks, homosexuals, psychiatrists, college deans, mothers-in-law, WASPs, New Englanders, Texans, New Yorkers, Southern Californians, Jewish American Princesses, and so on. The list is infinite. Can we actively hate every member of each of these groups? Of course not. The idea itself is ridiculous. And even if one *did* hate one or another of these groups about which we tell jokes, the joke-telling is likely to wreak the very least possible damage to the victims. Social or economic repression, physical assault, even pogroms or assassination would be far worse. As Davies (1990) puts it:

> ethnic jokes in general are not a good indicator of the joke-tellers' feelings toward the butts of their jokes, which may range from dislike and hostility to amity and affection. People do not necessarily dislike those whom they disesteem, and the throwers of custard pies do not regard their targets in the same way that those who hurl rocks or grenades do. (323)

While most such jokes are told by and for people of the "in-group," the results sometime "spill over to the target groups" where "it stings, but only verbally" (Schutz 1989: 175). And if the joke-teller is a public figure, serious repercussions occur.

Shortly after the 1976 Republican National Convention, Earl Butz, Secretary of Agriculture, was flying first class in an airplane with Sonny Bono, Pat Boone, and John Dean, later to be a leading figure in the Watergate scandal.

> After Butz had initiated the conversation with a joke about sexual intercourse between a dog and a skunk, discussion soon turned to politics. Boone asked why the party of Lincoln was not able to attract blacks. Butz responded, "I'll tell you what coloreds want.... First, a tight pussy; second, loose shoes; and third a warm place to shit" (Klumpp and Hollihan 1979: 20)

This was not the first time the loquacious secretary had gotten into trouble with his humor. In November 1974 he was asked about the Pope's stand on birth control. He responded in a fake Italian accent: "He no playa the game, he no maka the rules" (Butz 1976). This remark angered a number of Italians and Catholics.

Butz did not realize, at the time of his comments on blacks, above, that Dean was at the time working as a reporter for *Rolling Stone*. Dean dutifully reported Butz's racial slurs, which were mentioned in the publication, and subsequently published literally in at least two newspapers (Klumpp and Hollihan 1979). The scandal began to rub off on President Ford, who, reportedly against his wishes, had to ask Butz to resign. As he was cleaning out his office, Butz told a reporter: "You know, I don't know how many times I told that joke, and everywhere—political groups, church groups, nobody took offense, and nobody should. I like humor. I'm human" ("Exit Earl" 1976).

Of course, it is my thesis that humor directed at specific characteristics of ethnic and other groups does spring from the natural aggressiveness and competitiveness of the human psyche. But couched within the humor frame, the hostility is reduced to *play*, and satisfies our basic urge to "win" over anyone or any thing in a purely *symbolic* way. And usually when we practice this "play aggression" we expect to be performing it among like-minded fellows. As Schutz (1989) says, "the primary purpose of the [ethnic] humor is an in-group cementing of the fellowship of the members..." (175).

Jokes about groups, be they ethnic, racial, professional, or national make fun of some *characteristic* of the particular group. Now, it seems to matter what we call this characteristic. Many writers refer to the *stereotype* of the "stupid" Pole, the "canny" Jew, the "militaristic" German, and so forth. Others complain that to speak in terms of "stereotypes" is to conclude that people have an absolute belief in these "mental shortcuts," that they are "universal" and inherent to a particular group. Davies (1990), as do I as mentioned above, prefers the term "comic script."

He points out that "there are many comic ethnic scripts for which there is no corresponding significant and seriously held stereotype and there are many ethnic stereotypes that have had serious consequences but have not given rise to jokes" (6–7). As one example, for instance, the Germans are branded with the comic script of "militarism," although most German men now shun military service, whereas Japan, who fought most ferociously in World War II, whose soldiers often preferred death to surrender and committed horrid war crimes on victims and prisoners, mostly escape jokes making fun of Japanese militarism.

> An American soldier married a German war bride. They got along well until it came to the question of how to raise the children. He wanted them to grow up and go into business; she wanted them to grow up to invade Poland.

The above joke would suffer seriously from substituting "Japanese" for "German" war bride and "Manchuria" for "Poland."

As noted in an earlier chapter, many writers object to the theory of humor labeled as "superiority," "aggression," "conflict," and so on. One of the most notable and prolific of these dissenters is Christie Davies. He says in a footnote to the introduction of his book:

> My own main criticisms are that those who seek conflict, hostility, and aggression in and behind jokes (a) confuse the element of aggression inherent in many forms

of play involving competition, rivalry, etc. with the "real world" aggression of pogroms, riots wars.... (b) use these terms as a ragbag explanation of why jokes exist, without discriminating between types of conflict, reasons why a conflict exists, intensity of conflict, etc. In consequence, they are able to shuttle between the individual, social psychological, and social uses of the terms in a superficial and misleading way and tend to exaggerate the level of conflict and its importance for the joke-tellers. (1990: 326)

I insist that I am guiltless of charge (a), above; I concede that the conflict in humor is symbolic, that it is play. I do not imply that joke-tellers are potential pogrom-instigators, rioters, or warriors; but that the conflict is *real* and is based upon the particular kind of nervous system we have inherited from our biological ancestors over millions of years of evolution. And in the sense that it is symbolic and "playful," it remains largely "unconscious." By specifying what I mean by playful and symbolic, just above, I mean to also escape from Davies's charge (b) in the quote above.

I wish to state my position as clearly as I can. My point is that humor consists of basically two elements: one is conflict, contest, competition, aggression, hostility, or whatever synonym you wish. The other is "sudden perception" of the result of the contest, a "win" and a "loss." And that *the substraction of the first element from the text of a so-called humorous incident or story* makes the humor *vanish*, whereas the loss of "suddenness" can eliminate or greatly reduce the humor.

Now, in order to understand who "wins" and who "loses," we must be able to understand the joke. That is, we must be able to cognitively comprehend the content of the joke, or whatever; and then we must be able to understand what happens in the "punch line" that makes for a sudden "victory" and/or a sudden "defeat." Telling a joke whose audience does not "get it" can be a frustrating and unrewarding experience. While speaking to a local parent/teacher/student audience in a nearby small town I used a joke as example.

In 1961 Aristotle Onassis, the Greek shipping Tycoon, was shopping for a house to buy in the Los Angeles area. One house he visited was that of the late silent screen star, Buster Keaton. While Mr. Onassis stood in the courtyard gazing at the back of the mansion, his photographer, who accompanied Mr. Onassis everywhere and chronicled his travels, took a picture of his boss, with the house in the background. He entitled the picture, "Aristotle Contemplating the Home of Buster."

The joke met with mystified silence; the audience had never heard of the famous Rembrandt painting, *Aristotle Contemplating the Bust of Homer*, on which the joke was a reverse pun.

And this brings me to the point about what makes ethnic, racial, etc. humor such a popular commodity: the comic scripts we all associate with each group makes for a kind of shorthand, a use of common knowledge to make the jokes understandable. When one starts by saying, "There are these two Poles in a bar..." we adopt the play frame that informs us, "This joke is probably going to be concerned with *stupidity*." We don't have to be told, "There were these two really stupid guys in a bar..." And when we hear "This guy goes to Confession and tells the priest..." we automatically cue up what in our apperceptive mass is associated with the comic script "Catholic" (confessed sins, penance, Hail Mary's, forgiveness, catechisms, etc.). The opening of the joke, thus, prepares us for fun, for symbolism, for exaggeration, for unreality, for the chance to laugh at a foible or two of a kind of person whom we know pretty well. It does not matter that we do not nor need not believe in and/or hate the Pole for his alleged stupidity or the Catholic for his sectarian beliefs and practices. We *know* the comic script and delight in the sudden deprecation based thereon.

Thus, with the exception of my discussion of the pun in chapter 6, I leave the speculation (or refusal to speculate) on the motives (and the direction and intensity of those motives) of joke-tellers and their listeners to others. I do not wish to link certain kinds of jokes with certain sociological events or political movements at particular points in time, a task which Davies (1990) has accomplished so formidably. As an empiricist I am always looking for data more forcefully linking cause and effect. I have been skeptical of assertions of social/political/economic geneses of humor types ever since Gerald Walker argued in a 1957 *Esquire* piece that the so-called sick humor (Bloody Mary's, etc.) was a unique and distinct product of 1950s America. (See chapter 3 for my discussion of the topic.)

In his discussion of the Polish joke, Bier begins:

> The persistence of the "Polish joke" is a puzzling question in any theory of American humor. Since it is a subset of ethnic jokes and of derogatory humor in general, including sexist humor, we may be best advised to place it, first, in its historic context to better gauge the anomaly it has become. (1988)

I believe that the "Polish joke" need *not* be put into any historical perspective to understand it's persistence or even its existence. Sydney Harris (1972) has pointed out that every civilized group has had its own "out-group" to ridicule. Citing linguist Mario Pei, he points out:

The earliest Slavs called the neighboring Germans "Nemets," which means "mute" or "dumb." On the other hand, the word "slaves" comes from Slavs who were captured in battle. In France syphilis is called "the English disease;" in England it is called "the French disease." The English invented the term "to Welsh," a term meaning to renege on an obligation and thus an insult to the Welsh people. (1972)

Harris points out that up in Wisconsin, where he spent his summers, the "Polish joke" is replaced by the "Belgian joke," owing to the large minority there of folks of Belgian descent, mostly farmers.

Most Polish jokes seem to make fun of Poles' intelligence, or lack thereof. The Pole's doctor told him that, to keep from having more children, he should use condoms. The doctor gave him a supply, telling him that he should put one on his organ each time he had intercourse with his wife. After the Pole's wife became pregnant, the doctor asked how it happened. The Pole replied, "I guess she got pregnant because we don't have an organ; so I put a condom on our piano each time we had sex."

Stupidity seems to be a very popular trait for comic ridicule in "out-groups." Davies (1990) provides a two-page chart of who finds whom stupid in what language, and what language the butts speak and what is the relationship between the language of the joke-tellers and the language of their butts. For instance, the Brits and Australians joke about Irish stupidity; the French and Dutch about the Belgians; the Italians about the southern Italians; the Canadians about the Newfies (Newfound-landers); the Spanish about the Yucatecos; West Canadians about the Ukrainians, the Irish about the Kerrymen, and so forth (52–53). For some reason he leaves off from the list the Italians as butts, although he provides at least one joke that so ridicules Italians as stupid:

An Irishman decided to become a Pole and asked an American surgeon if he could achieve such a difficult transformation. The surgeon said that he could but warned that it would be necessary to cut out a quarter of his brain. The Irishman agreed to this and went to the hospital for the operation. As he was coming round from the anaesthetic he saw that the surgeon was sitting next to his bed holding his head in his hands and looking haggard and distraught. Realizing that his patient was conscious again, the surgeon said: "I'm afraid I've made a terrible mistake; instead of cutting out a quarter of your brain, I cut out three quarters."

"Oh, no," screamed the patient, "Mama mia!"(63)

Of course, "stupid" jokes are very versatile, and can be used with numerous butts, depending upon the joke-teller, the audience, and their relationships to the butts.

They had to drop drivers' education from the curriculum at Georgia Tech. The mule died. (Told at the University of Georgia by UGA students; could be told on A&M at Texas, etc.)

Know how a Techie has been using your word-processor?
The "white-out" is still on the screen (ditto, above).

What do you get when you cross a Georgia Tech grad with a gorilla?
A retarded gorilla. (Substitute for "Georgia Tech grad" just about any kind of person you want to demean).

Poles and Italians are demeaned not just for their stupidity; they also get it for what Davies calls "dirtiness."

Why are there so many Italians in America?
One swam over and the others walked over on the oil slick.

Why does a Polish funeral require only two pallbearers?
There are only two handles on a garbage can.

Other "ethnic" groups are ridiculed for other characteristics or stereotypes which make for humorous scripts. As already mentioned, the Germans (but not the Japanese) are well known for aggressive militarism; the Italians (at least when it comes to their armed forces) are known for cowardice, as are Arabs (especially Egyptians); known for their "canniness" and sharp dealing when it comes to money are the Jews (taken up later in this chapter) and the Scots.

The Germans have instigated much war in recent history, and the strong role which the military has had in German governance over the years has contributed to the comic script of the Germans as aggressively militaristic and extremely "right-wing" on the political conservatism/liberalism scale. To hyperbolize the extreme conservatism of a politician or writer one often hears that "He is two steps to the right of Adolph Hitler."

I recently heard on my car radio a Larry King rebroadcast. He was welcoming a "liberal" journalist to the show, and noted that his guest might have some difficulty during the program since Pat Buchanan, a confirmed conservative who ran for the Presidential nomination of the Republican party in 1992, would be joining the show later. The liberal journalist replied that most people had an exaggerated notion of the imagined conservatism of Buchanan, since they got most of their information about Pat from his televised speech before the Republican Convention.

The journalist quipped that they would know Buchanan better "if they had read Buchanan's speech in the original German."

A man working in a German factory making perambulators learned from his wife that she was pregnant. She urged him to swipe a "pram" from his factory, since they would soon need one and could not afford to buy one. The German factory worker told his wife he would never be able to get away with it, whereupon she urged him to bring home one small piece at a time, then assemble it when all the parts were secured. The man did so, and after three months had all the parts down in his basement. One night he went down to construct the perambulator. After six frustrating hours he strode upstairs and confessed to his wife, "It's no use. No matter how I put it together, it still comes out a machine gun."

Klaus Meyers, introduced on TV's *Caroline's Comedy Hour* as "Germany's number one comedian," strolls onstage "here in America just six weeks." "My biggest obstacle," he lisps in a German accent, "is overcoming the image of my German race." He giggles to himself, nervously. "One wonders, could people laugh at one such as these." He pauses. Then: "Vell—let me assure you—ve have vays to make you loff."

Humor directed at *groups* would have to include "racial humor." I will deal with it briefly.

"Race" and "ethnicity" differ in a number of ways, of course. For purposes of arguing this book's thesis, however, racial humor is quite akin to ethnic humor since it ridicules the target race (or members thereof) for particular stereotypical attitudes, behaviors, or activities believed or thought to be inherent to that particular race. However, while the "stereotype" of an *ethnic* group can be more a "comic script" and not actually believed by those enjoying jokes about the group's script, with *race* the stereotype may be much more strongly believed and acted upon in more deliberate, non-joke ways.

For instance, Davies (1990) writes briefly about some of the comic scripts used to ridicule American blacks, the largest and perhaps most discriminated against racial minority in the United States. He identifies two major stereotypes and/or comic scripts used in anti-black humor, most of which is generated by southern U. S. whites: blacks' supposed tendency to steal chickens and their supposed cowardice when danger looms.

The chicken-stealing of blacks, Davies says, is highly related to the low economic status imposed on blacks by southern whites; unable to afford the more expensive food (meaning meat), the impoverished black must settle for chicken—which he still cannot afford to buy and thus must steal from his white neighbors.

Farmer, at night: "Who's that bumpin' around out there in my chicken house?"

Voice from chicken house: "Dey ain't nobody heah but us chickens, boss!"

Davies suggests that black cowardice jokes may have been begun by southern whites to make fun of the blacks who had to remain at their most humble and meek around white folks who would otherwise lynch them or burn them out of their meager homes. He also implies that the large number of "black cowardice" jokes that came into being shortly after World War I were prompted by the perception of some that black soldiers in the war showed less courage than did whites (which the evidence does not widely support); and that the high percentage of blacks assigned to "work" or "service" units (as opposed to *combat* units such as rifle companies) compared to that of whites may have also been a partial cause.

At any rate, there exist many jokes featuring the fearful black man, ready to run at the slightest glimmer of physical danger. For years this comic script was exercised and reinforced in American films by the antics of the black character actor "Stepin' Fetchit."

Quite often a member of a ridiculed group can enjoy the joke against his/her own group because of an ability to always shrug it off with a "there are those in our group like that, but not me" rationalization. I, myself, do not feel included when "absentminded professors" or "boring professors" are pilloried. I can shrug and say, "Yes, there are absentminded and boring members of my profession, but I am not like that." And the "play frame" of the joke allows this kind of wriggling off the hook.

And any first-quarter student of the "cognitive dissonance" theory can understand and explain the phenomenon. If two dissonant (that is, conflicting) propositions are forced into one's consciousness, some psychological or physical change must be made to stanch the discomfort of these two conflicting, grating ideas. If the two proposition are, "I am a professor" and "The joke about Professor X is funny because it exposes the comic script of Professors as being absentminded," the professor hearing the joke has at least five alternatives. The professor can (1) temporarily "forget" (use selective memory) he/she *is* a professor; (2) consciously or unconsciously exclude him/herself from the rank of "those other professors" who really *are* absentminded; (3) selectively perceive the joke as not making "absentmindedness" a comic script (bigots "mis-understand" humor that ridicules bigotry; see Cooper and Jahoda 1947); (4) enjoy the joke, recognizing and acknowledging (good-naturedly, as in "having a good sense of humor") his/her own occasional funny lapses of memory; or (5) become offended, saying something to the effect that "Tain't funny, McGee!" and warning the jokester to not make light of his profession.

Research shows that a common tactic, when one's group is made fun of, is not to include oneself among those ridiculed. The "joke frame" makes this possible, it seems to me, and different "joke frames" could produce different psychological results from the "same" joke. For in-stance, let us once again consider the matter over which Earl Butz was fired in 1976, mentioned above.

Although Butz called his remark a joke, it was considered by many as more of a general slur on all black men. Review his words:

> I'll tell you what coloreds want.... First, a tight pussy; second, loose shoes; and third a warm place to shit.

The literal, grammatical, and syntactical implications of these words and sentences is that Butz believes this description to be true of *all* black men; he seems to be saying what he believes. Ridiculous assumption or not, that is the implication of the words imbedded in that grammar and syntax.

But suppose Butz had said, without any prompting question from Pat Boone:

> I heard a good one back in Omaha last week. Seems this city councilman was working late in the office one night when the colored janitor enters. "Jim," the official says to the janitor, "don't ever get involved with politics. It'll drive you nuts." "Politics? Boss, I tells you dis—I is only innerested in three things: loose shoes,..."

A black man, especially a middle-class black man, could conceivably laugh and think, "Yeah, there are some n——s just like that."

Such a "You don't mean *me*" tactic can be used most successfully with anti-American jibes.

In the first place, there are no comic scripts which generally refer to Americans specifically and to the exclusion of other nationalities/groups. Begin a story about a Frenchman (especially a Parisian Frenchman) and you are not surprised to hear involved the comic script of "lover" (or even "kinky lover"); stories involving "Greeks" are apt to invoke the comic script of sodomy or hubris.

But Americans are not so well pigeonholed.

Oh, there are specific areas to which Americans are vulnerable to ridicule, of course. But not to the degree that the French are stuck as lovers, the Greeks as sodomites, the Poles and Kerrymen as stupid, the Germans as militarists, the Arabs and Italians as cowards, and so on. The Americans are a polyglot mixture that resists easy "stereotyping." But we Americans have our faults, and they are recognizable and become comic scripts to varying degrees.

> What do you call a person who speaks three languages? Trilingual.
>
> What do you call a person who speaks two languages? Bilingual.
>
> What do you call a person who speaks only one language? American.

Sure, we all recognize the fact that Americans refuse to learn foreign languages. But an American can get in his car and drive hundreds, maybe even thousands of miles in one direction and remain in a territory where English is the predominant language; overseas you could drive 1000 miles in Europe and pass through nineteen countries. Americans can easily rationalize monolingualism.

We suffer from the "ugly American" image, the Yank who tours foreign countries, dragging with him his own culture (or, expecting to find it wherever he travels), draped in cameras, outlandishly dressed, overbearing, shouting in English the more to make himself understood, and so on. But there is hardly a substantial body of joke literature about this creature, whom most "regular" Americans would dislike, also.

I recently viewed a comic routine of a Canadian chap. He came on and said something to the effect that:

> I'm from Canada. Canada is a funny country. A pack of cigarettes there costs seven dollars; but a heart transplant is *free*!

Was he making fun of his native country? Of course not. The real basis of the joke lurks in the misplaced values of our own country, America; it rebukes the United States for its own lack of humanity. In contrast to Canada, who makes medical service available to all people and continues a determined campaign to eliminate the deadly and dyscosmetic practice of cigarette smoking, the United States allows bargain-basement pricing of tobacco products (after governmental subsidizing of the growing and harvesting of the noxious weed), and allows its poorest citizens to die without even knowing they *need* a heart transplant because they can't afford to go to a doctor for a checkup.

The quip by the Canadian would not be funny in Sweden. Talk about "Only in America!"

A show celebrating the twentieth anniversary of The Comedy Store was televised in 1993. Appearing on the stage, among others, was Tamayo Otsuki, a female Japanese comic. Early in her act she reports that "Like Barney [the m.c.] say, I am from Osaka, Japan—and I come to America because I am lazy." This quip got a good laugh from the recent American anger over some Japanese business tycoons referring to Americans as generally lazy in comparison to Japanese; not exactly an American stereotype, but a timely and opportunistic ploy by Ms. Otsuki.

Most of us belong to at least one "reference group," an identifiable group based upon one or more common characteristics with which members feel a bond and a loyalty, a group which supports the individual members in observing common attitudes and behaviors. Individual adherence to group norms might vary from one's willingness to die for one's country or religious affiliation to the camaraderie felt among American men because of their love of the game of golf. Whether one can enjoy humor directed at one's reference group probably depends upon many factors, one of which would be the degree of intensity of dedication to the group's goals and ways of thinking and behaving. Religious fanatics rarely regard as funny jokes or cartoons aimed at their beliefs or practices. Not so for golfers.

Jones drove off on the eighteenth tee with his foursome, hitting a tremendous slice which disappeared to his right through the trees and across the highway. Taking his penalty, he teed up another ball and finished the round with his friends. Ten minutes later he was having a cold beer in the clubhouse with his fellow players, when a state patrolman entered the nineteenth hole and asked, "Who sliced that tee shot off the eighteenth a few minutes ago?"

"Why, I did," Jones confessed. "What happened?"

"What happened?" said the cop. "Your ball went across the highway, crashed through the window of a house there. This scared the dog, who ran out through the screen door onto the highway. A motorist, to miss the dog, swerved off the road and wrecked his car."

"My God," said Jones, "That's terrible. Is there anything I can do?"

"Yes, I think so," replied the policeman. "You could close up your stance, lighten your grip, and keep your head down more."

The evidence about enjoying humor ridiculing one's own and other, rival reference groups does not lead to firm conclusions. Two studies (Priest 1966; Priest and Abrahams 1970) found that American political partisans rated humor directed at their party and candidates less funny than humor directed at rival parties and candidates thereof, *but still found "funniness" in humor directed at their interest group.* Gruner (1972) found that supporters of Richard Nixon were better able to identify the critical theses of satires directed against his rival, George McGovern, than those directed against Nixon, himself. But Nixon supporters were able to recognize the anti-Nixon barbs, also, only in lesser numbers. LaFave (1967) argues that the "reference group" theory of humor appreciation seems to work in explaining religious, political, and anti-Semitic jokes, but not for anti-black jokes.

My own empirical research has disclosed that satires such as those by Art Buchwald (and others, as by Art Hoppe) argue theses intended by their creators that are completely "missed" by U. S. college students (see Gruner 1965, 1966, 1967a, 1971, 1987a, 1987b, 1988a, 1988b, 1992b; Pokorny and Gruner 1969). Further research (Gruner 1983, 1985) has disclosed that two factors that prevent college students from perceiving the intents of satirists are *low verbal intelligence* (as measured by the Scholastic Aptitude Test) and *high authoritarianism* as measured by the short form Rokeach scale. Other studies (Gruner 1972; Priest 1966; Priest and Abrahams 1970) indicate that, for *political* satire, political partisanship can interfere with the understanding of satires directed at one's own preferred candidate for office. A number of studies (Gruner 1989a, 1989b, 1990, 1992a, 1992b; Gruner and Gruner 1991; Gruner, Gruner, and Travillion 1991; Gruner and Nobles 1992) and others in process and forthcoming, have failed to reliably show any other factors which might help explain student's inability to perceive the satirical intent of satires.

However, my inclusion of the two Buchwald pieces, above, was based on the firm belief that anyone interested enough to pick up this book and to read this far would easily understand who are the "losers" in those columns, and who laughs along in sympathy with the winners.

In present-day America a movement is afoot that ebbs and flows in popularity, strength, and attention from the mass media. This movement, properly or improperly termed "Political Correctness" (or, PC for short) would eradicate from language, humorous or not, any words or phrases that would bring the slightest irritation to the most sensitive members of the group referred to in a politically *incorrect* manner. A recent flap at the University of Pennsylvania involved a case where a white male dorm resident yelled at some noisy black females frisking about on the green-sward late at night outside his window; he called them "water buffalos." This event created enough tempest to fill every teapot in the state of Pennsylvania.

Such PC-action is often directed at humor. I have made up a slide show to demonstrate, with humor, how humans practice *selective perception* in the communication process. Several cartoons in the collection show men looking at attractive women; the "thought balloons" over their heads show the same women in the men's minds' eyes: naked. When I have demonstrated this slide show at scholarly meetings I usually have to face several flinty-eyed feminists who complain bitterly about my "sexist" slides. It does no good that I admit that the cartoons are, indeed, "sexist," but that it is not the women who are demeaned by the cartoonists: it is the lust-filled *males* who are exposed, practicing the usual male foible of undressing every attractive woman "with his eyes." These complaining ladies not only dislike the cartoon humor, they don't even *understand* it.

The PC critics, it seems to me, would do themselves and their fellows more lasting good if they would preach, not censorship, but accommodation. It is unfortunately true that humor bristles with sharp barbs. And humor is not going to disappear from the face of the earth (unless the human race decides to vaporize itself). As Schutz says:

> Dirty jokes are a staple of popular humor.... Whatever the esthetic and moral judgment of them, ethnic jokes, comic insults, and dirty jokes are the popular humor of America. (1989: 167)

We all learn, as we grow up, that, being human, we have to take a certain amount of kidding, for faults and mistakes. We must become, at least to some degree, "good sports."

I am over six feet tall, with quite skinny legs. When I played basketball for Pincknevyille Community High School, several teammates hung on me the nickname of "Stems." Later, in college, some of my frat brothers made fun of the same skinny limbs by calling me "Pigeon." Blowing my stack, even resorting to fisticuffs, was obviously "out" for me. I learned to live with my nicknames. And, you know, I never once had a goal stymied, or spent an hour on a psychiatrist's couch as a result of that schoolboy ridicule.

How much more amicably could we all live if we possessed the breadth of "sense of humor" claimed personally by Raskin (1992). His paper defines that particularly human property, "sense of humor," about as well as any I have come across. In the next few paragraphs I hope to commit the unpardonable act of rendering in lay terms his concept which he defined in more scholarly terms.

Raskin says that simple cognition is important to the sense of humor. If you lack the intelligence and/or the knowledge to understand the comic scripts involved, and how they clash and switch at the punch line, your ability to perceive some humor will be limited. But he is most concerned (and so am I) with the breadth of topics which each of us will voluntarily welcome as a comic script. He makes basically two points:

1. There are two kinds of talk, "real" talk for communication ("It's ten o'clock") and "unreal" talk which we use for play, fantasy, etc., which is "untrue."
2. Humor uses "unreal" and "untrue" talk (earlier called the "play frame"). When we enter the "play frame" together, we absolutely massacre the teleological fallacy: animals talk, think, wear clothes, operate equipment, live in houses, etc. Drunks can walk up the sides of buildings, people can drop dead instantly, Martians land in Times Square, man-eating plants single out *vegetarian* jungle explorers for their next meal, and so on.
3. People with no sense of humor treat every subject with solemnity; they speak *only* to communicate with "real" talk.
4. Raskin (and I) can snuggle into a "play frame" and use the "untrue" language of humor to enjoy making fun of *any* topic.
5. In between the people in 3 and 4 are those who choose not to see a comic script in *some* topics: Little Morons, feminist topics, one's religion, and so on.

It would certainly be a different and more pleasant world to live in if everyone could and would find mirth in every human concept imaginable; of course, such a situation is quite improbable, given man's basic nature.

But even if we could reach such a utopia, random feelings and occurrences could intercede. As Raskin concludes in his paper:

> if you have strong feelings about a subject you will not appreciate a joke about it. Such a situation removes certain scripts from humor circulation for a person, and thus partially handicaps this person's sense of humor, sometimes temporarily. (9)

A specific area of ethnic humor that has received much attention from humor scholars is Jewish humor.

On 8 July 1992 I was attending an international conference on humor in Paris, France, sponsored by the International Society for Humor Studies and the University of Paris' CORHUM (*Comique le Rire et l'Humour*). In one sectional meeting on national and ethnic humor I attended, Professor Richard Raskin of Aarhus University, Denmark, presented a scholarly paper on the history of two "Jewish jokes." During his presentation he tried to draw a distinction between "Jewish jokes," which he defined as "jokes told by Jews among themselves" and "anti-Semitic jokes" (jokes *about* Jews told by and to non-Jews).

I later had the opportunity to converse with Professor Raskin and, because I was relatively ignorant on the subject, told him a joke I had recently heard, and asked him if he would classify it as a "Jewish joke" or an "anti-Semitic joke." The joke:

> A young Jewish professional on a business trip goes down to his hotel bar one evening for a drink. Seeing an attractive young lady several barstools away, he buys her a drink, which she acknowledges with a warm smile and inviting look. He moves down to a stool next to her and they begin to get quite friendly. After a few minutes of quite pleasant conversation, the young lady confesses: "Look, you're a nice guy and I don't want to mislead you—but I'm a pro, and I'll go up to your room with you, but it will cost you $100.00."
>
> After a brief thinking period the young man replies, "Heck, why not; let's go."
>
> On the way up the young couple keep up a continual conversation during which each discovers that the other is Jewish. After getting to the man's room the guy proposes: "Look, since we're both Jewish, I don't see why you can't give me a little discount."
>
> The young woman denies that she ever makes such a deal, but they banter back and forth over the price for some minutes. Finally the young woman relents: "OK, since we *are* both Jewish, I will give *you* a 20 percent discount. But I want you to know that at these prices *I'm making no profit at all!*"

Professor Raskin laughed heartily at the joke. But when I asked him if he thought it were "Jewish" or "anti-Semitic," he could only scratch his chin and reply, "I am not at all sure which it is."

And so it is with "Jewish humor." People disagree on what it is. Some even deny that it exists!

The Public Broadcasting System in 1992 produced a ninety-minute TV program entitled "The World of Jewish Humor," one part of the *Great Performances* series. In that program Mr. Shelley Berman, Jewish comedian, denied that "Jewish humor" was a distinct type of humor. Milton Berle, his colleague, also cast doubt on the distinctiveness of the classification. Ben-Amos (1973) has also argued that there is no such thing as "Jewish humor." In addition, Oring (1992), in a much more scholarly way, proposes serious doubts that what has been called "Jewish humor" exists, or at least that it has a history going farther back than the early-nineteenth century.

But the plethora of books on Jewish humor, both collections and critical analyses, seem evidence that the genre does exist; furthermore, international conferences devoted to the subject have been held in 1984 (Tel Aviv), 1986 (New York), and 1988 (Tel Aviv again), arguing for the existence of Jewish humor as a distinct entity, as well as do a number of scholarly papers and articles. One entire issue (1991, vol. 4, no. 1) of *Humor: International Journal of Humor Research* was devoted to the topic, under the guest editorship of Avner Ziv.

In that issue of *Humor*, Ziv gives what he himself believes to be the three main characteristics of Jewish humor:

1. An intellectual dimension: a desire to distort the reality, to alter it and make it laughable (and thus less frightening and threatening)....

2. A social dimension: trying to maintain internal cohesiveness and identity. By comparing "us" with "them" it is possible to show that even if "they" are stronger, "we" can still win, mainly by using our wits.

3. An emotional aspect: helping one to see oneself as one is, namely far from perfect. Making fun of some unsavory aspects of one's behavior or personality might help in accepting them. It can even show that they are not so terrible: the proof—I can even laugh at them. Another emotional aspect related to self-disparagement is the sympathy one earns from others, and being accepted is, and was for two thousand years, a serious problem for a wandering people. (146)

It is interesting to note that this definition of Ziv's differs somewhat from his earlier (1984) attempt, "Jewish humor can be defined as humor created by Jews, intended mainly for Jews, and which reflects special aspects of Jewish life" (11). This particular definition followed his general definition of "humor" as "a form of social communication with an intent to amuse, and a special cognitive and emotional nature, that causes a physiological reaction" (9). Both of Ziv's definitions seem to rule out "visual humor" or "physical humor" such as slapstick, or the humor to be found in the accidental physical, mental, or social misfortunes of human beings. Very few people trip themselves, stumble against a flimsy aboveground swimming pool, flatten one side of the pool, and allow all the water and children therein to cascade out onto the lawn in order to create "a form of social communication with an intent to amuse." Granted, these are the kind of videotaped misadventures which the producers of such TV shows as *America's Funniest Home Videos* deliberately present for our enjoyment, but that is not the usual intent of the original protagonists of these taped vignettes.

A 1984 effort by Davies (in Ziv, 1984) attempts to loosely delineate between and among three kinds of jokes: "Jewish," "anti-Semitic," and what he calls "Hebredonian" (this latter indicating jokes that are kind of ambidextrous: can interchange Jewish terms with Scottish terms, making the jokes "Caledonian"). I say "loosely delineate" because Davies himself admits early on (75) that "jokes involving Jews cannot always be easily or conclusively sorted into these three categories."

Davies opens his argument by providing two jokes which he says are irrevocably Jewish, and any attempt to convert them to *goyische* would be to do irreparable harm to their humor.

> For twenty years the same customer visited a certain Jewish restaurant and, without fail, always ordered the same dish—borscht! In all that time he never once complained about the food or service—the model customer.
>
> One evening, when the waiter had served the customary plate, the customer called him back to the table.
>
> "Waiter, taste this borscht!"
>
> "Why, what's the matter with it?"
>
> "Just taste it."
>
> "Listen, it's too cold, it doesn't taste right, whatever, I'll take it back and bring you another serving."
>
> "Taste the borscht!"
>
> "Why should I taste? You don't want it you don't want it. So I'll bring you a change. Why should I argue with a good customer?"
>
> The customer, his face dark with fury, stood up. "For the last time, *taste the borscht!*"
>
> Intimidated, the waiter sat down. "All right, if you insist." He looked around. "Where's the spoon?"
>
> "Ah-*hah!*" exploded the customer.
>
> * * *
>
> Mrs. Kotchin and Mrs. Mishkin sat rocking on the porch of Villa Lipshitz, a Catskill resort, when a young man approached.

"*Gottenyu*! exclaimed Mrs. Kotchin. "Look at that boy! Did you ever see such a big nose? Such shifty eyes? Such a crooked mouth?"

In a freezing voice, Mrs. Mishkin replied, "It so happens, you are talking about my son."

"Well," said Mrs. Kotchin, "on *him* it's becoming."

I demur from this exercise in classification. I feel that the borscht joke could just as well feature a gentile Russian in a nonethnic restaurant. Or why not an American ordering goulash in a Hungarian restaurant in New York? As far as I am concerned, the humor comes from the great lengths that the angry diner goes to in order to demonstrate that the waiter has mistakenly failed to provide the customer with eating utensils, not any particular element of "Jewishness."

Additionally, I believe that the names (and even the gender) of Mrs. Kotchin and Mrs. Mishkin could be altered without detracting from the humorousness of the joke.

Davies does better at illustrating Jewish-and-Jewish-only humor with examples applauding (but also mocking) Jewish accomplishments and talents, such as intelligence:

A man was approached in the street in Moscow and asked,

"Are you Jewish?"

"No," he replied, "I simply *look* intelligent."

Davies makes a better case for the inclusiveness and the mutual exclusivity of the "Hebredonian" and the anti-Semitic through exemplification.

For example, he cites the joke about the child rescued from drowning; his mother (or, aunt) confronts the child's rescuer and demands to know what happened to the youngster's cap. This works as well as a Jewish or a Scottish joke. The anti-Semitic jokes Davies explains as those showing Jews to be "diabolically cunning swindlers and enemies of society," the stereotypes in which the tried-and-true anti-Semite believes in his bones. He cites as the prime examples of this type those jokes, so ubiquitous mostly in the early part of the twentieth century, the many jokes portraying Jews as arsonists-for-profit.

In the popular collection by Novak and Waldoks (1981) it is argued that Jewish humor can be divided into two great historical golden ages, the "traditional" nineteenth-century humor typical of eastern Europe, and the more modern, twentieth-century brand. The "traditional" humor, they say, has roots going back to the medieval Purim *shpils*, or comic plays based on the story of Esther and other Bible stories.

Novak and Waldoks hedge on trying to define "Jewish humor." They tell us on page xx that it is *not* "escapist, slapstick, physical, cruel, polite or gentle," and that it does not "attack the weak or infirm." But then they admittedly contradict themselves by pointing out that the Marx Brothers used slapstick, Jerry Lewis and Sid Caesar are physical, Don Rickles is cruel, Sam Levenson is polite, and Danny Kaye is playful.

They offer broad statements of what they think Jewish humor *is*, which I truncate here: it "is substantive; it is *about* something.... can be sarcastic, complaining, resigned, or descriptive.... tends to be antiauthoritarian. It ridicules.... frequently has a critical edge which creates discomfort in making its point.... Jewish humor mocks everyone—including God."

In his *Encyclopedia of Jewish Humor* Spalding (1969) more critically defines Jewish humor.

> The typical old-time Jewish joke was often a sardonic, even merciless self-derogation that bordered on the masochistic.... It seems to me that the reason is plain enough: the narrator recognizes himself for what he is—a simple human being, subject to all the foibles of mortal mind and frailties of the flesh. And because he has moral and intellectual courage to recognize and then ridicule his own weaknesses, he sees no reason to spare the sensibilities of his adversaries for their own deficiencies. Therein lies the key to the difference between the Jewish and the anti-Semitic joke: the latter emphasizes the faults but never the virtues of the Jew. Nor should we forget that the target of the true Jewish joke is not necessarily an anti-Semite, as many believe, nor even a despotic government. Derision is more often directed at another Jew....(xv–xvi)

Nevo (1991) did a quantitative study of the matter. He presented jokes to students and asked them to rate the jokes on "Jewishness." The jokes contained either *no* "elements of Jewishness," or one, two, three, or four "Jewish elements." These "Jewish elements" were Jewish *names* (Moishele, Itsik, etc.), Jewish *roles* (Rabbi, Shamash, etc.), Jewish "cultural content" (Talmud, Midrash, etc.), or Jewish *language* (Yiddish, Hebrew words, dialect, etc.), Jewish *locations* (Synagogue, Cheder, etc.), Jewish *stereotypes* (mercantilism, stinginess, nose length, etc.). Nevo found that jokes without specific Jewish content were not rated as very Jewish, but, with each addition of a "Jewish element," the ratings of "Jewishness" went up.

Spalding makes that particular distinction, also. Spalding insists that only jokes that are funny because of specifically Jewish content and *not* jokes with mere Jewish characters make up "Jewish humor." For instance, he quotes a joke often told as "Jewish:"

On an El Al airliner from Tel Aviv to New York an elderly man is seated next to a proud new mother with an infant in her arms. The man lifts the baby's blanket, peeks at its face and exclaims, "*Oy vay!* What a monstrosity. Never in my life did I even see such an ugly baby!"

The mother is outraged. "How dare you!" she shrieks; then continues to berate the gentleman in a high-pitched scream. The stewardess hurries over to quiet things down. The young lady screams, "He insulted me!" The stewardess asks the gentleman to change seats several rows away, to which he agrees. Then turning to the mother, she says "Now, Little Mother, please calm down.

I will go back and bring you a nice cup of hot tea with lemon—and I'll bring a banana for your monkey."

Spalding rightly declares that this bit of cruelty could occur between people of any ethnicity/nationality on any national airline. It is not *necessarily* Jewish. On the other hand, he does provide an example of what he means by a joke with strictly Jewish content:

Rosie's Mama answers her phone. It is Rosie.

"Mama, I got married!" says Rosie.

"*Mazel Tov!*" replies Mama.

"I might as well tell you, he's a *goy*."

"So he's a *goy*! I'm prejudiced?"

"But Mama, he's also a Negro."

"All right, he's a *schwartzeh*. By me everybody should be so tolerant."

"Well, frankly, Mama, he's unemployed."

"*Nu*, so you'll support him. A wife should help her husband."

"But, Mama, we have no place to live."

"Don't worry, Rosie, darling. You'll stay right here in our house."

"But you only have one bedroom."

"That's all right. You and your new husband can sleep in the bedroom and Papa can sleep on the sofa in the living room."

"Yes, but, Mama, where will you sleep?"

"Rosie, dear, about me you got nothing to worry. The minute I'm hanging up *I'll drop dead*" ("*I'm sticking my head into the oven*," in another version).

As you can easily see, each of the two jokes, above, contain considerable aggression, thus a winner and a loser each, but only the latter is made funny because of it's uniquely Jewish content.

But for the central purpose of this book, when it comes to "Jewish jokes," as far as fitting into the "laughing = winning" theory, it matters not at all whether the joke can be considered "anti-Semitic" or simply

Jewish jokes told by Jews about and/or to other Jews. I do not even have to get into the argument over the *existence* of "Jewish humor" (which pleases me); for the joke always makes fun of (ridicules, if you please) some aspect of "Jewishness," or at least ridicules the stereotypes most of the world carries in their collective consciousness; either that, or else the joke champions some supposed "negative" Jewish stereotype as superior to (ridiculing of) some other person, group, or concept.

Mintz (in Ziv, 1984) dissects "Rabbi vs. Priest" Jewish stories into four categories. There is *critical humor*, told on members of other groups, that are highly critical, "relying upon negative ethnic stereotypes;" secondly, there is *self-deprecating* humor, critical of one's own group and accepting of the "negative stereotype;" third, he speaks of *realistic humor* which is "less critical" and, fourth, he considers *ironic humor*, which he defines as more "positive" than "negative." Mintz admits that the first two types utilize aggression, criticism, and so on (what I am calling "a winner and a loser"), but hedges in his description of the latter two as "more positive." But let's look at some of Mintz's examples to see how "positive" they are.

Mintz calls *realistic* and "without much criticism" those jokes about conversion to Christianity or intermarriage with Gentiles. One example: "A new [formerly Jewish] Christian impresses the priest with his knowledge of Christian holidays, until he gets to Easter, which he describes as 'celebrating Jesus's emergence from the cave, the spotting of his shadow, and his return for six more weeks of winter.'" My response: this joke may show "little criticism," but our new Christian has made a monumentally stupid *mistake* (and fool of himself) over which he ought to be roundly embarrassed (and at which his audience should be at least dumbfounded). Without this mistake the joke is not a joke.

To illustrate *ironic humor* Mintz gives us a string of "Rabbi/Priest confrontations," where the Jew triumphs (always at the expense of the *loser* Gentile). Mintz claims these "feature a gentle, but pointed confrontation between a rabbi and a priest..." One example:

Priest to rabbi during interfaith banquet: "When are you going to give up your antiquated customs and eat some of this delicious ham?"

Rabbi: "At your wedding, Father."

Good squelch. A win/lose situation. Rabbi 1, Priest 0.

Gentiles enjoy jokes ridiculing the stereotypical Jewish traits just as they enjoy jokes ridiculing the stereotypical Scot, Irish, German, Italian, Arab, and so on. But, again, such enjoyment is usually quite innocent, and not intended as actual harm; for, to repeat: if one truly despised a particular ethnic group, ridicule would be the least deadly weapon available to operationalize that hatred. Again, a stereotype is merely a very handy kind of shorthand to provide the essential framework for understanding the content of a joke. Most gentiles who enjoy Jewish jokes are hardly anti-Semitic; and any "real" anti-Semite might enjoy Jewish jokes, but would hardly restrict his anti-Semitic behavior/attitudes to telling and/or laughing at them.

One feature of Jewish humor is supposedly the great extent to which it is used *by* Jews to make fun *of* Jews and Jewishness. Because of this feature Jewish humor has been labeled masochistic. Most writers deny this label. Much Jewish humor does engage in what we could call self-deprecation. But much Jewish humor ridicules non-Jewish people, institutions, and governments, also. And the Jewish penchant for self-derogation, at least according to Spalding, shows that, because the Jew has "the moral and intellectual courage to recognize and then ridicule his own weaknesses, he sees no reason to spare the sensibilities of his adversaries for their own deficiencies."

Another reason for Jewish self-derogation in their humor is given as a defense mechanism. It is "a good offense is the best defense" kind of ploy. As Martin Grotjahn has said, "One can almost see how a witty Jewish man carefully and cautiously takes a sharp dagger out of his enemy's hands, sharpens it so that it can split a hair in midair, polishes it until it shines brightly, stabs himself with it, then returns it gallantly to the anti-Semite with the silent reproach: Now see whether you can do it half as well" (in Novak and Waldoks, 85).

This image of Jewish self-immolation is disputed by Davies (1991) who argues:

> This [Grotjahn's] is a vivid but misleading image, for the point of getting hold of the dagger is not only to demonstrate superior dexterity but to switch daggers, so that an innocuous rather than a potentially envenomed weapon is used. This is a tactic that has both frustrated and infuriated anti-Semites (see Crosland 1922: 18; Hitler 1974: 287), who see Jewish humor as humanizing those whom they wish to demonize and as making a people whom they seek to represent as a malign threat appear comically harmless. (203)

Davies's argument here has a modern and empirical counterpart. Norman Lear intended his TV situation comedy, *All in the Family*, as a positive force in ameliorating the climate of racial and religious bigotry in the United States. He expected that the ridiculing of Archie Bunker's blatant prejudices would make these attitudes seem ludicrous and without merit. But what the program achieved was creation of an image of Archie as a "loveable bigot" (Surlin 1973). Viewers inclined to initially agree with Bunker's point of view usually thought that he *won* the ideological arguments he had with his son-in-law, "Meathead." And even viewers who disagreed with Archie tended to "like" him, despite his offensive views of blacks, Jews, and so on. Vidmar and Rokeach (1974) later also studied the reactions of American and Canadian viewers to *All in the Family* and concluded the same as did Surlin. They begin the last paragraph of their article with, "On balance the study seems to support more the critics who have argued that *All in the Family* has harmful effects."

Davies (1991) also effectively argues that the fact that Jews tell jokes ridiculing Jews and Jewishness does not make for masochism or self-hatred. He points out empirical studies showing (1990) that many ethnic minorities tell jokes on their own groups, usually enjoying such jokes more than jokes about rival majority groups.

As stated early in this section, "Jewish humor," whether considered anti-Semitic or self-deprecatory, makes fun of so-called Jewish shortcomings, although they can be considered from another light. Davies quotes Mendel (1970) as declaring that such jokes are a defiant "This is the way we are, the way we always have been, and the way we always will be!"

But let us go back to the question posed at the beginning of this chapter, which we might re-phrase here as, "Just when is a 'Jewish joke' anti-Semitic and when is it a within-group enjoyment of the group's own 'Jewishness,' whether that means self-deprecation or not?" Or put another, more popular and common way, "When does a 'Jewish joke' cause 'laughing-*at*' and when does it cause 'laughing-*with*'?"

Among others, Saper (1991) provides a useful paradigm from cognitive-behavioral psychology for judging the answers to these questions. He proposes using the standard SORC model—where S stands for the stimulus (joke), R stands for the response (laughter, anger, petulance, puzzlement, etc.), O stands for organismic variables intervening between

S and *R* (such as tastes, preferences, personality, attitudes, etc. of the participants. The *C* stands for the consequences, both short- and long-term that tend to follow the joke-telling.

For the *S* to be a "Jewish" joke, it would have to contain "Jewish elements" (Nevo 1991). The *O* would refer to such as who is telling the joke to whom, for what purposes, with what attitudes, and so on. The *R* would be the attitudinal and behavioral responses of the listener(s). The *C* would be the more lasting effects of the joke-sharing. Take the following joke as an example:

> Manischevsky and Goldstein are about to face a Nazi firing squad. The SS officer offers the two condemned men blindfolds, which Manischevsky accepts with a nod of the head. Goldstein, however, demurs: "No, I tink not." His friend remonstrates against him: "Please, Izzy, don't make trouble."

Now if this joke (S) is told by a Jew-hating neo-Nazi, with the intent of demonstrating (once again) how spineless are Jewish men (O), and if it is enjoyed by another neo-Nazi (O, again) who laughs at this reminder of how cowardly he "knows" Jews behave (R), the joke is anti-Semitic; and the (C) is likely to be a strengthening in the belief of both bigots that Jews really are "yellow."

If, on the other hand, the joke-teller is a Jew, sharing the joke with another Jew, both are likely to smile and think: "Yes, that's us—peaceful and thoughtful to the end; we are really too dang nice for our own good."

But to reiterate, either of the two extremes of SORC, above, fit neatly into the laughing = winning theme of this work.

But, as also mentioned earlier in this chapter, many jokes with Jewish content champion Jewish characteristics, sometimes to the detriment of others. A few examples from Davies (1991):

> An elderly Jewish man walks into a jewelry store to buy his wife a present. "How much is this?" he asks the clerk, pointing to a sterling silver crucifix.
>
> "That's six hundred dollars, sir," replies the clerk.
>
> "Nice," says the man. "And without the acrobat?"

Some "Jewish humor" uses a "Jewish" comic script or trait to demean non-Jews and "uplift" Jews. Jews, for instance, are universally recognized for intelligence and desire for intellectual enrichment. A modern joke emphasizing this Jewish quality, while at the same time denigrating a nominally "superior" gentile, is the story of the teacher in a small, expensive private secondary school who has only one Jewish boy in his class. One day this gentile teacher tires of the Jew's continued superior achievement over his gentile classmates. "Isaac," the teacher scolds the boy, "You are the very embodiment of your people's greedy proclivities. Here you are, your parents pay the same tuition as do those of the other boys, and you must always take advantage of the situation and learn twice as much as anyone!"

One can hardly end a chapter like this without considering the phenomenon of the Jewish American Princess (JAP) jokes; especially as they have been associated with the "Jewish Mother" joke.

The JAP is a single, materialistic, overly-made-up, spoiled, pampered, over-indulged, whiny, nouveau-riche bitch; she may or may not be Jewish, but usually is, and she can be at once a voracious slut or a haughty, sexless tease. More than anything else, she is "defined by" the jokes about her:

> What's a JAP's favorite w(h)ine?
> "Aren't we going to Miami this year?"
>
> Why does a JAP close her eyes during sex?
> "To daydream about shopping" (or, "She can't stand to see a guy having fun.")
>
> What do you call a JAP nymphomaniac?
> "One who simply must have a man at least once a month."
>
> How do you know when a JAP has an orgasm?
> "She drops her nail file."

Obviously these are jokes ridiculing JAPs. The JAP is the loser, and the joke-sharers (if they enjoy the joke[s]) are the winners. But are they relatively innocent of real malice, or do they create real victims among the young women who seem to match the JAP stereotype? Are they merely innocuous, hyperbolized portrait-scraps of mythical beings too abominable to lead a living, breathing existence? Or do they create real or imagined misery to those they supposedly vilify? In compliance with the SORC model of joke consumption, I would say that it all depends on whom you ask these questions.

Spencer (1989) argues that JAP-baiting, especially on selected U.S. college campuses, has caused widespread heightening of anti-Semitism in both thought and deed. I invite you to read his own complete argument, but quote only his conclusion:

JAP-baiting on the college campus is far from harmless fun. It is a pernicious form of humor that communicates and reinforces a stereotype that is sexist and anti-Jewish in sentiment. It serves as an outlet for campus tensions of gender, race and ethnicity, region of origin, social class, and peer membership. The JAP is the scapegoat for these tensions, her harassment is masked in humor, and the activity is perceived as harmless fun directed at women who deserve no better. Humor, in this sense, serves as the primary mechanism for labeling, stereotyping, and communicating prejudice. (1989)

Spencer is supported by Mimi Alperin (1989), whose speech (later printed and distributed as a brochure by the Miami Chapter of the American Jewish Committee), was printed without editorial comment in *Humor*. To Alperin, the JAP joke is a dangerous and damning trend that threatens the status of Jews, men or women.

What once were considered harmless, in-group jokes told largely by Jewish comics to mostly Jewish audiences have escalated into an epidemic of hurtful, often hateful attacks of JAP-baiting, particularly on college campuses. I and many other Jewish women never thought the jokes were either funny or harmless.

Whereas Spencer and Alperin rail against the JAP joke for dangerously exacerbating anti-Semitism, Davies (1990) dismisses their argument with a "pooh-pooh" and then proceeds to an excellent explanation of just why Jewish men make up and enjoy jokes ridiculing both young Jewish women (JAPs, if you will) and the older, married, "Jewish mother." Davies in general dismisses ethnic humor as a serious tool of the bigot. He says that JAP jokes "are of indisputably Jewish origin and that the non-Jews who enjoy them are far more likely to be philo-Semitic devotees of Jewish humor in general than anti-Semites in disguise." Jokes are only forms of *playful* aggression (my point, exactly), and for its own sake. Once in a great while one single individual *might* choose the joke form to express his scorn for an out-group, but humor can be ambiguous enough to allow any individual to decide for him/herself what message it conveys. And hate and bigotry can be more clearly and forcefully expressed in less indirect verbal and nonverbal forms.

After dispensing with the alleged dire consequences of humor directed at Jewish women, Davies goes on to make an intriguing, insightful, and compelling (to me) case for the raison d'être for the propensity of Jewish males to make up the many jokes about their female counterparts. His argument is supported by both his findings from sociology and his conclusions based upon his research in humor.

First, the Jewish man is compelled by an inner sense of duty and constant pressure from his peers to marry within his religion. There are many jokes ridiculing the Jew who tries to "assimilate" into gentile society, either by name-changing, adopting a gentile religion or even marrying a gentile. The result of such pressure: "Jewish women have become the subject of jokes because for Jewish men they represent duty as against temptation" (369).

Second, the Jewish male is restrained both by custom and homegrown humor from the kind of aggressiveness found so commonly in gentile hooligans. He is not known as a fighter, a gang-joiner, a "tough guy." To prove his point, he quotes two items from *American Jewish* (1980):

> When did you last hear of someone being afraid to go into a Jewish neighborhood in case he was mugged by an accountant? Can you imagine one *schwartze* saying to another, "Let's get out of here. I don't like the look of those four Jews hanging around on the corner."

Third, Davies points out, although Jews have a strong liking for jokes in which gentiles get comically drunk, Jews themselves abhor drunkenness among themselves. For a Jew, drunk is not cute nor comical; it is unacceptable. There are numerous jokes about drunken Americans, Irish, Finns, Brits, and so on, but jokes on drunken Jews are well-nigh nonexistent.

So: Jewish men are home-loving, sober, diligent, peaceable, "thoroughly enmeshed in a familistic way of life," and do not "escape from this into an all-male subculture, characterized by drinking, brawling, and delinquency." Unable to "escape" their women, they joke about them.

I have truncated and, probably, oversimplified Davies's case here, and you are invited to peruse the entire brief he spreads on the pages of *Humor*. His conclusion is an apt summary of his position:

> The Jewish sense of family duty has prevailed over temptation, and the inevitable result is jokes that mock the moral guardians of the Jewish world—Jewish mothers and present and future wives. Far from being an index of misogyny and patriarchy, Jewish jokes about women (in contrast to, say, jokes about Irish and Australian men) are a wry acknowledgement of the powerful and legitimized influence that Jewish women exercise, especially when contrasted with the womenfolk of other ethnic and religious communities. It is the man who *does not* and in a sense cannot leave his wife at home and casually "go out with the lads and get drunk" who is going to tell jokes about the women who "prevent" him from doing so. Jewish women should reflect that the alternative to hard-joking Jewish men is Andy Capp.

If it is true, as so many writers on Jewish humor assert, that the special humor of "the chosen people" came from the many years of being an oppressed minority, and who now make up a psychologically distanced "guest minority" in one country or another, has Jewish "independence," achieved through their own nation of Israel, caused Jews to cease enjoying self-deprecating humor? Is it possible that, after a long armed struggle to establish a nation, and then two lightning wars in which the enemy is quickly dispensed with, that Jewish humor should take a turn toward "Jewish superiority?" This question was recently asked by Nevo (1986), who attempted an empirical study to provide answers.

Nevo conducted two studies with Israeli Jew and Arab students in situations where they both rated humor presented to them and also *generated* humor in standardized cartoon-completion exercises. His general conclusion was that "As for the present study, it might be said that there is no evidence that Jews in Israel laugh at themselves more than Arabs do, and there is some evidence to the contrary" (199). One particular finding of importance: when laughing at "their group," individuals appeared to be laughing at *other individuals in the group* and not necessarily at themselves. This phenomenon seems quite sensible. For instance, as I have said, I am a professor, and I still enjoy jokes denigrating the "absentminded professor." Why? Because I do not consider myself among the absentminded! I likewise enjoy jokes ridiculing the typical "boring professor":

Professor, lecturing: "Who is smoking back there in the back rows?"

Student, from back: "Nobody! That's just the *fog* we're in!"

Certainly I do not consider myself boring; it's those other guys that put their students to sleep. Because of my training and what I teach, I consider myself something of a psychologist. I enjoy jokes such as: "Psychologist: one who would father a set of twins, have one baptized, and keep the other for a control" (or, "A man who pulls *habits* out of *rats*"). These jokes do not touch me. I am not so slavishly devoted to the experimental method, and I do not run rats through mazes.

But regardless who is being laughed at and who is doing the laughing-at, there is still a winner and a loser.

On this business of self-deprecating humor, Nevo concludes the report of his empirical study like a good scientist: "Laughing at oneself is a concept that should be studied more carefully, giving attention to active and passive modes of expression, and various definitions of self."

5

Sexual, Sexist, and Scatological Humor

*We must not, of course, compare words said in public
with deeds committed in secret. Persons who indulge
in indecent talk would certainly shrink at performing
openly the acts of which they speak.*
—E. A. Westermarck, *The History of Human Marriage*

Sexual and/or profane humor is often considered a unique "type" of humor. Indeed, as we shall see in the final chapter of this book, it is common for researchers to divide humor into types such as "aggressive," "nonaggressive," and "sexual." Does "sexual" or "scatological" humor differ significantly from other kinds of humor? If so, is the difference merely in content, or in both content and form, or in the psychological mechanism of achieving laughter? This chapter argues forcefully for the "only content" difference.

Part of my preparation for writing this chapter was to reread G. Legman's two volumes (1968, 1975) on *Rationale of the Dirty Joke*. These two tomes constitute nearly 2,000 pages and literally hundreds of "dirty" jokes (I did not count them). Let us begin here by considering a joke *not* included by Legman:

A visitor to a large hospital was being shown around by a friend of his, an orderly. As they passed a patient's room they observed the male patient on his bed vigorously masturbating. The orderly answered his friend's shocked expression with, "That guy has a rare disease; the only known cure is to have as many orgasms as physically possible."

Further down the hall they observed in another patient's room a male patient having sexual intercourse with an attractive nurse under him; she is wearing only her nurse's cap. Again, the orderly interprets the puzzled look on the face of his friend. "This guy has the same problem as the guy masturbating back there."

"But why," asks the visitor, "does the guy back there have to jerk off while this other gentleman gets to fuck this lovely nurse?"

"Oh," replies the orderly, "*this* guy has Blue Cross/Blue Shield."

Is this a "sexual joke?" Is it "dirty?" Is it "sexist?" It *must* be "sexual," most would say. It concerns sexual activity; in fact, two forms of such activity. It uses the sexual words "masturbate," "sexual intercourse," "orgasms," and even the "dirty" slang words/phrases "jerking off" and "fuck."

Of course, it would be most easy to classify this joke as *sexual*. It does contain sexual content. It is concerned with sexual activity. A sensitive joke-teller might refrain from telling it in mixed company of non-friends for fear of embarrassing or antagonizing, especially with words like "jerk off" and "fuck" as part of the joke.

But: what makes this joke funny? Who is the butt? Who wins, and who loses, according to our theory?

Well, you would *not* consider this joke funny unless you were aware of a familiar truism concerning medical care in America which serves as a standard comic script: people who can pay their own way for medical care (through insurance or otherwise) generally receive better medical treatment and care than do those who cannot. We who enjoy this joke's reminder of our two-valued (and unfair?) system of medical care are the winners; the system itself is the loser. The joke, like most jokes, advances the comic script to ridiculous lengths of hyperbole. There are no illnesses whose cure rely upon repeated orgasms; even if there were, hospitals would not abandon nonpaying patients to the self-help treatment of masturbation and then assign nurses to prostitute themselves for the benefit of paying customers. But in the "play frame" of the joke, the comic script "makes sense." We understand that those who can pay get the best, and those who cannot get the rest.

This comic script of medical care/medical payment is a common one. Art Buchwald (1979: 89–91) wrote a satirical column employing it. In it, Art goes to a hospital to visit a friend. The hospital staff, desperate for customers to fill its beds, rush Art into a room, strip him, and clothe him in a "backdoor" hospital gown; they subject him to an interview by a doctor making rounds with a an entourage of interns and residents, then roll him into the operating room for exploratory surgery since Art "doesn't know what his problem is." Buchwald can only halt the madness by screaming that he has no insurance and can't pay for his hospital stay. He is dressed and bum-rushed out the door in jig time.

What's the point? Here we have a comic script; it becomes the basis for both a great "dirty" (at least sexual) joke to be told and sniggered over with close friends, and at the same time can be used for a column that can be printed in a "family newspaper." And this simple incidence illustrates the thesis of this chapter: sexual, sexist, and scatological humor uses the same kinds of comic scripts as does *non*sexual, *non*sexist, and *non*scatological humor. "Dirty" jokes differ from "clean" jokes only in subject matter and language, not in form or technique; both "types" of jokes follow the formula of a contest, resulting in both a winner and a loser. Toddlers may get laughs and think it is hilariously funny to merely say naughty words, like "poopoo" and "caca", but they outgrow this phase quickly and must early on have their dirt in the form of jokes, with winners and losers.

In wading through Legman's two thousand pages for my second time I did not encounter a single dirty joke (which I understood; some were in foreign languages) that did not fit the theory of humor propounded in this book. In fact, I can make the same statement about all the humor I have encountered since beginning its serious study in 1955 (as I wrote earlier). And at the end of this book I shall issue a challenge to anyone who believes he/she can provide an example of humor which can *not* be shown to fit the "laughing = winning" formula. (And, by the way, I agree with Legman that "dirty jokes" are some of the most hostile and aggressive in existence; but I cannot agree with his Freudian interpretative schema, including as the basis of jokes women's "penis envy," boys' fear of castration by the father, competition with Dad for sex with Mom, etc.)

Reaction to humor is both intellectual and emotional. We must, in order to enjoy a joke, be able to cognitively, intellectually understand its content and the comic scripts involved and their relationships to the "punch line;" but much of the reaction to a joke is also emotional. Because of the emotional factor in humor, various researchers have been interested in its relationship to similar emotion not caused or affected by humor. So, before progressing on to analysis of various dirty jokes, a brief overview of some of the research on the relationship of humor to other-related emotion is in order.

Canton, Bryant, and Zillman (1974) exposed college students to written material that increased their general emotional level (excitation) with either a "positive" or "negative" hedonic tone, then had them rate humorous material. The general excitation, whether "positive" or "negative," enhanced the ratings of the humor.

Strickland (1959) experimentally induced in his subjects either *anger* or *sexual desire*, then exposed them to either *hostile* or *sexual* humor. Those who were angered rated the hostile humor higher than did the control group; those who were sexually aroused appreciated more greatly the sexual humor than did the controls.

Dworkin and Efran (1967) deliberately angered subjects and then exposed them to either "hostile" comedy album cuts or "nonhostile" (actually, "less hostile;" see final chapter) clips. Both "types" of humor decreased hostility (further proof that the "nonhostile" humor was misnamed) in the angered subjects. The subjects rated the "hostile" humor as slightly more funny than the "nonhostile," which supports a bias of mine: usually, everything else being equal, the more hostile the humor, the funnier.

Byrne (1956) found that the more hostile his neruopsychiatric subjects were, the more they enjoyed humor.

Prerost and Brewer (1977) exposed angered subjects to two kinds of "hostile" humor: one called "threatening," the other called "nonthreatening." They found that the hostile but *non*threatening humor decreased anger the most, and was rated as funniest by the experimental subjects.

Baron and Ball (1974) angered subjects, and then exposed them to allegedly (see final chapter) "nonhostile" humor; this supposedly innocent humor decreased subjects' anger. Again, I take this as further evidence that the "innocent" humor contained *tendency*.

Berkowitz (1970) either did or did not have subjects angered by the behavior of an applicant for a dorm supervisory job. He then exposed them to hostile humor. He found that the hostile humor increased hostile responses to the applicant later, whether they had been angered or not!

Singer, Golob, and Levine (1967) had subjects view either cruel, aggressive art or "nonaggressive" art, and then view and rate some aggressive humor. They found that those who had viewed the aggressive art rated the aggressive humor as less funny than did those who viewed the nonaggressive art; they concluded that the aggressive art had revulsed the subjects toward aggression in general, and thus they rated the aggressive humor as less funny (they appreciated less the aggressive content of the humor).

Three other studies, by Singer (1968) Landy and Mettee (1969), and Mueller and Donnerstein (1977) found evidence that appreciation of aggressive humor could reduce aggressive mood states.

Baron (1978) paired up the angering of male subjects and their exposure to either *exploitative* or *nonexploitative* sexual humor. An explanation of what Baron meant by these two kinds of sexual humor is in order here.

Nonexploitative sexual humor depicted sexual activity in which the female actors in the stories were not duped, lied to, "tricked," and so on; that is, they were engaging in sexual activity voluntarily while "knowing what they were doing." Example:

> A young woman [is pictured] sitting across the table from a physician. She is seen remarking, "Have I had any side effects from the Pill? Only promiscuity."
>
> (She freely confesses her "sin" [thereby becoming our "loser"] without any wily questioning by the doctor.)

Exploitative sexual humor in the study "took advantage" of females' vulnerability, cupidity, naïveté, stupidity, and so on, as in:

> A young man and young woman are shown seated on a bed. The young man is busily removing the woman's bra.
>
> She remarks, "Explain again how this is going to help end the war in Vietnam."

Baron found that the exposure of the angered males to the *exploitative*, but not to the *non*exploitative humor, reduced their anger. That is, it was the humor that most blatantly aggressed against exploited persons that was effective in reducing subjects' hostility.

So there does seem to be a link between anger/frustration/ aggression *and* aggressive humor. Some would say that human aggression and human aggressive humor ought to be related in a causal manner. It makes perfect sense, especially according to the laughing = winning theory, for the greater appreciation of hostile humor to occur after being angered, for instance. In simple terms, a person is (1) angered (denied something he/she wants, or else given something [like undeserved hostile criticism] he/she does not want) and next (2) is exposed to humor where someone else "gets it" (providing the subject with what he/she does want [laughter at a ridiculed other]). What aggression hath given, aggression hath taken away. Why is this important?

Well, my reason for briefly reviewing the research above (with hope that I have not oversimplified too much) is to go on and review some other research that links sexual *humor* with aggression, and sexual *feelings* with aggressiveness!

We humans (and, specifically, we Americans, perhaps) have "romanticized" sex as somehow part and parcel of romantic love. Ideal sex is characterized as the physical joining which serves as the counterpart to the emotional and spiritual bonding of "true love." We tend to abhor and warn the young against "sex without love." Women, more than men, consider sex more "special" when accompanied by mutual emotional commitment. It is for these reasons that we may be surprised, disturbed, even revolted by observing the behavior at our zoo's primate house on a warm and sunny day.

Best-selling author Camille Paglia (*Sexual Personae*, 1990) insightfully describes human society's schizophrenic muddling with the animal and the divine spark:

> Like art, sex is fraught with symbols. Family romance means that adult sex is always representation, ritualistic acting out of vanished realities. A perfectly human eroticism may be impossible. Somewhere in every family romance is hostility and aggression, the homicidal wishes of the unconscious. Children are monsters of unbridled egotism and will, for they spring directly from nature, hostile intimations of immorality. We carry that daemonic will within us forever. Most people conceal it with acquired ethical precepts and meet it only in their dreams, which they hastily forget upon waking. The will-to-power is innate, but the sexual scripts of family romance are learned. Human beings are the only creatures in whom consciousness is so entangled with animal instinct. In Western culture, there can never be a purely physical or anxiety-free sexual encounter. Every attraction, pattern of touch, every orgasm is shaped by psychic shadows. (4)

Later (23) she puts the case more bluntly and more succinctly: "Modern feminism's most naïve formulation is its assertion that rape is a crime of violence but not of sex, that it is merely power masquerading as sex. But sex *is* power, and all power is inherently aggressive."

Is there any evidence in our empirical study of humor that might support in any way the assertions of Paglia? It seems that there is.

Prerost (1972) artificially angered student subjects at Western Illinois University. After assurances that the subjects were, indeed, angry, he had them rate jokes classified by a group of judges as "neutral," "aggressive," and "sexual." Remember, now, Prerost made the subjects *angry*; he did not attempt to arouse them sexually by having them judge "obscene" pictures or steamy passages from erotic literature. These people were rendered mad, not horny.

The ratings of the humor by the angered students made for an interesting pattern. Instead of rating the "hostile" humor as funniest, as expected, they rated the *sexual* humor as funniest! Another aspect of that pattern was telling. The non-angered females rated the "neutral" humor highest, the "hostile" humor second-funniest, and the "sexual" humor *least* funny. This order of ratings was just the opposite that of the males who, both angered and not, preferred the sexual, then the hostile, and then the neutral least. But something interesting happened to the women who were made angry in the experimental manipulation: their humor preferences reversed so as to resemble those of the males. The *angered* females gave highest ratings to the sexual humor and lowest ratings to the neutral humor!

Prerost offered an explanation for his findings:

Apparently the two humor types (aggressive and sexual) are very closely related, especially for males.... the results do strongly indicate that humor is a natural vehicle for expression of an aggressive mood.... Other forms of humor were preferred by females to sexual humor when they were in nonaggressive moods, but once they were aroused, sexual humor became their preferred choice.(286–287)

His concluding sentence:

It seems highly probable that the two arousal states of sex and aggression are highly similar, and further research dealing with the aggressive aspects of sexual humor and the commonality of mood state is clearly indicated.

One is tempted to commit the post hoc analysis fallacy and imply that perhaps college women really enjoy sexual humor but, when in full control of their faculties, refuse to make public this acknowledgement, under the socially-approved sanction of "nice girls don't think like that" syndrome; but that, further, when they are emotionally energized, allow this appreciation to slip out without the censor of the cooler impediment of reason.

Prerost took himself at his word on the imperative to do further research in this area. In a later study (1976) he once again induced anger in college students, then had them rate both sexual and nonsexual humor. Angering the subjects caused them to rate both types of humor higher than did the non-angry, but their ratings rose higher on the sexual humor. When he measured the subjects' mood states after the exposure to the humor, only the angered students who had been exposed to the sexual humor showed a reduction in affect. Prerost concluded:

The sexual humor did produce a reduction or catharsis of the aggressive mood state. Sexual humor like aggressive humor must provide impulse expression of aggressiveness; expression through appreciation of the sexual humor satisfied the mood. This was particularly true of the females.... The fact that sexual humor produced a cathartic reaction in this study supports the contention that the aggressive and sexual mood states are similar. (776)

In the Baron (1978) study mentioned above, the men rated the humor on "funniness," but also rated each item on amount of *sexuality*. On the average, those who were angered rated the jokes higher on sexual content than did the non-angered control subjects. Here is a further link between anger and sexual perception.

Barclay and Haber (1965) angered (or did not anger) college students and then had them write responses to male- or female-dominant Thematic Apperception Tests (TAT) pictures. Their analysis allowed them to conclude, "A strong linkage was demonstrated between aggressive and sexual motivation. In many aspects of the study they were parallel in effect" (472).

In a follow-up study, Barclay (1970) angered sorority and fraternity members at Michigan State University and then had them respond to male-dominant and female-dominant pictures from the TAT. The angered students responded with higher sexual motivations in their writings. Barclay wrote in his summary, "It was concluded that increases in aggressiveness cause increases in sexuality for males and females, regardless of E[xperimenter]'s sex."

The fact that aroused aggressiveness/anger is empirically linked to enjoyment of sexual humor, again, is not surprising, in light of the laughing = winning theory and the thesis of this chapter. The angered person is more likely than a placid one to delight in perceiving the ridicule (within a sexual context) of some fictitious man or woman, some group, some organization, some idea, and so on.

Much sexual humor ridicules either a male or "maleness," or a female or "femaleness," a natural condition since most of us are divided along the male/female parameter. Such a division gives rise to the name "sexist" humor. Studies of appreciation of sexual humor *by* sex have generally shown either that males appreciate sexual humor more than do females, or else males more greatly enjoy anti-female sexual humor while females prefer anti-male sexual humor (Sekeres and Clark 1980; Chapman and Gadfield 1976; Love and Deckers 1989; Losco and Epstein 1975; Priest and Wilhelm 1974).

I turn now to a sampling of sexual jokes to show how they fit the laughing = winning theory. The corpus from which to choose such jokes is huge, but I will try to include one or two from each major category developed by Legman for his two-volume "rationale" for the genre. Legman's taxonomy allows for fifteen major groupings of dirty jokes by subject matter: Children, Fools, Animals, The Male Approach, The Sadistic Concept, Women, Premarital Sexual Acts, Marriage, Adultery, Homosexuality, Prostitution, Disease and Disgust, Castration, Dysphemism and Cursing and Insults, and Scatology. These categories he subdivides into 77 subgroupings, and these subgroupings are further divided into another 178 specific types. One might wonder at the great diversity that one man can find in dirty jokes!

Two common themes in sexual jokes regarding *children* are (1) the child's unexpectedly mature understanding/activity regarding sex or (2) the things a child will do or say because of sexual ignorance. An example of the form:

> Little Johnny, age seven, is in love with Mary, the little girl next door. He approaches Mary's father and explains that he and Mary plan to marry. Mary's Dad is amused.
>
> "What are you going to do for money?" he asks.
>
> "I have my allowance," explains Johnny, "and Mary has six dollars in her bank."
>
> "That's OK for now, Johnny," the father says, "but what will you do when you start having children?"
>
> "Well," said Johnny, "we've had pretty good luck so far."

Winners: we who enjoy the joke; loser: Mary's Dad, flabbergasted suddenly with the prospect that his little girl has been having regular sexual intercourse at such a tender age! (Johnny can also be considered a "loser;" he has let the cat out of the bag and is now liable for retribution.)

When talking about sexual matters, children can "innocently" say the darndest things:

> A little boy says to his mother: "Mama, guess what I saw Daddy and the maid doing on the bed!" "Be quiet," warns Mom. Then, after a moment's reflection: "You wait to tell me until Mama asks you to."
>
> At the dinner table that night she asks her son, "Now Jimmy, what were you going to tell me this morning?"
>
> "Nothing; only that I saw Daddy and the maid on the bed together, doing just like you and Uncle Tom did last summer when Daddy was gone fishing."

Winners: us, again. Losers: Mom, on whom the embarrassing tables have been turned; Dad, for being "ratted on," and also for learning that he has been cuckolded.

Legman begins his chapter on "The Fool" (series 1): "Probably the most important element in understanding any joke is to grasp clearly and from the beginning *who is the butt.* This not only means determining which of the characters in the story receives the hostile impact of the punch line (so well named), but whether, for that matter, the butt is actually any character in the story at all." For instance, a very famous "fool" jokes goes:

> A man is shipwrecked on a desert island for ten years.
>
> One day a beautiful, naked young woman is washed up on the shore. The man revives her and she says, "Now that you've been so good to me I'm going to give you something you have not had for ten years."
>
> "You mean to tell me," the man says, "that there's some beer in that barrel?"

We win again, laughing at the fool's stupidity; the fool, himself, is the loser by showing his foolishness. But one can also consider that this man's choice of beer over sex just might represent a "typical" *male* response, making it gender-specific and thus "sexist."

> "I have a good joke on you," one friend tells another.
>
> "I was walking by your house last night; your bedroom shade was open and I saw you screwing your wife."
>
> "Hah!" responds the friend. "The joke's on *you.* I wasn't even home last night."

Winner: the usual; loser: the stupid cuckold, who thinks he is a winner!

Legman claims that most "Animal" jokes are anthropomorphic (that is, they actually represent human behavior in disguise):

> A hen finds an assortment of beautifully colored Easter eggs. She arranges them in a nest and begins sitting on them.
>
> The rooster comes along and peeks at the eggs; livid, he runs across the barnyard and beats up on the male peacock.

We laugh at the jealous, mistaken rooster (the loser), of course; but chickens do not have the ability to reason that offspring of a different hue spring from male loins not one's own—only humans do this.

Some "animal" jokes are best thought of as "animal/human" stories:

> A ventriloquist at a summer camp is amazing the neighboring farmhands with his abilities. He has the horse say "Hello, Captain," and the cow moo "Oh my aching teats!" He then looks thoughtfully at the nearby flock of sheep; a farmhand blurts

out, "Listen if that little ewe at the edge of the flock says anything, she's a goddam liar!"

And we enjoy the unconscious confession of the loutish farmhand that he has been committing sodomy with the ewe.

What Legman refers to as "The Male Approach" is that jokes are created *by* men *for* men; inherent in this setup is that most jokes demean *females*. Part of "The Male Approach" is that women are nearly always available to almost any man, and she need only be asked. Thus are women humorously demeaned:

> An ex-boxer who is very successful with women is asked his secret. "I just stand on the corner and say to gals who walk by, "'Say, wanna fuck?'"
> "But don't you get lots of slaps in the face for that approach?"
> "Sure do. But you'd be surprised how much fucking I get, too!"

Legman quotes a very popular, oft-quoted bit of doggerel that argues for the impossibility of verbal rape. Entitled "Ode to the Four-Letter Word," it goes:

> Though a lady repel your advance, she'll be kind
> As long as you *intimate* what's on your mind.
> You may tell her you're *hungry*, you need to be *swung*;
> You may ask her to see how your etchings are hung;
> You may mention the ashes *that need to be hauled*,
> *Put the lid on her saucepan*; even *lay*'s not too bald.
> But the moment you're forthright, get ready to duck,
> For the girl isn't born yet who'll stand for 'Let's ——.'

In the category of "The Sadistic Concept" Legman includes jokes about *rape*:

> A bellboy is on trial for raping the chambermaid; it is alleged that he caught her head out the window while she was watching a parade, locking her head there by pulling down the window, and having intercourse with her from behind. "Why did you not scream for help?," asks the Judge. "Well, Your Honor, I didn't want people to think I was cheering for a *Republican* parade."

As usual, *we* win as the poor maid shows her lack of judgment by valuing petty politics over personal ravishment; we are even left ripe for the interpretation that, since she demurred from screaming for a petty reason, she actually *enjoyed* the rape (a male chauvinist comic script for many "rape stories").

The comic scripts that men choose for jokes about women include that in which women are desirous of large male organs on their lovers. Legman ascribes this female desire to the Freudian notion of the female's "penis envy," a concept in which I do not believe. Instead, I see these jokes as making fun of the sluttishness of women who would place great importance on such a matter.

> A woman is told that the men in the East have penises that are short and thick, while men in the West have penises that are long and thin. She says she would prefer a man who was born in the East but who has lived in the West a long, long time.

Included in "Women" jokes are those where the female misinterprets an innocent remark for a sexual invitation:

> A young man with a sore throat goes to the doctor's house in the early evening. The doctor's pretty young wife opens the door. "Is the doctor in," the young man hoarsely whispers. "No," the wife whispers back, "come right in."

> A young couple are walking in the park on a summer eve.
> The young man looks at the wet grass and exclaims, "Some dew."
> The young woman replies, "If you're asking, yes I *do*."

Jokes concerning "Premarital Sexual Acts" typically involve the unmarried, thus the young. These jokes make fun of the inexperience, discovery, disappointment, interruptions, and awkwardness involved in youthful attempts at sexual gratification.

> A man slides his hand up a girl's leg in a bar. She slaps his hand away, saying "No, you don't. Tits first."

Here we laugh at the girl's crude revelation that she is experienced at the petting game, and, like most females, "consider[s] the handling of their breasts by men as more than a venial familiarity and, in general, this is considered a proper preliminary to more 'serious' genital caresses" (Legman 1: 400).

> *He*: "It's so dark I can't see my hand in front of my face."
> *She*: "That's OK. I know where it is." (Or: "You know damn well your hand's not in front of your face.")

Certainly not fighting him off, she reveals complicity in the dirty deed.

Legman includes the subtopic of "birth control" and the results of not using it under "Premarital Sexual Acts":

> A girl tells her father that her rich boyfriend has gotten her pregnant. The father rushes to the young man's house and threatens to kill him. "Now, don't get excited," says the young man. "I plan to do right by your daughter.
> If it's a boy, I will settle on her $200,000.00; if it's a girl, I will settle on her $150,000.00. Do you think that's fair?"
> The father replies, "And if it's a miscarriage, will you give her another chance?"

Here we laugh at the greedy father, willing to be bought off in order to forgive sexual promiscuity—and even willing to continue to prostitute his daughter in case the first deal falls through!

Jokes about "Marriage," according to Legman's classification scheme, include jokes about "the mother-in-law" (which always means the mother of the bride) and "the forbidding mother." Occasionally incest jokes appear in this category:

> A girl wants to marry one of the neighbor's sons, but her father warns her privately, "You can't marry that boy. Whatever you do, don't tell your mother, but that boy is your half-brother."
> This happens with three different boys, and the girl eventually realizes that she will not be able to marry anyone in the neighborhood, so she tells her mother the situation.
> "Daughter," says the mother, "you get yore marryin'-cap on. That man you call 'Paw' ain't no kin of your'n at all."

We may cluck our tongues at the lecherous father, but we wind up laughing at the cuckold when we learn of his wife's return treachery.

Also inherent in the "Marriage" category of jokes are the many utilizing the common comic script of the traditional desire of the man to marry a female virgin.

> A rich old widower chooses as his young second bride a sweet near-adolescent raised all her life in a convent, to assure himself of acquiring a virgin. After the wedding they hie themselves to a luxurious hotel for their wedding night. As they pass through the lobby the young bride notices several beautiful, exotically dressed young women present, and asks her new husband who they are. Told they are "prostitutes," the young woman asks "But what are prostitutes?" Her wizened old husband replies, "They are women who will let men possess them sexually for a price; some charge a hundred dollars or more per man."
> "A hundred dollars!" exclaims the girl. "I never dreamed men paid so much. The priests only gave us girls an apple."

Is it necessary to point out that the ancient gentleman expecting a pure virgin is the one who comes out the loser in this story?

It comes only naturally that Legman follows analysis of jokes on "Marriage" with jokes on "Adultery." One of my favorites concerns a man discussing with his wife her possibilities should he die first:

> "If I *did* go first, would you remarry?"
> "Well, probably."
> "Well, would you live with him here—in *our* house?"
> "I imagine I would."
> "Would you sleep with him—in *our* bed?"
> "I suppose I would."
> "Well, would you let him drive my sports car?"
> "No. He can't drive a stick shift."
> (Or: "Would you let him use *my* golf clubs?
> "No. He's left-handed.")

Here, of course, the wife is the loser for accidentally revealing her infidelity. And we get a laugh *on* her *and* the cuckolded hubby.

The "Mother-in-Law" can get involved in cases involving adultery:

> A husband away on a trip telegraphs his wife that he will be home that evening. When he arrives he finds her in bed with another man. He moves to a hotel and begins divorce proceedings. The wife's mother comes to see him.
> "It's all a misunderstanding. I have the explanation. I went to see Elsie, and she did not get your telegram."

Here we can snigger at the mother-in-law, overly-protective of her daughter, somewhat demeaning toward her son-in-law, and totally *stupid* in thinking that her "explanation" would mollify the cuckolded husband.

Legman's analysis of "Homosexuality" jokes begins the second series. Not all of these jokes ridicule homosexuality or specific practitioners of the life style.

> A man confesses to his psychiatrist that he enjoys sexual intercourse with horses.
> The shrink asks, "Male horses, or female horses?"
> "*Female* horses," the patient indignantly replies. "You think I'm queer or somethin'?"

Here our laughter is directed at the man who is deluded by the idea that, he is normal so long as he has sexual relations only with female horses.

Other jokes openly ridicule the various practices in which homosexuals engage:

> Two homosexuals are having an argument. One screams at the other, "Well, you can just kiss my ass!" The other replies, "This is a fight, Dearie. Let's keep romance out of it." (Or, "I will not. I'm not ready yet to make up.")

> Two homosexuals in a car collide with a pickup truck.
> One of the two runs over to the pickup, screaming epithets at the big, hairy brute of a driver, who turns on the homosexual and mutters, "You can kiss my hairy ass, you goddam cocksucker."
> The homosexual runs back to his car and tells his companion, "I think everything's going to be all right. He's willing to settle out of court."

Both lesbians and male homosexuals are ridiculed in the old saw:

> A queer picked up a lesbian and took her to his hotel room, where they argued all night over who should do what, with what, and to whom.

Jokes about "the satisfied client" of "Prostitution" stories often ridicule the client, not the prostitute.

> An elderly client at a whorehouse insists on a particular girl even though she is occupied. The madam asks, "What does she have that my other girls don't?" "Patience," replies the old guy.

Here it is the (at least) semi-impotence of the elderly gentleman that is suddenly revealed as a comic script. Paradoxically, the joke makes the "patient prostitute" seem like less of a real professional, who would ordinarily prompt a client to climax as soon as possible so as to be able to move on to her next "trick."

A "prostitute joke" can become social commentary:

> A man is picked up by a prostitute and taken to her apartment. He finds it full of books, college pennants, and diplomas on the wall. He asks, "Are these your diplomas?"
> "Yep," she responds. I got my B.A. at Tufts, my M.A. at Columbia, and my Ph.D. at Oxford." The man is puzzled.
> "Then how did your get into your present business?"
> Her reply: "Just lucky, I guess."

The girl's answer may be taken to mean that she enjoys sex a great deal, and is thus "happy with her work;" but the emphasis here on books and degrees argues the proposition that so many bright, young, and well-educated people cannot find financially rewarding employment in the fields for which they have been educated. If Oxford Ph.D.'s in the United States regularly stepped into jobs paying a hundred thousand dollars a year, our "joke" becomes a tragic puzzle. This joke is a criticism of "the system."

Often in "Prostitution" jokes we find the butt to be the "John" who patronizes the whore.

> A visitor to a bordello complains that he has little money.
>
> He is told that he can only afford their oldest "girl," and she and he retire to her room. They begin their tryst in the dark at the man's request, so that he need not look at the unattractive old strumpet. As they start, she says, "How is it?" and he replies, "Awful. It's really rough in here."
>
> She squirms away, saying "Here, I'll take care of that."
>
> After a few moments he is back in her; he says, "Hey, now, that's more like it—smooth and slick. What did you do?"
>
> The old girl cackled, "I just scraped off the scabs and let the pus flow."
>
> (One can understand why this is from the second series, Legman's really dirty "dirty jokes.")

Prostitution can serve as the subject matter in a joke in order to make fun of others besides the girl and her client.

> A salesman is having lunch with a new client, and the subject of the University of Alabama somehow enters the conversation. The salesman laughs and says, "The only ones who go to the University of Alabama are football players and whores."
>
> The client bristles: "My *wife* attended Alabama!"
>
> The salesman gulps. "And what position did she play?"

Here we laugh at the embarrassed and business-wounded salesman who makes a valiant but futile (and stupid) attempt to recover. One more:

> An "ugly American" arrives in London and enters a cab.
>
> "Take me to Soho, Driver," he says, "where the action is. I understand there are three whores on every street corner there."
>
> "Roigt you are, Guv," replies the cabbie. "There *used* to be three on every corner, but nowadays the average is down to two, what with you Yanks marryin' 'em and takin' 'em home to the States."

And prostitution becomes the vehicle to "run down" another loudmouthed, ill-mannered jerk.

Prostitute jokes, like any "dirty" joke, can involve punning and wordplay:

What do you call the children of prostitutes? Brothel's sprouts.

We take up the *pun* in the next chapter.

Legman gets really nasty when he comes to "Disease and Disgust" in series 2. He includes here "The Fear of Touch" which occurs in many sexual situations.

A "little old lady" and a "little old man" are in bed.

She says, "Honey, let's make love." He replies, "I can't.

I don't have a condom." She insists: "Hey, come on, we're too damned old to get pregnant."

"I know that," he says, "but I'm afraid that if I get it wet, my arthritis will flare up."

Here we laugh at the aged and the problems associated with their aging. But another reason to "fear touch" is related to the danger of venereal disease:

A married man asks another if he ever "cheats" on his wife.

"Sure do," replied the other. "But," says the first, "does your conscience never bother you?"

"Certainly," was the cheater's reply, "but only for nine days. If everything is OK after that..."

The cheater is the amusing butt because he knowingly practices a dangerous game *and freely makes public his stupid actions*.

Two Army corporals decide to patronize a local whore known far and wide as "Susie-Q." A buddy warns them to stay away from her since she has *syphilis*. Not knowing what "syphilis" is, they look it up in a dictionary. Discovering that it is "a disease of the privates," they decide it is safe to screw Susie-Q after all, since they are *corporals*.

Here the comic script, again, is *stupidity*. The slight play on the word "privates" is not significant enough to classify the joke as *ethnic* or *sexual*.

A common comic script is the price one must pay for one's sexual pleasure through the ravages of venereal disease.

A man has intercourse with a woman during his travels in Asia. Experiencing trouble, he goes to a doctor, who tells him that he has leprosy and that his penis must be amputated. The distraught man seeks a second opinion, an old and wise Chinese medical man, who examines him and says, "No have to amputate penis," which makes the poor traveler smile in relief.

The doctor continues: "Penis fall off by itself in three weeks."

We chuckle at the terrible fate of our hero, above, especially since he is (1) in bad trouble, then (2) briefly and apparently out of trouble, and (3) plunged right back into disaster.

A joke also used by Legman for illustrating "The Male Approach" appears in "Disease and Disgust."

A guy is frustrated by his girl's persistent refusal to "go all the way." One night he drives ten miles out of town, then stops and tells her, "Ok, now it's fuck or walk home." She walks.

The next week he has a date with her again. He drives out *twenty* miles this time, with the same offer and the same choice by the girl.

The next week he drives her *forty* miles out of town, then repeats his multiple-choice offer. She consents, and they have sex in his back seat. Afterward, over cigarettes, he chides her: "Now, don't you feel a fool for taking those two long walks home?"

She replies: "I figure I would walk ten miles, even twenty miles—but I'll be damned if I'll walk *forty* miles just to keep a friend of mine from getting the clap."

This joke offers up a smug male chauvinistic bastard on whom the tables have suddenly been turned. He thought he had just won, but now he (and we) know that he has been a huge loser.

In covering jokes regarding "Castration," Legman delves deeply into Freudian theory which I will not bother to repeat here. Some of his examples fulfill his open threat that some of the series 2 book would be stomach-churning. I limit myself to the more palatable of jokes on this topic.

A trooper arrives at the scene of an auto accident. A young woman was thrown from the vehicle and killed; the male driver is still safely strapped into his seat. The trooper berates the young man for allowing his girl friend to ride unbelted.

"Get off my case," the young man says, "and go over and look at what she has in her hand."

It appears that the young man did not get off scot-free in the accident, but lost an important part of his anatomy as a result of their well-named "joy ride". The feeling that "he had it coming" allows us to laugh at his plight even more carefreely.

A famous and often-collected limerick has to do with the female castration of males.

> There was a young Queen of Baroda
> Who built a new kind of pagoda.
> > The walls of its halls
> > Were festooned with the balls
> And the tools of the fools that bestrode her.

As is usual with limericks, clever rhyming beguiles us. But any laughs must be on our poor "fools" who thought they were getting something for nothing (and wound up with nothing for something!).

Legman includes one other limerick on the topic:

> There was a young couple named Kelly
> Who had to live belly to belly.
> > Because once, in their haste,
> > They used library paste
> Instead of petroleum jelly.

Making "the beast with two backs" has more than once been described as a ludicrous position for humans to get themselves into, but being stuck that way for some time by glue is hilarious.

Legman's "Dysphemism and Insults" concerns some material that might be included in the next chapter of this book, but the topic is covered here since the tricky language is of the "dirty" variety and involves such as insults and curses.

> A woman in a pet shop asks about buying a porcupine.
>
> The clerk tells her that there are two kinds of porcupines, the Rocky Mountain and the Canadian. Asked the difference, the clerk says "The difference is in length of pricks; in the Rocky Mountain it's about three inches, in the Canadian it's more like five inches."
>
> The woman is offended and outraged by the clerk's response, and she calls in the manager to complain. The manager assures her that the clerk did not mean to say anything impolite. "He was just talking about the *quills'* length on the two varieties. As a matter of fact," added the manager, "their pricks are about the same size."

Here we have the same bad/good/bad again technique of the joke, above, regarding leprosy and the loss of the penis. The lady is "offended" by the clerk; the manager soothes her feelings with a logical explanation; then violates her sensibilities by using the horrid word "prick" with its true slang denotation.

In Legman's last classification of dirty jokes, "Scatology," he includes jokes involving the human rump (rear-end, ass, arse, etc.) One such joke deftly skewers an attempted put-down with a quick riposte:

> The loser in a card game quits; in a final dig at the winner, a bald man, the loser runs his hand over the winner's bald pate and murmurs, "Frank, your bald head feels exactly like my wife's ass."
>
> Frank takes a feel of his own head and replies, "By God—you know, you're *right!*"

Traditionally, angry people often lay on their enemies the curse of something (at least verbally) "shoved" (up the rectum of the rival). This is a well-worn comic script:

> A customer in a restaurant calls the waiter over and tells him, "Take this steak back to the chef and tell him to stick it up his arse!"
>
> "Sorry, Sir," replies the waiter, "but your steak will have to get in line behind one pork chop and a coconut pie ahead of you."

This "lineup" makes for a highly amusing picture of the embattled cook.

Scatology jokes can also invoke the comic script of *stupidity* combined with reference to acts ordinarily unmentionable:

> A man with constipation returns to his doctor with the same old complaint. The doctor asks, "Didn't you take those suppositories I gave you?"
>
> "Sure did," replies the patient, "and they did me no good at all. And, in the bargain, they *tasted* terrible."
>
> Shocked, the doctor asks, "You mean you swallowed them?"
>
> "Of course I swallowed them, Doc. What the hell did you expect me to do with them—shove 'em up my *ass?*"

I have now concluded exemplifying Legman's fifteen divisions of "the dirty joke." I am not sure into which classification it should be placed, but I wish to include one last story I picked up in my travels through the ubiquitous muck of filthy humor extant today while working on this chapter. The subject matter is sex, but the object of ridicule is the *conceited nature* of both a young man and a young woman.

> The arrogant young couple are engaging in sexual intercourse, when the girl says, "I'm really tight, am I not?"
>
> The guy replies, "I'd say that you're presently well-filled."

There seems to be little doubt that sexual humor is one of the most prevalent and best-enjoyed kinds of humor. As Ruch and Hehl (1988) point out, "Sexual themes apparently are one of the most prominent contents in Humour. Sex as a salient ingredient in humour was stressed by many humour theorists...and appeared in nearly all factorial investigations in this realm too...."

One reason for the popularity of sexual humor, of course, is that it is entertaining. When the people telling and hearing the jokes together know each other well enough to not be offended by the content or the language of such humor, they can relax and laugh at the sexual antics as much as they like. Another possible reason for the popularity of sexual humor is the featured point of this chapter: much sexual humor can also profit in humorousness by its active ingredient of *aggression*. That is, if both aggression and sexual content *each* make for good jokes, a combination of the two adds up to double enjoyment. And the saving social grace of being able to enjoy right up front two socially suppressed activities (sex and aggression) is that they are couched in the "harmless" context of the jokes' "play frame." Ziv and Gadish (1990) demonstrated that, for instance, more "affect" and more aggression is allowed in overt expression when the respondents are urged to "use humor" in writing stories explaining ambiguous TAT pictures.

But then, enjoyment of such humor can be dampened under some social conditions.

For instance, Young and Frye (1966) had experimental conditions set up for groups to be exposed to sexual humor in same-sex groups. As *male* groups were getting underway, the experimenters had a female student confederate enter the room on the pretext that she mistakenly came "at the wrong time" but begged to be allowed to take part in the experiment since she could not stay for the (later) all-female session. She was allowed to join the group of males. All sat in a circle so that each subject could see all the other subjects' reactions.

When the one female laughed at the sex jokes, the men did too. But when the female showed embarrassment, such as burying her face in her hands and lowering her head to her desk, the laughter of the males was inhibited.

Legman insists that the telling of dirty jokes has another function other than just enjoyment: a functional one, as far as the male is concerned. He likens telling sexual jokes in the presence of females to "verbal rape." If the women don't laugh, they can be teased as "poor sports." If they do laugh (even if against their will) they show positive affect in the presence of words that create pictures in the mind of sexual *activity*. By forcing females, thus, to show pleasure in the presence of symbolic sexual behavior, the male joke-teller batters away at the female's natural reluctance to engage in actual promiscuous sex.

At least one study (Davis and Farina 1970) lends support to this "sex humor as verbal rape" supposition. They had male college students come into the lab and evaluate provocative sexual material. The subjects' actual ratings of the sexy material were secured in two different ways.

A sexually attractive female graduate student administered the experiment. In one condition she was dressed, made-up, and behaved in a highly sexually attractive manner; in the other she was dressed plainly, used no makeup, and behaved completely "all business." Call the conditions "hi-sexy" and "lo-sexy."

The female confederate would hand the humorous materials to the male subject and then either (1) have the subject tell *her* his ratings, which she would dutifully record, or (2) let the subject write down his responses and place his papers into an "anonymous" receptacle in the lab. While the subject was completing his task in this no-tell-her condition, she sat apart from him, with her back to the subject, apparently engrossed in another task.

In other words, she was either "hi" or "lo" in sex appeal, and either received directly the subjects' ratings or did not. It is obvious, then, that the subject would *know* whether the female experimenter would become aware of his ratings of the humor.

Davis and Farina found that, in the "lo-sexy" condition, the subjects' ratings of the humor did not differ, whether the lady directly received the subjects' ratings or not. But, in the "hi-sexy" condition, the ratings of the humor were significantly higher when the subjects knew the female received and understood their ratings. They explain these results as subjects' motivation to show sexual interest in the sexy experimenter by rating the sexy humor higher.

Telling sexual jokes and expressing appreciation for them in the presence of females may be rooted in the (conscious or unconscious) attempt of the male to enhance opportunity for sexual activity. Since it has been some time since I was of the age and unmarried state that I, personally, might have been interested in such machinations, it is difficult to remember if such a supposition was true in my case or not. But the idea does "make sense," and is supported somewhat by research.

Another study is pertinent to this point. Bill and Naus (1992) had students read and evaluate a number of described incidents, several of which were classified as "sexist" incidents. The "sexist" incidents were scattered randomly throughout the entire set of described events.

College students rated the incidents on several scales, including one measuring "funniness" and one measuring "sexism."

What they found, basically, was that the more "funny" an incident was rated, the lower it was rated on "sexism." This finding coincides with the *All in the Family* studies which found that Archie Bunker, by being "funny," came across as a *"loveable* bigot," and with the motivation of the Nazis to stifle Jewish humor so as to not "humanize" the Jews.

It might be that making sex "funny" reduces its solemnity, its "seriousness," its dread; and thus perhaps results in less resistance to and more practicing of sexual activity.

Does this not seem like a hypothesis deserving of further research?

6

The Special Case of Puns:
Word*play* is a Game to be Won, Too

A pun is the lowest form of wit.

—John Dennis

*A pun is the lowest form of humor—when you
don't think of it first.*

—Oscar Levant

What we call a *pun*, the Greeks had a word for: *paronomasia*, or,
roughly translated, "equal word." As Lederer (1988, 1990) points out,
there are three major types of puns: the homograph, the homophone, and
the double-sound pun.

The homograph (Greek: "same writing") employs a word or words
with two or more meanings. The multiple meanings are represented by
the same word, spelled the same way:

Who was the first man to bear arms? Adam. He had two.

How did Samson die? From fallen arches.

The young woman wished her boyfriend would give her a ring.

Show me Nixon's grave and I'll show you a Republican plot.

Here we have "arms" standing for both *human appendages* and *weap-
ons*; "arches" standing for both *foot structure* and *architectural support*; "ring" meaning *telephone call* and *engagement ring*; and "plot"
meaning both *burial site* and *scheme*.

The homophone (Greek: "same sound") combines two words of different meanings *and* spellings but which sound alike.

131

What is black and white and red (read) all over?

A newspaper.

A bloody zebra.

A young man with a squeaking shoe decided to become a songwriter since he had music in his sole.

A tourist from Czechoslovakia was killed in an auto accident in the United States. His remains were cremated and sent home via parcel post. His immediate family was wired the message: "The Czech is in the mail."

The "double-sound pun" can be more complicated. It can be a word that *puns* on a *pun*. Richard Lederer gives us one in the title of his book, *Get Thee to a Punnery*. "Punnery" is a pun on "nunnery" which, again, is a pun on Hamlet's use of "nunnery" which could, in his time, mean either a "house of ill refute," as Archie Bunker called it, or "housing for nuns."

Lederer reports that Oliver Wendell Holmes punned with the words "physician" and "fevers" in, "As a physician, I am grateful for small fevers." And the irrepressible Groucho Marx punned on two words in the conclusion of his, "After shooting an elephant in Africa I had a hard time getting the tusks out, but in Alabama the Tuscaloosa."

But now, down to business.

I have put off the burden of proving that puns and other "plays on words" resulting in humor fit quite nicely within the "laughing = winning" formula proposed by this book until the matter could be taken up now in a separate chapter.

The argument will be divided into two parts. As pointed out by Duncan (1985) when discussing "The Superiority Theory of Humor at Work," the humorous process involves

the *initiator* [who] is the person who tells the joke or begins the humorous act. The *target* is the person to whom the joke is told, and the *focus* or *butt* is the person at whose expense the humor is directed. Individuals or groups who observe or hear the joke are the *publics*.

Part 1 considers the pun from the standpoint of its *initiator*, or inventor, and who it is that represents his/her target and/or butt; part 2 will consider the extant pun that is gathered by others and dispensed either orally or visually (in print) for the enjoyment of others.

Part 1 first asks the question, "*Why* do people create puns?"

Let's consider the question as multiple-choice.

a. Punsters develop the verbal habit as children and, as with smoking, find it hard to quit.

b. Punning is a disease of the mind with an as-yet-undiscovered cause.

c. Punsters succumb to their art through peer pressure.

d. Some people just unconsciously make puns without realizing it.

e. Punsters go to special schools and are taught punning through Skinnerian behavior modification.

f. The mother of every known punster was terrorized by a *Webster's Dictionary* while pregnant with him/her.

f. The Devil makes them do it.

g. None of the above.

I opt for *g*. I argue that one who deliberately creates puns for those around him/her does so in order to show off how damn clever and smart he/she is. I ask you: what other possible motive could exist that would drive a person to utter truncated riddles which are more likely to elicit groans and grousings over "bad puns."

In his essay, "Pardon the Pun," Buffington (in Moger, 1988) affirms my point:

> There truly is a love-hate relationship with puns. You love them if you create them—and hate it if someone beats you to the punch. It's like, "I wish I said that." So, what do you do when you hear a pun? Groan. Although it's music to the punster's ear, that simple groan is a pseudo-putdown. The groan protects you, because you just found yourself one-upped by the guy with the superior vocabulary, and indirectly informs him that you won't put up with his showing off. To say the very least, knowledge of language is a prerequisite to effective punning. (85)

As the two quotations heading this chapter indicate, it is only those unable to pun well that "look down" on punning. As Jonathan Swift wrote: "Punning is a talent which no man affects to despise but he that is without it." Edgar Allen Poe made the same point: "Of puns it has been said that they who most dislike them are least able to utter them."

Joseph Addison (*The Spectator*, no. 61) wrote that "The seeds of punning are in the minds of all men, and though they may be subdued by reason, reflection, and good sense, they will be very apt to shoot up in the greatest genius, that is not broken and cultivated by the rules of Art." All good testimony to the free-wheeling intelligence of punsters.

Evans (1978: 565) argues that "punning is often an instrument of wit and even by themselves puns often surprise us with that 'fine excess' which Keats saw as the essence of poetry. Certainly some very witty men—Charles Lamb, Thomas Hood, and, above all, Shakespeare—have been addicted to punning."

Charles Lamb, mentioned in the paragraph above, one of the best essayists and letter-writers to use the English language, loved and practiced punnery: "A pun is a noble thing per se. It fills the mind; it is as perfect as a sonnet; better" (in a letter to Samuel Taylor Coleridge). Macready is quoted (in the *Journal*, 9 January 1834) as saying of the writer: "I noted one odd saying of Lamb's that 'the last breath he drew in he wished might be through a pipe and exhaled in a pun.'" (Lamb was as much addicted to tobacco as he was to punning.)

Alan L. Otten, in the report of his study of the puns of Shakespeare, "The Pun Never Sets..." (in Moger, 1988), calculated the frequency with which the Bard injected punnery into his earlier as compared and contrasted with his later plays. His hypothesis was that the *young* Shakespeare, in an effort to dazzle his contemporaries with his literateness despite his youth, used many puns as proof of his linguistic mastery; but that, as he matured and gained acceptance, he would feel much less the need to impress his audiences and his critics of his versatility. He concludes, in part:

> When you make a diagram of the plays by the years in which they appeared and apply these percentages, you will end up with a gradually descending curve, the descent being more rapid at the beginning. This, in the main, corroborates our hypothesis. In the exuberance of youth, his brain thick with teeming fancies, his mind impressed with the euphuistic style of the day, Shakespeare simply revelled in his mastery of the language and was no doubt eager to show that whatever others could do, he, at any rate, could go one better. (141–42)

Contemporary punster/writer/lawyer Harvey C. Gordon has produced two books (1980, 1981) of puns. He refers to the people toward which his puns are originally directed as *victims*. He recommends:

> When a pun is told [with a straight face] it is not unusual for at least one person in the group not to know what hit him until someone groans it to his attention. (If no one in the group catches the pun, be sure to stop the conversation, smile, and tell everyone what a great play on words they just missed!) (1981: 118)

In both his books Gordon gives several examples of puns he has "cracked" in the presence of friends, acquaintances, waitresses, and business associates. After several of them he relates the negative consequences inflicted upon him by his victims' either verbal or actual behavior. It is well that Gordon subtitles his original book and it's second edition "How To Lose Friends and Agonize People."

Such direct person-to-person punning obviously involves the punster as the *initiator*; and the person(s) hearing the created pun are just as obviously the *public* (they are the first and only people to hear the pun). But they are also the butt(s)! They are the victims of one-upmanship, of a clever verbal riposte that demonstrates the surprising and momentary *verbal superiority* of the punster! They hear the pun which, at first blush, does not "make sense." They suspect a verbal puzzle. Turning on the brainpower, putting some thought into the little riddle, they then "get it"; they figure out the hidden, second meaning, and it's verbal logic within the context of the statement. Then, because they have spent mental energy for no other purpose than to find that they have been "defeated" (as well as "tricked") they either maintain a flabbergasted silence, "groan," or make a face ("groan visually"). It is the straight-faced punster, the *initiator*, who laughs inwardly at his/her own cleverness ("I won! One point for me!").

I argue that the pun descended from the *conundrum*, or "punning riddle," which, in turn, descended from the common *riddle* with its "I-know-the-answer-and-you-don't" contest nature. In the common and early riddle the riddler hopes to demonstrate superior knowledge to the "riddlee." In the *conundrum* he not only "defeats" his riddlee, but "tricks" him by using a word or phrase with a double meaning; and unless the "riddlee" is knowledgeable or crafty enough to come up with the strange and nonobvious meaning, he is beaten—and "unfairly tricked." No wonder he would groan. And the pun is a natural descendant of the riddle—an *abbreviated* riddle without the question/answer format. Instead of asking "What did the toothless termite ask in the tavern?" and, getting a no-answer shrug, stating "He asked 'Is this bar tender here,'" the punster just says "Hear about the termite who entered a tavern and asked 'Is the bar tender here?'"

Perhaps you have lingering doubts about the *contest nature* of the pun. The competitive nature of that humor form is best seen in direct person-to-person punning and counterpunning, a form not often seen. Consider these contests:

Joe: Oh, heck. I left my wristwatch upstairs.

Moe: That's OK. It'll run down.

Joe: I doubt it. It's a winding staircase.

Don: I went to see the movie *Jaws*.

Ron: I hear it's expensive. Did it cost you an arm and leg?

Don: No, but it *did* cost me a fin.

Ron: But you can afford it, with your present wage scale.

Bill: I saw some deer off U.S. 78 yesterday.

Phil: Any doe?

Bill: Yes. Three bucks.

Phil: I don't believe you. You're just saying that for fawn.

Bill: No, really. I'm not just blowing my horns.

Barry: I'm broke. Bought some cattle futures and got a bum steer.

Larry: Oh, quit your beefing.

Barry: I don't think you herd me. I'm penniless!

Larry: A penny saved is a penniless to spend.

Jill: This coffee tastes like mud.

Jane: That fits. It was ground today.

Jill: Well it can't perk me up this morning.

Jane: That's because you're such a drip.

Jill: Cracks like that could make me dislike you in an instant.

Jane: Oh, simmer down. Your boiling over.

Jill: Sometimes I feel like decaffeinating you.

Jane: You're not strong enough.

Bob: The cops arrested a streaker yesterday.

Rob: Could then pin anything on him?

Bob: Naw. The guy claimed he was hauled in on a bum wrap.

Rob: You'd think the case was supported by the bare facts.

Bob: We can probably hear more about the case tonight on the TV nudescast.

Rob: Tomorrow's nudespaper might have more details.

Here the one-upmanship competition of the pun comes into full view.

Punning has long been associated with intelligence. As *Chicago Sun-Times* columnist Robert J. Herguth, wrote in his "Foreword" to Gordon's second edition of *PUNishment*: "...people with rapier wits and high I.Q.'s can be singled out instantly, because they plunk homespun puns into even the most serious chats. Puns are to words what Bach is to music, what Rembrandt is to canvas, what a French chef is to pot roast."

It was Freud (1905: 143) who, writing about "innocent" jokes involving wordplay, contradicted himself (on *innocent*): "The motive force for the production of innocent jokes is not infrequently an ambitious urge to show one's cleverness to display oneself—an instinct that may be equated with exhibitionism in the sexual field." And Grotjahn chimes in: "A pun offers a challenge to the skillful word juggler, which is its redeeming feature. The listener admires the pun more for the effort and ingenuity which goes into it than because he enjoys the wit" (1966: 79–80). And, although he and I disagree on the details of the main reasons for puns' inclusion as humor, Harvey Mindess (1971) joins our chorus in highlighting the nature of the punning act:

> It is founded…on the fundamental enterprise itself: the twisting of words to convey unexpected thought….the exercise amounts to a rudimentary creative process, for it involves nascent ideation—new images and ideas being formed out of old dull parts. (89)

Another Freudian, Edmund Bergler (1956), supports the punster-as-aggressor hypothesis: "The inveterate punster, although he no longer runs the risk of being hanged, is still a nuisance; the helpless listener feels that he has been made the victim of a cheap trick, and resents it" (120).

So much for the lively art of original, person-to-person punning in conversation. On to part 2.

In this part we consider the pun which comes from an *initiator* predominantly anonymous and unenvisioned. These are the "secondhand" puns we hear and repeat, those we find in "joke books," in magazines such as *Readers' Digest*, in books devoted exclusively to the collecting of puns, and on the walls of public places. In most of these the *public* and the *butt* are one and the same, as in the punning of part 1. In this case both the "winning" and the "losing" become more obscure. When encountering a pun in a *Readers' Digest* "Toward More Picturesque Speech" or being told "a good one" by a friend, we *expect* a small verbal puzzle, as explained above. We hear/read the pun, experience the brief moment of indecision, of "puzzlement," then solve the riddle successfully *and without having been defeated by a tangible, recognizable verbal adversary.* By solving the verbal riddle, without having been "defeated" by anyone, the target/public becomes the *winner*. Human problem-solving is a self-satisfying behavior. This obscuring of the distinction between "winner" and "loser" is probably responsible for the classification of so many wordplay stimuli as "innocent" or "nonhostile."

Now: why does the "winning" target/public in some cases "groan," and in other cases *laugh*? The truth is, the vast majority of puns one is

likely to come across in humor books are not funny. There is hardly a
snicker in a carload of them. They might even be considered as not belonging at all to the class of *humorous* stimuli. But then there is that
occasional pun that comes across as a sheer delight.

It is a matter of *quality*. Let us consider this characteristic in terms of
the laughing = winning paradigm.

If the heard/read pun is a "bad" (read "poor," "strained," "overworked,"
"flat," or "trite") pun, it presents the target/public with puzzle-solving
work they consider "not worth the effort." The unconscious verdict of
the target/public is: "This crummy pun was more like work than play.
Being work, not play, I have missed 'getting what I want.'" Result:
groannnnnn. The groan signifies *loss*.

On the other hand, if the pun is a "good" one, the target/public is
more likely to laugh with pleasure in sharing the witty insight of the
anonymous, clever and impersonal punster. The unconscious response
is, "The solving of this little puzzle resulted in jolly good fun! This was
a good one!"

I must have read or heard a million or more puns in my lifetime, and,
just recently, in preparing for this chapter, had read a number of books
devoted to the genre. My reading included a book of verbal witticisms
entitled *Puniana* and published in 1866. Many of the puns, in riddle
(question/answer) form, fall into the "groan" category; and some reflect
1866-era language and content that the 1990s would find in poor taste:

> Why is a black man out for a holiday like a bandy-legged Emperor? Because the
> knee-grows out. [Ne-gro's out]

> Why is a nigger like a door? Because he is so palpably made for an egress [a
> Negress].

Others which "fall flat" merely show their datedness as to historical
period:

> Why was *Uncle Tom's Cabin* not written by a female's hand?

> Because it was written by Mrs. Beecher's toe [Mrs. Beecher Stowe].

In my opinion, the vast majority of puns one finds in books are of the
"groan" variety. They are "not worth" figuring out. They are just plain
"not funny," just as other figures of speech, such as analogy, metaphor,
simile, and personification are not funny.

But there is always the occasional pun that is worth telling and repeating because "figuring it out" and sharing in its brilliance brings sheer delight. I currently am spreading as far and wide as I can the following:

> The goalie of the Los Angeles hockey team had showered after the game and was walking from the arena to his car. A young man stopped him with a request for an autograph of his game program. While the goalie was accommodating the request, the young man explained that he was a real fan of the goalie and his team, and was actually from the goalie's hometown. The goalie then said, "That's great. Say, I was just going to get something to eat. Why don't you come along and let me buy you some supper, and we can talk about the old hometown?" The youngster said thanks a lot, but his Dad was waiting for him nearby in the car. "That's OK," said the goalie, "ask him to come along. I'll buy him a bite to eat, too!" So it was agreed. The three had a nice supper, and, over coffee, the conversation became quite *spiritual*. After all, present was the Father, the Son, and the Goalie Host.

One of my favorite moments in radio broadcasting was the BBC show, "My Word," presented on Public Broadcasting (now, alas, canceled). One feature of the program pits one member of each team in an applause-eliciting contest providing the "origin" of a famous saying or quotation given them during the program. The stories which the contestants create generally end in a pun on the quotation. Recently one contestant was given the task of providing the background for "Old soldiers never die, they only fade away."

The gentleman who was presented this task, in his measured and cultured British accent, told the story of his encounter with the lady who scrubbed the floors and stairs of his office building, a woman known in England as a "charwoman," or just plain "char." Ascending the outdoor steps, he happened to step on the char's wrist, which evoked his apology and started a conversation, in which the char related to him that she had "sold her body" to a medical association for fifteen quid, for a research project on "obesity." She said all she had to do to earn the money was to demonstrate annually that she weighed "at least eighteen stone." Noting that the woman was "thin as a rail," the storyteller asked her how she was able to prove such an obvious fib. The char replied that she had her friend, Ada, who weighed a good *nineteen stone*, go to the weigh-in in her place. Asked by the gentleman how she could get away with such chicanery, the char replied that the actual sale of her body had been made seventeen years previously, and the hefty Ada has gone in for the mandatory annual weigh-in once each year since, and the medical authorities had not caught on to the scheme yet. At this point the storyteller came to his conclusion: it just goes to show you that "Old sold chars never die, they only evade away."

My retelling of this lengthy story, leading up to a most clever pun, never fails to draw at least an amused smile.

Jokes and puns can be considered a form of *art*, if we can accept the kind of definitions of that word we find in dictionaries, such as "the disposition or modification of things by human skill, to answer the purpose intended (meaning *art* as opposed to *nature*)....creative work generally, or its principles; the making or doing of things that have form and beauty; ....products of creative work....[the product of] skill, dexterity, or the power of performing certain actions, acquired by experience, study, or observation," and so on.

If puns are then to be considered an art form, we should ordinarily expect only a very few to succeed abundantly. Of the millions of paintings, drawings, and sculptures crafted by human minds and hands, do not only a relatively *few* reach the acclaim accorded those displayed in the world's great museums and sold at the highest prices in competitive auctions? Do not only a tiny percentage of humans talented in music, dance, singing, acting, and writing attain their goal of making a successful vocation from their abilities? And if, as Harry Reasoner said in a CBS TV special in 1967 , there is a thin line between a public speaker's achieving "eloquence" and "letting off hot air," why should we *not* expect that most puns (and jokes) would be ineffective as humor?

But in experimental studies, even the weakest of jokes and the poorest of puns usually are reported as having been rated somewhere in the "humorous" range, no matter how lowly. I suspect that such ratings as "low humorous" might result from the scaling methods used. If a study employed, for instance, a simple twenty-point linear scale bookended by, say, "not funny" and "the funniest ever," *some* respondents are going to make checkmarks above the "0" or "1" end simply because the stimuli is *worded* as a joke or pun—it *looks* like it should be funny. This will produce an *average* rating somewhere in the "humorous" range.

To counter this kind of "lack of a floor" rating, I use a scale whose bottom is "just not funny," but with "just plain stupid" one notch below that. And I get lots of checkmarks on these choices. Some scales only seem to have "floors," when what they really need are basements.

In addition to puns (a) whose initiator is the winner and the target/ public is the loser, and those (b) whose initiator is obfuscated by anonymity and the target/public is *either* the winner or loser (depending upon the quality of the pun), there is a third winner/loser configuration: this occurs when the initiator is *neutral*, the target/public is the *winner*, and the *loser(s)* exist as an element in the *content* of the pun.

The reader may recognize this third configuration as the same as that for the ordinary *joke*. And, indeed, that is how such "puns" operate, psychologically. In fact, I would classify them more as "jokes" (involving "wordplay") than "puns," but the examples below I quote from books specifically devoted to the art form of *the pun*.

For example:

He (dejectedly): You've played the deuce with my heart.

She (archly): Well, didn't you play the knave?

[Clever pun-upmanship, but a *put-down* of he by she. He loses, she wins, and we, the target/public laugh (and win) along with she.]

Pat: What do you suppose became of all those love triangles you hear about?

Pete: Most of them turn into wrecktangles, I guess.

[We win; the losers? Those anonymous poor devils who gamble on love "three ways.]

Gert: I didn't see John at the dance last night but I hear he acted the part of a thoroughbred.

Trude: What part?

[Trude cleverly skewers John, the horse's a——, to our delight.]

John: Don't you think I'm rather good looking?

Jane: In a way.

John: What kind of a way?

Jane: Away off.

[This time it is "Jane" who shoots conceited John down in flames for us!]

Dopey Dan is so dumb he thinks rhubarb is a French street.

[Clever punster hyperbolizes Dopey's stupidity for our pleasure.]

Ruth rode in my new cycle car
In the seat in back of me;
I took a bump at fifty-five,
And rode on Ruthlessly.

[Mayhem is almost always funny; we love it.]

There was a little lawyer man
Who gently smiled as he began
The widow's husband's will to scan;
And thinking of his coming fee,
He said to her quite tenderly,
"You have a nice fat legacy."
Next morning as he lay in bed
With bandages on his broken head
He wondered what-in-heck he said.
[And an unintended homophone reaps horrible revenge from a feminist activist.]

Puns and "wordplay" can combine with sexual and hostile content to make a good joke. Legman offers a great many, including Senator Hoare is delivering a long speech against a certain bill, standing first with his left hand and then his right hand in his pants pocket. His opponent rises and remarks, "The Senator from Massachusetts seems to be leaving no stone unturned to prevent the passage of this bill" (1975: 290).

In limiting my classifications of pun quality to "good" and "bad," I perhaps oversimplify. Marino (1988) proposes *three* classes, the third being "beautiful." But, apparently, what he would call "beautiful" or "very good" are esoteric quibbles unrecognizable by 99 44/100 percent of the literate population. Marino admits that it would take an "appreciative audience" to hear Hamlet's "very good pun," a remark made to his father's apparent ghost: "Thou com'st in such a questionable shape/That I will speake to thee." Very few of the great unwashed would consider this one a rousing crowd-pleaser. Another example he provides is the not-so-hilarious use of *hende* in Chaucer's *The Miller's Tale*; and how many people are you acquainted with who know many different Middle English meanings of that word that would make it such a side-splitter?

If for no other reason than some will accuse me of deliberately avoiding its analysis, I will now deal with the "elephant joke." Not all elephant jokes involve *punning*, of course, but some do.

How do elephants make love in the water? They take off their trunks.

What do you do with an elephant with three balls? Walk him deliberately and pitch to the rhinoceros. [And elephant jokes can be *sexual*.]

Oring (1992) reproduced these in his collection his article "To Skin an Elephant" in which he tries to *explain* elephant jokes. In this effort he first attacks the psychoanalytical conclusion of Abrahams and Dundes (1969) that "the elephant is an ambivalent father figure," but that this father figure "In reality [is] the black man (perceived as a sexual threat) that stands hidden behind the image of the elephant" (17). I can only concur with Oring's conclusion that this explanation from Freudian Monsterland holds no water.

Next, Oring shows that the particular riddle form of the typical elephant joke does not fit the rules and conventions of "traditional riddles" as defined by such folklorists as Taylor (1943) and Georges and Dundes (1963). Oring never quite explains why he wishes to point out that "elephant jokes" are not "traditional" riddles in structure, but I quite agree with such a declassification of the pachyderm pun. After all, if the *content* is so lacking in logic, why should the *form* need to match tradition?

But although I agree with Oring in dismissing the murky Freudian interpretations of the content, and that the elephant joke's format is hardly "traditional," we differ on the psychology behind the little darlings.

Gerald Walker argued (falsely) in a popular mens' magazine that the explosion of "sick jokes" (Bloody Mary's, etc.) was a unique product of the angst-ridden social/political/economic climate uniquely inherent to the 1950s United States. Oring makes the same kind of argument for the chronological topicality of the elephant joke:

> The elephant joke craze exploded in 1963. Coincidental with the emergence of the jokes was the emergence of the counterculture [of the sixties]....The jokes both augur and reflect something of the spirit of what came to animate this era. (1957: 26–27)

Oring's argument on the origin of elephant jokes is a difficult one to *prove*, of course. I would like to propose another theory (equally difficult to prove, probably) of why elephantiasis enveloped our joke-world in 1963. I am older than Oring, and thus remember one of the best motion picture sight gags in history, which could very well have been the spark that eventually stirred up the herd of elephants that stampeded across our consciousness in those times.

The late, great Jimmy Durante starred in the *1962* movie *Jumbo*, the title referring to the huge elephant which that movie featured. Toward the end of the movie, Durante is trying to sneak the elephant, unseen, out of the area. As he leads this huge behemoth around a circus tent he and his long-nosed charge are suddenly confronted by a large crowd, featuring several policemen. One of the cops shouts at him something to the effect of, "Where do you think you're goin' with that *elephant*?" Jimmy's response is to back up against the trunk of the elephant, spread his arms out to his sides in an effort to hide the beast, and blurt back, wide-eyed and innocent-faced, "*What* elephant?"

Now, I don't know how far back into vaudeville and theater this particular comic script (treating a creature or object of humongous size as if size can be completely disregarded) might go, but can't you just imagine one or more comedy writers, professional or otherwise, as a result of the success of the "Jumbo" sight gag, latching onto this script as one to be played for laughs to an extent limited only to one's imagination? The script of "hiding the elephant" by all sorts of ridiculous means has seen heavy service:

> How do you know when an elephant has been in your fridge?
> Footprints in the cheesecake.

> How can you tell when an elephant is with you in the bathtub?
> You can smell the peanuts on his breath.

> Why do elephants wear green sneakers?
> So they can hide in the grass.

> Why did the elephant marry the ant?
> Had to; it was a "shot-gun" wedding.
> [Jokes about elephants having sex with smaller creatures, by the way, are old enough for long white beards.]

> Why do elephants paint their toenails red?
> So they can hide in cherry trees.

> How do you get six elephants into a Honda?
> Three in front, three in back.

Once you have extant "disregard the elephant's size" riddle/jokes, then the pachyderm can spread out to become the subject of other silly, stupid comparisons. You can forget the original script because you have a "genre" of "Elephant Jokes." Elephants (and related concepts and animals) can become the subjects of riddles/jokes/puns using other comic scripts. The usual form is that of the riddle, usually with a nonsensical answer, which is often a play on words, or a pun— a *conundrum*.

What does an elephant use for a vibrator? An epileptic.

What do you get when you cross an elephant with an M.D. specialist in skin disorders? A pachydermitologist.

The conundrum, the wacky word-playing riddle, has been with us a long time. As noted above, *Puniana* provided dozens of punning riddles from the middle of the nineteenth century. During the 1930s and 40s the "Little Moron" semi-riddles (Hear about the Little Moron who.... No? Then I'll tell you...) served as popular content for the technique. The "knock-knock" joke, a kind of riddle, also has had a long history. The question/answer, riddle format has been popular for jokes ethnic or not (What did the priest and the rabbi discuss? Sects). Derogatory jokes directed at particular human types have used the popular riddle form; only the *content* changes:

Why did the Georgia Tech student stay out all night? He stopped outside a whore-house and waited for the light to turn green.

What does the blonde say when you blow in her ear? Thanks for the refill.

How many southern Californians does it take to screw in a light bulb? Southern Californians don't screw in light bulbs; they screw in hot tubs.

What is gray and comes in a bottle? Liquid Elephant.

(Liquid Elephant does not yet exist; but in an age in which nearly anything can be liquified, Liquid Elephant, if possible, could very well be gray.)

What did the elephant say to Marcel Marceau? Nothing, since he did not know sign language. (Elephants use no human language at all, but if they *did*, they might still be deficient in the language of mime.)

To summarize: *creators* of puns and punning riddles do so in order to "defeat" their targets/publics with brilliant verbal exhibitionism. But, rare is the case when an acquaintance "makes up" an original "elephant joke" (or other great pun) on the spot in order to "stump" us. Much more commonly we hear someone's pun or elephant joke repeated by a second (or umpteenth) party, or else read it as an anonymous publication. With the aggressive, smart-ass initiator hidden from our perception, the non-sensical little puzzler *does* lose some of the obviously competitive nature of the win/lose situation prevalent in play. This disguising of the *intent* of the original punster by making the pun's creator *anonymous* must surely give rise to the idea, as Freud contended, you can have non-tendentious ("harmless" or "neutral") wit, whereas the puns actually owe for their effect their ancestors, the riddle and the conundrum. Puns are word*play*.

And as even Oring (1992: 28) admits, "Humor, first and foremost, appears to be a subspecies of *play*" (my emphasis). I agree. And *play* must involve a winner and a loser, or it isn't much fun. Otherwise, why do we always keep score?

I conclude this chapter with an interesting personal example of "Hey, look at me!" punning.

At the 1994 conference of the International Society for Humor Studies at Ithaca College in New York State we took one afternoon off for a bus-and-walking tour of three nearby state parks which featured magnificent waterfalls cascading down to beautiful Lake Cayuga. As we trudged up a path toward one waterfall a young linguist from South America (I think Brazil) touched me on the shoulder and pointed to a sign that read "Pedestrian Path Only."

"Please, Sir," he began, "what does mean 'pedestrian?'"

"It means 'person walking,'" I replied. "Comes from 'pedal,' meaning 'foot-operated?'"

"Ah, yes," he smiled with understanding.

A little farther up the path we encountered a small group leading two dogs on leashes. After a bit the young man from Brazil once again touched my shoulder. "Pardon, Sir, but in English isn't foot of dog 'paw'?"

"Yes," I replied, "A dog's foot is called a 'paw.'"

The linguist smiled wryly. "Then," he said, "this is also *paw*destrian path!"

I turned on him with mock anger. "You are showing off!" I said. "You are showing us how clever you are by *punning*!"

"Yes," he agreed, beaming from ear to ear with pride and self-satisfaction. "I am in America at humor conference three days and I pun in *English*!"

7

The Mirage of "Innocent" Humor

*We do not err because truth is difficult to see. It
is visible at a glance. We err because this is
more comfortable.*

—Alexander Solzhenitsyn

Writers on the subject of humor, with the possibly unique exception of
Max Eastman (1921, 1936), all agree that *much* humor can be accu-
rately described as aggressive, hostile, deprecating, bellicose; that people
delight in that kind of humor finds its source in our human tendency to be
mean, malicious, unkind, maybe downright nasty—in a word, "superior." A particularly nasty, yet humorous anti-Catholic riddle currently
is making the rounds:

> How do you get a nun pregnant?
> Dress her up like an altar boy.

But most modern writers remonstrate against the notion that *all* humor
can be explained as resulting from "superiority." These writers argue for
a class of humorous events, some which actually produce laughter, as
"innocent." Sometimes the term "innocent" is replaced by other terms,
such as "nonhostile," "neutral," or "nonsense." These writers usually
emphasize that with "innocent" humor the impetus to laugh comes, not
from the *content* of the humorous event, but the *form alone* (usually the
wording). Included in this category might be something like:

> When asked how birds know when they should fly south,
> one third-grader replied: "It's a family tradition."

Now, any reasonably intelligent English-speaking human could detect
that the "Catholic nun" riddle, above, contains fairly hostile content

whereas the one-liner about bird migration is, by comparison, quite "innocent": however, notice that, without the naivete (could we say "ignorance" or even "stupidity?") of the young speaker, the jest loses every bit of humor it might be said to contain (really good "hostile" jokes are almost always a lot funnier than even good "innocent" jokes such as the "family tradition" gaff.)

In 1989 a group meeting at Indiana University were discussing the relation of humor to metaphor which they were studying with the use of computers. Another topic was that of "slippage humor," defined (in one way) as the kind of humor it is *not*: it is "contrasted with aggression-based humor." Their first example:

> the casual remark made by David Moser while wandering in Harvard Square near the music store Briggs & Briggs: "If Harvard Square were Harvard Cube, Briggs & Briggs would be Briggs & Briggs & Briggs." (420)

I assume that Harvard Cube is in the nature of a *pun*, and as a pun it is quite a verbal display of superior intelligence; but I doubt that many nightclubbers or borscht-belt audiences would get much of a laugh over it.

I can understand the desire of writers who continue to persist in arguing for the existence of "harmless," "innocent," "neutral," humor without "tendency." The very idea that the precious joy of laughter stems from a basically *mean* and "antisocial" psychological characteristic can disappoint the nobility of human spirit we all think we strive for. To ascribe degradation to humor "dehumanizes" us. People want to believe that we are fallen angels, not risen brutes. We prefer not to see the truth in the anthropology volumes.

McGhee (1979) even stresses, in the opening chapter of his book (10) that "The difficulty with these views [concerning sexual, aggressive, or superiority themes] is that we can easily point to humorous events in which these themes are completely lacking." Interestingly enough, with an entire book ahead of him to write, he gives not one example of humor which he claims is lacking in such a theme.

Theorists arguing for humor that is completely bereft of hostile content (one technique for achieving the *competition* of the win/lose paradigm) often do a pretty good job of arguing *in theory* that degradation, superiority, etc. cannot be the source of *all* humor. They make persuasive cases for their point mainly, I believe, because they *want* to believe that it is so.

But they generally allow their argument to self-destruct by the unwise tactic of producing vulnerable *targets*. Unlike McGhee, above, they try to provide examples of their "innocent" humor.

Sigmund Freud was certainly not the first, but may have been the most famous writer who postulated the existence of "innocent" humor. But, as Martin Grotjahn (1957) has pointed out, Freud was unable to provide a single example of wit/jokes completely devoid of what Freud himself called "tendency."

Freud (1905, 1960) proposed that the *jest* differs from *jokes* (the latter of which depend for their effect on the criticizing of others). The jest prolongs "the yield of pleasure from play, but at the same time of silencing the objections raised by criticism which would not allow the pleasurable feeling to emerge." (129) He follows this description with an example. A doctor named Rokitansky is asked what professions his four sons now follow. Two of these were physicians, the other two were singers. Dr. Rokitansky's reply was, "Two heal and two howl" (129–130). We may applaud and receive pleasure from Dr. Rokitansky's clever use of alliteration, but let us not overlook the derogatory slur at his two singing sons. Few vocalists would appreciate being referred to as *"howlers."* The good doctor cleverly confesses his value-laden *contrast* between his sons: one pair performs the socially acceptable and highly rewarding work of medical practice while the other pair of offspring merely make unappetizing noises. Remove the epithet-nature of this "jest" and you remove any humor that may reside therein. Sulloway (1979) quotes the Rokitansky jest as (probably) typical of Freud's conception of that genre (jests).

Freud himself seems to argue *not* very forcefully for the existence of "innocent" humor, however; his approach is far from "straightforward." He ruminates at one point that, "The motive force for the production of innocent jokes is not infrequently *an ambitious urge to show one's cleverness*, to display oneself—an instinct that may be equated with exhibitionism in the sexual field." This to me sounds like "demonstrated superiority of verbal expression" which I brought up in the previous chapter. Freud at this point was referring to one pun which he repeated several times in his book: Heine has one of his characters, a poor lottery-agent, boast that the rich and famous Baron Rothschild had once treated him "as his equal—quite 'famillionairely.'" Yes, quite clever for a lowly lottery-agent, demonstrating his clever verbal gymnastics.

In his chapter entitled "To Skin An Elephant," Oring (1992) analyzes the so-called "elephant joke" and its relatives in an attempt to deliberately disprove the "aggressive" or "superiority" aspect of humor. To give but one example:

Q: Why are elephants gray?
A: To distinguish them from blueberries.

First of all, this is the common *riddle* form of wordplay. And let us consider the question, "Why do people pose riddles to other people?" Are people *motivated* to pose them? Of course. If they are *not* motivated to pose them, then what else *causes* them to pose riddles? Random selection of words, grammar, and syntax from one's apperceptive mass to speak/write in this particular way?

As I pointed out in the previous chapter, people are motivated to pose riddles for the purpose of "stumping" another person. The riddler hopes and expects the riddlee to *not know* the answer. Since the riddlee cannot give the answer, the riddler can then supply it, thus "winning" this minuscule "contest of wit."

Of course, when the riddle is an "elephant joke" or one of its cousins, it is classified as a conundrum, or "punning riddle." In this form the riddlee cannot reasonably be expected to know the answer (unless he/she has heard it before, which spoils things for the riddler); so the riddlee "gives up" (surrenders, admits defeat, etc.), only to learn that the "correct" answer is a ridiculous play on words which he/she could not possibly be expected to know. Thus he/she is not only "defeated," but "tricked" by foolish wordplay; this "trickery" plus the "play frame" of the well-known humorous riddle form softens the defeat; the riddlee may even smile in recognition of why the wordplay "works," thus making the riddlee *successful* in riddle-solving. We all like that. The reader might wish to review the previous chapter on this point.

One of the more prolonged attacks on the "humor-is-not-all-superiority-humbug" is by Morreall (1983).

He begins (10) by pointing out that the laughter of babies can have nothing to do with "superiority" since the baby cannot distinguish itself as a being separate from its surroundings (an argument also repeated by McGhee 1979). I am not sure how John came to this conclusion about babies, but I do know one thing for certain: babies do not laugh when *not getting exactly what they want* (in fact, when they want something they are *not* getting, they make sounds *much* less pleasant than laughter). And, contrariwise, each time a tiny baby is seen laughing, he/she is getting just exactly what he/she wants at that moment!

He mentions the laughter of the baby when *tickled*, and when playing the game of "peekaboo" as laughter unaffiliated with any superiority, aggression, or competition context (1979:10 and 1987:129). He thus avoids the evidence from anthropology and experimental studies, amply summarized by Koestler:

> Thus tickling a child will call out a wriggling and squirming response. But the child will laugh only—and this is the crux of the matter—if an additional condition is fulfilled: it must perceive the tickling *as a mock attack*, a caress in a mildly aggressive disguise. This is why people laugh only when tickled by others but not when they tickle themselves.... Not only must there be a second person to do the tickling, but her expression and attitude must be mock-aggressive—as mothers and nurses instinctively know. Battle cries like "peekaboo" and "bow-wow" pay guaranteed dividends.... Experiments in tickling of babies under one year old showed babies laughed fifteen times more often when tickled by their mothers than when they were tickled by strangers. For naturally the mock-attack will make the baby laugh only if it knows it is a mock-attack; and with strangers one never knows.... The rule of the game is "let me [baby] be just a little frightened so that I can enjoy the relief." (1964: 80–81)

(Note: some researchers specializing in humor development in children do not consider the child to enjoy *humor* until s/he can experience symbolic play, using symbols [language] at eighteen months to three years of age, as does McGhee [1979], while others consider the laughter of the younger child *humor* as coming from tickling, peekaboo and other games, that produce an "arousal jag" from pleasure at *mastery* [for instance, see Schultz 1976].)

Back to Morreall: he skips over rhyming and alliteration and puns without exemplifying why these techniques get laughs without superiority, but then does come up with an instance at which he had a hearty laugh. He opened his refrigerator one day to find a bowling ball there.

What's funny about a bowling ball in the fridge? Well, how did it get there? Did it start out as a grape in there and just evolve? Did it begin as a tiny "black hole" and generate it's own gravity, enough to attract sufficient inert matter to engender it's heavy, rounded self? Did an inept bowler from the alleys next door forcefully "gutter" one right out the building, through Morreall's open window and, bouncing, ricochet it into the fridge, absentmindedly left open by John?

Of course not. Someone deliberately and *stupidly* placed it there, hoping to "get a rise" out of Morreall. But it did not work. John quickly saw through the stupidity of this practical joke and had a good laugh over this failed attempt to "get John's goat." You cannot put one over on John!

In the same breath Morreall reports having a good chuckle over his sleepily pouring fresh coffee over his morning cereal.

This is a clear case of one part of a man laughing at another part of himself, such as Fry (1963) was quoted earlier as explaining. Ability to laugh at our own blunders is a marvelous way to transcend our mistakes, and is a quality most folks would count as part of "having a good sense of humor." And John Morreall certainly does possess such a quality sense of humor. John even later admits (Morreall 1989) that he would consider this event "a piece of relatively harmless bungling, and laugh"(13). After all, when we make a mistake such as pouring coffee onto our cereal or locking up our car with the keys in the ignition (and maybe even with the engine running?) we have few emotional options. We can become angry (with *ourselves*) and start kicking something or someone; we can slide into self pity and moan, "Why oh why must this happen to me?"; or we can look upon the absurdity of our mistakes, detach ourselves from and then *laugh at* them. Which option is the most sane?

Morreall thinks he would laugh in a movie showing a man, falling, who grabs for support, finds the handle of a slot machine, and pulls it as he crashes toward the floor, winding up hitting the jackpot (47). I would find that scenario funny, too, since the unsteady casinoite had accidentally and unexpectedly *beaten* the gambling establishment "at their own game." He not only makes a ridiculous picture of himself as he crashes to the deck, klutzy but unharmed; but he also turns the tables on the hard-to-beat casino operators.

John (on the same page) offers the scenario of seeing someone fall into a swimming pool, fully clothed, as one that might cause him to laugh for the event's "incongruity" alone, but that seeing a despised neighbor take the same splash in his new, expensive suit would "delight" him by the clotheshorse's "setback." But I daresay that few of us can hold back a feeling of mirth at seeing almost anyone get a sudden, accidental dunk in the pool fully dressed. And not because of simple incongruity—but because an incongruous and playfully disastrous accident has occurred—to someone else. Also, by the way, I can't think of anyone I know who would consider their own fall into a swimming pool while fully clothed a simple *incongruity*. The folks *I* know would consider such a dunking a disaster ranging from mild to quite serious (depending upon what is in one's pockets and how expensive and/or waterproof one's watch is)!

Beginning on page 61, Morreall concedes that, from here on, he will be writing only of humor funny because of and only because of *incongruity*. One such incongruity he mentions is the differences between customs of disparate cultures, and how they can seem "funny" if unfamiliar. He uses one Margaret Mead ethnocentrism as an example:

> A Plains Indian had just placed food on a new grave, when a white man looking on jocularly asked, "Do you expect the dead man to come up and eat that food?"
>
> To which the Indian responded, "As soon as your dead come up to smell the flowers you place on their graves."

The subject of this story is the incongruity of Plains Indian and "white" cultures, certainly, although such an incongruity need not be funny at all; but it is also a fine and clever "put-down" of a rude, insensitive, Caucasian clod. (The Indian *wins*.) And, incidentally, it also hints that our Euro-American flowers-on-the-grave custom seems a trifle ridiculous. (According to Panati's *Extraordinary Origins of Everyday Things* [1987] strewing both food *and* flowers on human graves was begun by Neanderthal Man.)

Morreall muses that "I can pass by a row of houses, all of one design, and then laugh on reaching a house of a completely different design" (64). I am not John's analyst, but I can empathize with such an experience. I would interpret it as, "After all those copycats, here is a house born of reactionary creativity! I applaud the owner, and share in his smug revolution against architectural conformity! The nonconformist wins, and I applaud!" I think my explanation is at least as credible as Morreall's; as we have seen earlier, simple incongruity is not funny. Incongruity *with a purpose* is.

Morreall (who is a philosophy professor) then gives us a string of examples which he claims are funny because of "incongruity" (alone), but which I would say definitely fall into the "win/lose" or "ridicule" class: the little TV *battles* between Ed Norton (Art Carney) and Ralph Cramden (Jackie Gleason) of TV's *The Honeymooners*; the combative tricks of the practical joke (pulling a chair from under someone) or the more elaborate hoaxes pulled on the unsuspecting, as on *Candid Camera*; the situation in which people either fail (which we love to see) or else succeed with little effort (with whom we laughingly empathize), and the two Englishmen on a train, one of whom says "I say, is this Wembley?" and the other replies, "No, Thursday." To which the first rejoins, "Me, too." This latter story amuses us by the dotty gentlemen's absolute failure to communicate, a defect which they perceive as perfect communion.

He goes on to produce a prodigious list of funny-only-because-of-"incongruity" laughter-producing phenomena: inferiority, such as physical deformity, underdevelopment, weakness, moral inferiority, failure, ignorance and stupidity (including the naivete of children), and sundry other human deficiencies that we laugh at as a result of superiority. He even mentions those kings of slapstick, Laurel and Hardy, as depending exclusively on "incongruity" for their slam-bang comedy effects. Morreall also so classifies the old radio/TV team of George Burns and Gracie Allen, without mentioning that each and every one of Gracie's "punch lines" reveal her stupidity, ignorance, and/or cupidity.

Morreall refers to mimicry, such as what professional comedians of the Rich Little genre perform, as "incongruity." Mimic comedians who make us laugh *do* entertain us by mimicking the voices and mannerisms of well-known others—but they do far more than just mimic. They "do" *comedy* in their mimicry roles. If a comic *only* mimics a well-known person, we might be entertained by that comic's skill, much as we are entertained by a really proficient juggler, acrobat, or dancer. But we will only laugh at that mimic when he/she "does" *comedy* in the mimicry act. When Dana Carvey "does" former President George Bush, he does not simply reproduce what George says and does; Carvey exaggerates Bush's manner of speaking, acting, and thinking by making fun of George Bush, as in his overly-simplistic "That's baaaaaaad!—That's go-o-o-o-o-od!" When Phil Hartman "does" President Clinton, he criticizes the president through exaggeration of his propensity for junk food, his womanizing, his ever-present smile, and so on. When Jim Carey facially mimics any celebrity, he does it in a way that makes a comic caricature of that celebrity, emphasizing and exaggerating the famous person's most laughable facial characteristics.

Rich Little impersonates "Tricky Dick" Nixon to perfection; but he does so in order to show us humorously most of the former President's baser qualities.

In 1972 impressionist David Frye recorded a comedy album entitled *I Am The President*. In a radio advertisement for the record Mr. Frye imitated several well-known persons as they talked about Frye's album. In the voice of President Nixon, Frye said, "I have heard Mr. Frye's new comedy album, *I Am The President.* But he is *not*—the president! I am the president!" (Emphasizing and ridiculing Nixon's megalomania). He has a comment "from Texas": (voice of Lyndon Johnson) "I listened—and it gave me—a hea—vy heart!" (ridiculing LBJ's maudlin folksiness). "From Alabama" we hear: "If any pseudo-intellectual-hippie lays David Frye's new album on my stereo—it's gonna be the last stereo he ever lays a record on!" (razzing Gov. George C. Wallace's militant stand against anything non-southern and/or non-white/middle class).

Mimicry or impersonation can be humorous or serious. Consider the vision of Arthur Koestler on this point:

> The impersonator is two different people at one time. If the result is degrading, the spectator will laugh. If he is led to sympathize or identify himself with the impersonated hero, he will experience that state of split-mindedness known as dramatic illusion or the magic of the stage.... The same dramatic devices may serve either a comic or a dramatic purpose;.... Rosalind in *As You Like It* and Leonora in *Fidelio* are both disguised as men, yet in one case the result is drama, in another comedy. (1964: 68)

Christopher Wilson (1979) devotes an entire chapter to "The Sense in Nonsense," which attempts to explain "innocent humor," which he defines as

> neither intended nor perceived to express sexual, aggressive, derisive, or other motivational meanings. The amusing properties of nonsense derive solely from its incongruous form.

I feel toward "nonsense" as humor much as Bill Fry and I feel toward "incongruity." Some nonsense is funny, but nonsense is not sufficient in and of itself to be funny. For instance, I think that the idea of the United States spending billions of dollars on the B-2 bomber is about as nonsensical a way of throwing money down a rathole as ever devised by Congress. But I don't think it's funny!

After introducing us to a theoretic formula involving Xs and Ms with various numberings, Wilson, unfortunately for his theory, gives us some examples: Spoonerisms such as "just received a blushing crow" and "our queer old dean" (for "just received a crushing blow" and "our dear old Queen)" both stupid, laughable human linguistic *mistakes*. He also includes amusement from naive and senseless questions from small children, such as "What does blue look like from behind?" and musings such as "It's strange that animals have holes in their skin precisely at the place where their eyes are." Wilson, himself, even, cannot avoid calling such ridiculous items "childish" and "*idiotic*" (My emphasis—*idiots* have amused Man from The Beginning). Another statement he includes as "innocent" nonsense is the phrase "(he) is better off dead," since no one may *be* at all, if dead. Again, this is a truly stupid remark, not just an incongruous nonsensical phrase. If it were not stupid, it would not be funny. Later in the chapter Wilson attempts to demonstrate "innocent" humor in "contrived jokes." His first three oxymoronic examples:

> I'd give my right hand to be ambidextrous.
> A verbal agreement isn't worth the paper it's written on.
> If Roosevelt were alive, he'd turn in his grave.

And then he throws in:

> Sleep faster. We need the pillows.

Let us please be reasonable! If you lost your right hand, ambidexterity would be impossible; verbal agreements are *not* set to paper; live people do not reside in graves in which to turn over; and no one can get more in sleep by sleeping faster. These "jokes" are funny because of the *stupidity* of their authors. Who could possibly imagine these statements coming from an intelligent, careful, thinking being? And these were the only "innocent" contrived jokes Wilson offers as examples.

He does cite, in that chapter, however, several studies that either used or "discovered" so-called innocent humor. One of these studies was by Rose Coser (1960).

Coser sat in on psychiatric hospital staff meetings and recorded events which elicited laughter. She claimed that only 16 percent of the humorous events were "innocent;" and by "innocent" she seems to imply "without a specific target." Reading her original report makes very hard work indeed of trying to perceive anything funny at all that went on in those meetings. I suspect that the events *taken out of the meeting context* could hardly be understood, let alone appreciated as humor. And Coser seems not to offer specific examples of "targetless" humor, unless it was (86–87) the one where a junior staff member mentioned in a report a patient, interested in genealogy, especially among prisoners of war in the American Revolution. A senior staff member interrupts with "What happened to the prisoners of war?", thus steering the meeting away from the topic at hand, something only a *senior* member of the staff could do (because of his superiority position). And it occurs to me that, if the senior staffer unilaterally decided to get the meeting "off the subject," this act could certainly be considered an act of exercising his *superiority*.

Similar to the study by Coser is that of Goodrich, Henry, and Goodrich (1954). Like Coser, they gathered laugh stimuli in psychiatric staff conferences, then classified the events. As in the Coser study, it is difficult to read their examples and understand why or how they could be "funny" (get laughs). Since they were not "jokes," the difficulty in understanding them comes from the fact that these stimuli for laughter were all out of context. They categorized the "laughs" (174 total) into three *forms*: Disparagement (85), Incongruity (81), and "Uncertainty"(8). I provide here their description of the various "incongruity" laugh-stimuli, rather than the actual examples (which are not at all clearly "funny"): "when objective reality is denied…when ideas appropriate only in nonclinical situations were brought into the clinical situation…violation of mores…when interpersonal relations were confused or ridiculed…when traditional values were altered…when propriety was endangered." All of these descriptions, to me, sound like they involve stupidity, irrationality, ignorance, aggressiveness, and/or norm-breaking! How do Goodrich et al. sum up their sampling of "incongruity" items? "All these examples represent a 'lifting of the veil,' a *trespassing* (my emphasis) on things not ordinarily mentioned in public in these forms." Again, this sounds like "trying to win," to me; perhaps these stimuli would best fit under the classifications of the various "freedoms" that Harvey Mindess (1971) insists we can categorize humor under, such as freedom from conformity, freedom from inferiority, from morality, and so on.

Middleton and Moland (1959) gathered jokes from black and white university students and classified them as either (1) ridiculing, (2) "harmless," (3) sexual, or (4) "cruel." They found only eleven of the jokes they gathered to be "harmless," which they defined as "consisting largely of puns and plays upon words." Cannily, they provide *no examples* of such "harmless" humor, but we have already seen how puns and plays on words can show cleverness (superiority) or stupidity (see chapter 6).

Singer (1968) exposed black subjects to (1) a recording which mobilized aggressive impulses towards segregationists or (2) a "neutral stimulus" and then had them listen to a black comedian using either hostile-to-whites humor or "neutral humor," or to a "control stimulus." Singer admits that the "theme of the neutral humor was international tension, nuclear destruction, and anxiety about death." This is *neutral*? The example given:

> You know it's a very dangerous thing. I mean, Kennedy told them to do it [nuclear bomb testing] underground...I mean all that fall-out. And you know who this really affects? Can you imagine a physical education instructor on television saying, "Now, take a deep breath." [laughter]
>
> But we...we just tested one. Did you see the paper today? We tested one underground. I go for that! [laughter]
>
> Which tomorrow you'll probably read that we have created a new problem: "fall-up." [laughter]
>
> But Kennedy is a wise and a brilliant man, testing those nuclear bombs underground. Let's face it. That's where the people are going to be. [laughter]

This example might be "innocent" in that it does not belittle blacks, but nuclear holocaust, mass homicide, and the prediction that we would all end up (six feet) underground are not really what I would call the themes of "innocent" or "harmless" humor!

Dworkin and Efran (1967) made respondents angry, then exposed them to either hostile humor, "nonhostile humor," or a nonhumorous recording. They tell us that the "nonhostile humor" came from six (rather antique) commercial comedy albums: by Nichols and May, Bill Cosby, the Smothers Brothers, Bob Newhart, Stan Freberg, and an album entitled *The First Nine Months Are The Hardest*. I was able to track down these albums and thus secure the specific cuts which Dworkin and Efran labeled "nonhostile." And Professor Dworkin actually lent me by mail the actual edited cuts they used in the experiment. Let me ask the reader if these comedy bits would be the least bit funny without a little honest hostility.

Band 2, side 2 of *Bill Cosby is a Very Funny Fellow, Right!* is entitled "Hoof and Mouth." Cosby begins by making fun of the movie, *Hud*, which "had no plot." He felt that the most interesting part of the movie came when cowboys herded all the sick cattle into a huge hole and shot them dead (Whee! How innocent!) He points out that the "shooters" were wearing rubber clothes to keep the contagious foam around the mouths of the cattle from splattering on the executioners themselves (more innocent fun). He even demonstrates that, if a rifleman *should* get contaminated by the infectious foam, he, the shooter himself, would be blown away (Bang!). Bill them mimics a conversation between two cows headed for the deadly pit. One cow wonders aloud what is going on. His buddy tells him that they are going into the pit to be shot because they got "the hoof and mouth." The first cow opines that he would just as soon avoid the Grim Reaper, and inquires as to how he just might manage that escape. His partner replies, "You could start by wiping that foam off yo' mouth." This sure is real innocent stuff. Could give a small kid nightmares.

Side 2, band 3 of *The Button Down Mind of Bob Newhart* has Bob on the phone as the head of a company that produces board games, such as Parcheesi and Monopoly. He answers a call from a fellow named Abner Doubleday, who has invented a brand-new game which he has named "baseball"; Ab apparently wants to sell Bob on the idea of producing the game for the American parlor (a ridiculously stupid idea on the face of it). Naturally (because this was Newhart's "format"), we hear Bob talking to Doubleday and responding to him on the phone. Bob, of course, has never heard of the game of "baseball," and wants Abner to describe it to see how it would fit into the family board game market. (Nonsensical, certainly, and a monumentally *stupid* idea, too.)

Bob asks how many couples can play the game, and learns that it is played by eighteen men, which dumbfounds Newhart. How can you get a gang like *that* into the family room? Bob learns that two men, a pitcher and catcher, throw the ball back and forth ("Is that all?"); but that, also, a man from the other side stands between them with a "bat" and tries to hit the ball—unless the pitch *is* "a ball!" Eventually Bob comes to the conclusion that he is the victim of a practical joke from another guy in the office having a little fun.

Now this is *non*sense, certainly. It does not make sense. It *would* make sense if baseball were unknown in today's telephone society and Abner Doubleday were alive and well and had just invented a game that he wanted to sell to a board game manufacturer. But how idiotic would a newly-resurrected Abner Doubleday have to be to even consider selling the national pastime as a board game, to be played in the living room? How stupid would it be to try to explain it over the telephone? Why would a Newhart/executive even *consider* further any "board game" that took eighteen men to play? This would take a great deal of naivete, also. Down in flames comes the "innocence" of this little monologue. [And, by the way, Abner Doubleday did not "invent" baseball. See Don Burnam (1975) *A Dictionary of Misinformation*.]

The First Nine Months are the Hardest is about, of course, having a baby. It was directed by Carl Reiner.

Side 1, band 2 is a dialogue between the expectant parents and is entitled "The Due Date." She tells Hubby that, according to her doctor, the baby is due 8 August. Hubby wants to know how the doctor can know the exact date. She tells him it's because she told the doctor "when she didn't" and "when *we*…" He asks "When we *what*." She repeats in a louder voice, "*When we*…" (She is too embarrassed to even say "made love," "had sex," etc.; and the embarrassment of others is always fun, isn't it!)

Hubby finally catches on. But now *he* is upset. "You told him *when we*…?!?!!?" We now perceive that *he* is embarrassed to have someone know the exact date he *did it*. How shameful! But later, we find that the doctor's knowledge of the exact date of their shameful act is not the root cause of our hero's discomfiture. He is afraid the news will get back to his mother!

How can we *not* laugh at a wimp who wishes his own mother to not know that he engages in the sordid business of sexual intercourse—and with his wife. (Also, thinking that Mom does not know is clue to his moronism.) How in the world would this conversation, which ordinarily would be a simple exchange of information between marrieds, come across as a "comic bit" unless one or the other (or both) partners suffered the pangs of some negative emotion, such as embarrassment, over the revelations? Once again we can dismiss "innocence" from a comic event.

A fourth bit of "nonhostile" humor used by Dworken and Efran was side 1, band 3 of *Golden Hits of the Smothers Brothers* (volume 2). This cut is entitled "My Old Man." The general tenor of the piece is the sibling rivalry motif which has been the Smothers Brothers' steady bread and butter over the years (brother-against-brother competition is always so *innocent*). Dworken and Efran edited from the band several really vicious brotherly cuts from the piece, leaving only the one song they sing.

The song, "My Old Man," is one in which they aggressively put down each other off and on, interrupting each other from one verse to another. "My Old Man," the hero of the song, in the first verse is "a sailor" and "wears a sailor suit." In the next verse he becomes "an anthropologist" who "wears an anthropologist's suit [should such a garment exist];" here, working the four-syllable word into musical space for only a two-syllable word (sailor) requires a slight mangling of the musical rendition. In the next verse he becomes "a refrigerator repairman," requiring *eight* syllables to crowd into room previously on for two. In this verse "My Old Man" also switches from reading the "Sunday news" to *Playboy*, a faintly shameful act to be caught at back in the 1950s. In the fourth verse, Dick makes "My Old Man" a "cotton-pickin,' finger-lickin', chicken plucker," jamming a full seventeen syllables into the space composed for two. And Tommy issues a warning over possibly making a mistake on "plucker" (presumably by a careless substituting of the you-know-which F-word).

The editing of this Smothers Brothers routine left it unusually unfunny for me, although the "live" audience responded with much laughter. I suppose you had, like the audience, to *see* the bit on stage to get the full impact of the mugging, and so forth.

Side 1, cut 2 of *The Best of the Stan Freberg Shows* (volume 2), presents Stan's interview with "The Abominable Snowman." The band begins with a bit of self-disparaging humor: Freberg admits that he has sponsored himself in his own show—for the huge sum of $100.00 (thus "cheapening" himself). The interview with the Yeti involves mostly making fun of the creature for his size, and so on. He wears size twenty-three sneakers, which make it difficult for him to "tippy-toe" up on victims; he has four pairs in different colors, the only "ensembles" available to him for his fashion statements. When asked to demonstrate his trade, "terrorizing mountain climbers," the Yeti has Freberg turn his back and close his eyes, whereupon the ten-and-one-half-foot monster releases a horrendous roar, which instantly turns Freberg's hair white; then Freberg takes his leave as our monster spots a mountain climber that he must rush off and terrorize. We hear in the distance the Yeti emitting his blood-curdling roar, and the subsequent receding death scream of the mountain climber as he cascades (harmlessly, of course) down the mountainside. Pretty innocent stuff, huh?

The comedy bit used by Dworkin and Efran which seemed the least funny was "The Physical" by Nichols and May, because of it's more-than-usual-subtlety for this pair. Nichols comes to the office of a doctor, whom he discovers, to his discomfiture, is a woman. He is embarrassed to undress and get under a sheet for her examination of his troubled midsection. Unused to the physical ministrations of a female, he giggles uproariously when her hands on his abdomen bring out his ticklishness.

As she examines him (and questions him about his health, height, occupation, financial situation, etc.) it becomes gradually apparent that she is considering him as mate-material. She ends by telling him to get plenty of rest and come back and see her later—an hour later. The man's embarrassment, his ticklishness, and his final role as game for a predatory female hardly strike me as completely "nonhostile."

So much for the innocence of the humor used by Dworken and Efran.

Trice (1982) used cartoons rated as "aggressive" or "wordplay," but provided no examples for analysis.

Golub and Levine (1967) used three sets of four cartoons. Four were "high-aggressive," four were "low-aggressive," and four more were "nonsense (innocent)." They described these four "innocents":

9. A crab with a black and white checkered pattern on its shell is standing by the curb of a swanky hotel. A doorman nonchalantly motions to guide a guest toward the crab. The guest replies, "I'm afraid you misunderstood...I asked for a Checkered *Cab*."

10. Two tipplers coming home from a wild night on the town are gaily staggering up and down walls, as well as back and forth across the sidewalk and street.

11. While his surprised wife watches, a man paints his living room by holding a paint roller against a wall as he rides back and forth on a bicycle.

12. A "Robot Adding Machine" equipped with myriad dials and gauges is using an abacus to do its adding.

My analysis: yes, these cartoons certainly are nonsensical. But then so is our multitrillion dollar national debt; the United States' financial hole is about as bereft of any sense as the most fantastic of cartoons, and yet it is not a bit funny. In addition to nonsense, these cartoons carry the following baggage: (9) involves *stupidity*, a horrendous mistake made by the doorman, unthinkable though a "checkered crab" might be; if "checkered crabs" really existed, our doorman is guilty of grievous error; (10) ridicules *drunkenness*—in our world of entertainment only hopelessly drunk or moronic humans, or improbable cartoon characters such as The Roadrunner and Wile E. Coyote, may dangerously defy gravity and other natural laws and "get away with it" without bothering to think about the danger involved; (12), again, involves the stupidity of the paint-roller-wielding idiot husband who is being quite a trial for his poor, suffering wife; and (13) has an "Oh, how the mighty are fallen" moral—here is this marvelous machine, conceived by geniuses and constructed by the world's greatest engineers—and it can't do its own job without an abacus, a computing aid of so ancient a vintage that not even the *Encyclopedia Britannica* will speculate on its date of origin.

Singer, Gollob and Levine (1967) used four cartoons "containing minimal or no aggression." One was the "checkered crab" cartoon mentioned above. The other three:

1. A zoo keeper and a group of spectators stand in front of the cage marked "Laughing Hyena." They are all grinning widely. The zoo keeper comments, "Contagious, isn't it?
   [Here we have human beings forced to the realization that they are no better than these "lower animals." Low aggression, for sure, but degradation nonetheless.]
2. As a plumber plugs up the hole in a pipe with his finger, water pours out of his ear.
   [Completely nonsensical, of course; but what is all that water going through his head doing to his brain cells?]
3. An astounded woman looks down at a minuscule man, perhaps one-quarter her size. Looking up at her, he says, "Then I saw this bottle with a sign on it... 'Drink Me.'"
   [I don't know about you, but if I were suddenly shrunk to one-quarter the size of a woman, I think I would consider the "come-down" quite a catastrophe!]

Prerost and Brewer (1977) used four jokes they labeled as "non-aggressive." They provided in their report one example:

An obstetrician was telling of one of his unusual deliveries: "When I spanked the baby, instead of crying he began laughing. It was then I noticed he was holding a birth-control pill."

[What an extremely clever zygote to manage *becoming* this baby by somehow (miraculously) seizing The Pill which Mommy-to-be had swallowed to prevent his own creation, and to hang onto it, intact, for the nine-month gestation period. He really put one over on Mommy! Since he won so big, he has *earned* his big laugh.]

O'Connell (1960) used what he called "nonsense wit." The only example he provides: "Description of a cow followed by a couple of ducks: 'Milk and Quackers.'" Such puns are taken up in chapter 6.

In his book, Morreall cites Bradney (1957) as one who has "observed that people express *innocent* [my emphasis] jokes in situations that might otherwise lead to personal animosity, as when inconveniencing another person, or when disagreement arises." Bradney's study (for a degree thesis) was carried out in a large department store. She quotes Radcliffe-Brown (1952) on what kind of joking behavior he found in a primitive society and, thus, what *she* might expect to find in the department store:

> The joking relationship is a peculiar combination of friendliness and antagonism. The behaviour is such that in any other social context it would express and arouse hostility, but it is not meant seriously and must not be taken seriously. There is a pretence of hostility and a real friendliness. To put it another way—the relation is one of permitted disrespect.

This description seems to me to be what has been termed "playful aggression": aggression with a "play frame" hanging round it. Bradney describes what she found:

> The type and method of joking in the store are also similar to that found in primitive societies, although there is both a slightly wider variety of method and a very much wider variety of subject-matter.... Store joking is altogether less formalized.... a jovial manner of passing the day or commenting on the weather or some other matter of topical interest; mutual teasing about personal habits, appearance, love experience, morality, and, in particular, work and method of work; telling funny stories about members of the store and telling other funny stories in some way relevant to the subject of conversation.

The actual examples Bradney provides I would classify as "friendly ridicule." A porter interrupts two salesgirls by emptying their waste bin, and "excuses" his delay of their work with "Gets more like Christmas every day, don't it?" The piano department was moved often during the history of the store. When a customer asked for that department's whereabouts, one salesman replied, "If you'd be good enough to wait here, madam, it's sure to be passing by." A woman employee cracks to the liftman, "How's my best boyfriend today?" He replies (sarcastically), "I shall be all right now I've seen you!" A buyer, seeing a salesclerk operating in slow motion, remarks to another: "Miss—looks as if her heart's in her boots today! Don't you like work today, dear?" (this last sentence delivered to the slowpoke).

To repeat: I see elements of "win/lose" in all these examples, which would completely lack humor without that element of competition.

Morreall also mentions the study of Miller (1967) as one showing that "innocent" jokes can avoid personal animosity and oil the gears of group harmony. Miller studied the humor of a Chippewa Tribal Council and concluded that their humor was of two types, "ribbing" and "wisecracking." And he accepted the dictionary definitions of each: "*rib*: to tease a person; to make fun of or poke fun at; *wisecrack*: bright, smart, witty or sarcastic remark; an impertinence; a joke, esp. when it emphasizes another's shortcomings." He illustrated what he meant by the latter in quoting Professor Irwin Corey:

> To wind up an argument, the wife said, "And what's more, my mother says you're effeminate."
> The husband replied: "Compared to her, I am."

Nothing I find in Miller's article could I define as "innocent humor."

Strickland (1959) claims to have used eleven cartoons "representing neutral or nonsensical themes" in his study. These cartoons were selected "by type" by "fifteen judges." But Strickland (perhaps wisely) fails to provide any examples of this "harmless" humor for study and analysis by others.

Prerost (1975) also fails to provide examples of the "neutral" jokes he used, telling us only that they were chosen from a pool of 150 jokes by ten judges, and that "The twelve jokes scoring lowest on these two dimensions [aggressiveness and sexuality] were used as the neutral jokes." Here we find not even a denial that aggressiveness and/or sexuality was explicitly absent from the "neutral jokes;" only that they scored "lowest" in these two characteristics.

Leak (1974) used humor he classified as hostile wit, racial wit, humor, and "nonsense." He provides only one example of each. His example of nonsense: "My father and mother are first cousins," the new pupil explained to the teacher. "I guess that's why I look so much alike." Any humor from this little confession would have to stem from the pupil's *stupidity*, which we have come to expect of the issue of such obviously incestuous relationships.

Cantor, Bryant, and Zillman (1974) used various "types" of humor to find what funniness ratings they would receive under conditions of both positive and negative "hedonic tone." The one cartoon illustrative of what they called "nonsense wit"

> involved a variation on the cliché about the prospector searching for water in the desert. In this version, a Martian-type monster, apparently just having landed in

the desert, is seen crawling on all fours, with his antenna drooping and his tongue hanging out, and crying "Ammonia! Ammonia!"

Martians crawling through an earthly desert really is pretty nonsensical. But what makes the visual pun funny is that the poor devil is *dying* from lack of an element vital to his survival! Isn't imminent death *antiseptically benign*!

Landy and Mettee (1969) used cartoons, supposedly "hostile" and "nonhostile." They describe four of their "nonhostile" stimuli:

1. A little boy, standing with a puppy on a leash, says to his friend, "He's only four weeks old and he can already say 'arf.'"
2. A couple is seated on a couch, apparently after a date. The girl turns to the boy, who is seated with his right side closest to her and says, "Want to sit on this side, Lefty?"
3. Four salesmen, clad only in their underwear, are standing in a clothing store, strewn with empty clothes hangers. One comments to the others, "Most successful suit sale we ever had, I should say."
4. A train engineer, leaning out the window of a streamlined engine which is stopped at a station, asks a passerby, "Pardon me, but do you have the correct time?"

Analysis: In (1), the little boy undoubtedly and unintentionally reveals his own cupidity/naïveté/stupidity (pick one). Any intelligent, knowledgeable being would know that a puppy can say "Arf" at even a younger age! As for (2), the young lady slyly and subtly confesses to the kind of lusty streak which "nice" girls are not supposed to have (or at least, are not expected to openly display in so many words). The salesmen in (3) are either the most stupid or the most mercenary hucksters working the game; and either of these traits is stimulus enough for aggressive laughter. Can't you just *picture* each salesman removing his outer garments to turn over to a customer as he collects money and writes receipts for the merchandise? And we all know that if anyone in the world is supposed to carry and use a most accurate timepiece, it is the railroad engineer. But in (4), above, we have one that will slack off his professional responsibilities by taking the word of any old passerby as to what is the time. This gentleman has not done his job well.

Berkowitz (1970) used two four-minute cuts of professional comedy, one "hostile" and one "nonhostile." He identifies the comedy used only by source, so it is not analyzable here. I think I can take his word for it, though, that his four minutes of "Mr. Warmth" (Don Rickles) was in truth "hostile." But his so-called nonhostile humor came from George Carlin. I have seen/heard a lot of Carlin, and I can think of no four-minute abstract of his material that would not contain at least some hostility.

Goldstein, Mantell, Pope, and Derks (1988) used twenty "hostile" and twenty "nonhostile" jokes in their study. Their article gave no examples of jokes from either classification, but Pete Derks kindly provided me with a copy of their study's stimulus. One of the supposedly "nonhostile" jokes was the one at the beginning of this chapter involving birds migrating "as a family tradition."

Eight more of the remaining nineteen depend for their humor on the mere human *stupidity* involved:

> There was this little boy who never spoke a word his entire life. One day, when he was nine, he was sitting with his family at the dinner table and he said, "This roast beef stinks." His mother almost fell over and screamed, "How come you never said anything before?"
>
> Her son replied, "Up until now the food has been pretty good."
>
> [Could anyone imagine a boy so dull that all would be perfect for him for *nine years*? Or a family so simpleminded that they would allow a child to remain mute for nine years without seeking professional help? Those folks need a parenting class!]

> A doctor died and went to heaven. There was a long line to get into heaven. St. Peter was there and the doctor goes to the front of the line. St. Peter says to the doctor, "You have to go to the end of the line." Then he sees a man with a stethoscope around his neck go to the front of the line. The doctor quickly marches to the front of the line and says to St. Peter, "How come that doctor got in?" St. Peter answers, "That's no doctor, that's God; sometimes he thinks he is a doctor."
>
> [I heard a much better version of this joke; St. Pete won't allow the doctor to wear his surgical garb, but the doc sees a heavenly denizen wearing it. He complains, only to learn that "God sometimes like to 'play doctor.'" Here we have God demeaned as one misguided into the illusion that He is a mere (mortal) doctor. It is a possible play on "Doctors play God" by reversal.]

> Vernon, going on five, watched his mother put a clean diaper on his baby brother. When she didn't dust the infant with talcum powder, the boy shouted, "Wait, mother; you forgot to salt him."
>
> [A cute little mistake by Vernon, but a mistake nonetheless. No mistake, no funny.]

> A letter from camp. "Dear Mr. and Mrs. Black: Please send your son Bill eighteen candy bars immediately. Signed, his counselor."
>
> [Poor stupid, naïve Billy, expecting his folks to swallow that ridiculous artifice. Sounds like the note handed by a student to his teacher: "Please excuse Jimmy for being absent last week; he was sick. Signed: My Mommy."]

Operator: "Number, please."

Drunk in phone booth: "Number, heck, I want my peanuts."

[We relish stories of the stupid things drunks do, such as trying to get nuts from a pay phone.]

A moron was walking along the street, hampered by a cane that was several inches too long. "Why don't you cut a few inches off the bottom?" a friend suggested. "That wouldn't help," replied the moron. "Its the upper end that's too high."

[The label on this joke's protagonist tells us what to expect: idiocy. And we are not disappointed. Aren't we all glad we have morons around to laugh at?]

"Was it very crowded at the cabaret last night?"

"Not under my table."

[Again, a pathetic, tragic, pitiable—and hilarious stereotype: a drunk who so stupidly pollutes himself that he can't maintain himself in his chair.]

Another joke, a conversation between a child and its grandfather, partially relies on stupidity:

"Was the sermon good, Grandpa."

"Yep."

"What was it about?"

"Sin."

"Well, what did the minister say?"

"He's agin it."

["Stupid kid—what do you think he would say about sin?" Also: I detect a bit of aggressive truculence in this old man; the child obviously wishes to converse with its Grandpa, and Grandpa answers with the barest minimum of verbalization. Sour old coot!]

Self-pride turned to hubris can be laughable:

A mother proudly introduced her son to a charity committee friend. "This is my son, Drexel, Mrs. Crane. Isn't he a bright little boy?" The youngster, quite accustomed to being shown off in public, purred, "What was that clever thing I said yesterday, Mother?"

[Apparently the kid suffers from exaggerated pride; stupid lout can't even remember the clever thing he said a day ago!]

Another example:

Miss Sutherland took her class on a tour of the White House, and then asked the students to write their impressions of the visit. One boy wrote: "I was especially glad to have this opportunity to visit my future home."

[And aren't we certain that this smart aleck has a comeuppance coming? Conceited urchin!]

Both normal childish greed and poor parenting combine for laughs in the following:

> It was my son's first party at school, so I baked enough cookies for the twenty-five children in his class. When he returned home with the bag still half full of cookies, I asked him why. "I was full," he replied.
>
> [The greedy imp committed a social faux pas, to the great embarrassment of his mother, for not teaching her son better party manners.]

Children can sometimes confound their closed-minded elders, and the result is mirth.

> Mrs. Higby wanted to enter her child in a modern kindergarten, but the child was only four, and the age requirement was five. "I think," said the mother, "that she can pass the five-year-old test." "We shall see," said the teacher. Then to the child she said, "Dear, just say a few words that come into your mind." "Mother," said the four-year-old, "does the lady want logically-connected sentences of merely irrelevant words?"
>
> [Our little prodigy brandishes her verbal sagacity in a stunning riposte to skewer the teacher's habitual cynicism. Not really a dangerous encounter, but competitive enough to be humorous.]

Another turn of the tables by child against adult:

> "No, I don't get the best marks in school Daddy. Do you get the best salary at your office?"
>
> [Let's hope the kid did not get really physically abused for this little burst of "innocent" counterattack!]

Sex raises its ugly head, sort of, in three jokes:

> A pupil at a strict girls' school asked for permission to drive out with a gentleman. "You know the regulations of the institution," was the reply. "Are you engaged to him?"
>
> "No," she said, "but I expect to be before I get back."
>
> [The predatory, scheming female on the hunt for a man is a common butt of jokes the world over.]
>
> "I want a pair of shorts to wear around my gymnasium."
>
> "Certainly, Miss. What size is your gymnasium."
>
> [The humor comes from a verbal mistake where the clerk thinks he is asking about the size of a "private area" of the lady (a stupid mistake, as well as a social faux pas and a poor pun. Again, see chapter 6.)]

Dick: "Was that a new girl I saw you with last night?

Doc: "No, just the old one painted over.

[Ridiculed here is the tendency for women to put infinite trust in artificial makeup; reinforcement for the cultural saw that "No woman would trade beauty for brains."]

Finally, enforced poverty can drive men to desperate (and laughable) measures:

Usher, passing collection plate at church wedding:

"Yes, Ma'am, it is unusual, but the father of the bride requested it."

[And we laugh at this exaggerated example of another cultural stereotype, The Father of the Bride, required to bankrupt the family to officially and ceremoniously provide the means for his daughter to enter into a marriage which, in these days, may last anywhere from one to three years.]

The last "innocent" joke used by Goldstein et al. to be mentioned is a pun, and a double-barrelled one at that:

"Darn it, I left my watch upstairs."

"That's all right, it'll run down."

"No it won't. It's a winding stairway."

[The pugnacious effrontery of puns were taken up in chapter 6.]

Tucci (1989) used "self-deprecating," "aggressive," and "neutral" newspaper cartoons from Sunday supplement comic pages for his doctoral dissertation, twenty in each category. He had hypothesized that adolescents clinically defined as "depressive," "acting-out," or "normal" would rate the three "types" of cartoons differently. None of the eight hypotheses tested in this regard were supported. And it is little wonder. Although I did not secure for analysis the self-deprecating nor the "hostile" cartoons, I did secure from interlibrary loan Tucci's "neutral" cartoons. Dr. Tucci himself, then, corroborated my assumption that the cartoons I received were the actual stimuli he used. These are described and analyzed below.

First, a comment. Just because a comic strip is on the "comic pages" does not necessarily mean it is "funny." Some strips, such as *Judge Parker*, *Dick Tracy*, and *Mark Trail* are not even intended as comedy. Others that ordinarily we would think of as "comic" are often less "funny" than they are merely "interesting." I have been an avid reader of "the funnies" since long before New York's mayor, Fiorello LaGuardia, read them over the air during a city newspaper strike. And I notice that, many times, the cartoonist of a supposedly "funny" comic strip has merely "gone through the paces" and produced a strip with a beginning, middle, and end in order to "fill the space." Cartoonists run dry, use up all their comic twists, and just fail at being funny. Often a comic strip in its "later years" is something that a fan reads more as a habit than a seeking after true laughs. My own experience has been that, for instance, *Peanuts* was hilarious in it's first few years of syndication. But that, with the passage of time, the strip has become more and more bland, having run out of suitable material that made it funny originally—adultlike wisdom and truth unexpectedly coming from the mouths of babes. Also, Lucy has run out of ways to trick Charlie Brown into trying to kick the football she is holding for the "extra point," and Charlie himself has run out of ways to wreck his kite.

That having been said, let us look at Dr. Tucci's twenty "neutral" cartoons.

A *B.C.* cartoon (13 January 1985) has our caveman hero zipping down the road on his one-wheel vehicle, the one that goes by itself while the rider stands on the axle. A stone road sign warns BRIDGE OUT, and, sure enough, next panel shows an enormous dental bridge lying beside the road (a pun; see chapter 6). Another sign warns TOLL BRIDGE AHEAD, but another directs one to the right with "XACT CHANGE LANE. Our driver turns right and stops at a turnstile—a stupid one constructed by a stupid engineer/bureaucrat—a long stick across the road with a forked stick for a fulcrum and a basket on the off-road end. Our driver hurls eleven clams into the basket; the weight drags the basket to the ground and the end blocking the road correspondingly rises to let our hero pass. But now, of course, to make this *automatic* XACT CHANGE gate "work" again, some toll booth custodian will have to walk (or drive?) over, remove the weighty eleven clams, and thus *manually* reset the "automatic" device. A stupid invention devised by a stupid someone or other!

Four *Garfield* strips (not my favorite) from 29 January 1984, 25 November 1984, 30 December 1984, and 18 March 1984. One shows a sad Garfield on a rainy day with nothing good to watch on TV. So he uses his great imagination, in the last frame, to completely placate himself with an enormous daydream of play, fun, and gluttony (the latter his usual habit) under a sunny sky. The second has insomniac Garfield unable to sleep at 4:00 A.M. So he wakes up the house dog and his sleeping master,

Jon, with lights and noise, then gloatingly purrs that, "If I can't sleep neither will anyone else." Nice cat. The third one has our hero standing before a mirror and making all kinds of altruistic New Year's resolutions. Then he pauses, says to the mirror that "I don't like you *already*," and smashes the mirror to bits. In the last frame he pads away smiling, "Once again I've survived a new year with my vices intact." The fourth has Garfield's master attempting to finally give Garfield more food than he can eat. He prepares a table loaded and groaning under the heavy strain. Jon sics Garfield onto the gargantuan pile of food, says "He's either going to get sick on all that food, or he's going to burst trying," and picks up his own hamburger. In the last panel the pile of food is transformed into empty plates and a pile of bare bones. Garfield is crowded up against Jon's hamburger with the thought balloon, "Are you going to want the rest of that hamburger?" Jon's face is a wide-eyed picture of consternation. These four cartoons exemplify my prime reason for disliking *Garfield*. He is a rotten role model for both man and beast—but he also always wins!.

The Born Loser of 15 April 1984 takes his wife to the golf course for her virgin attempt at the game. She scores a hole-in-one from the first tee (Hubby: "I can't believe it!"), then asks for another ball. Asked why, she replies, "I think I've got the hang of it now." Born Loser "loses" again; his wife has done more on her first stroke than he has done in a lifetime of playing this frustrating game. And she is so ignorant (stupid?) that she think's she is just starting to understand the game!

Boner's Ark of 29 January 1984 has lovesick Priscilla Pig pursuing Duke (a male penguin?) and spilling out her heart to him; specifically, she declares what it is about him that makes Duke the "only one" for her. He turns to her and says, "Priscilla, you make me sick. You're fat and ugly and stupid! I can't stand you and I never want to see you again." Priscilla interprets this humiliating rejection as two reasons why she loves him: "Number one: you're always kidding around. Number two: you never mean what you say...Number three..." Duke can't believe the extent of the hated pig's cupidity. Really innocent strip.

The Lockhorns cartoon of 27 May 1984 continues the eternally long and extended domestic war between this husband and wife; she a nagging, jealous shrew, he a lazy, libidinous lecher with an eye for every pretty young female, and anything alcoholic. In this one the Mr. is sacked out in a hammock over a yard full of weeds; the Mrs. is bugging him with a sarcastic "Well, if you don't feel like cutting the grass, how about taking down the Christmas tree?" Sloth, shiftlessness, don't-give-a-damn attitude, and a sarcastic bitch of a ball-and-chain. Such utter neutrality in a cartoon!

In the once-funny cartoon *Peanuts* of 6 February 1983, Charlie Brown dupes Snoopy, sacked out on the peak of his doghouse roof, as usual, into believing that drinking two cups of hot chocolate and then putting the empty cups on his feet will keep him warm the whole winter night. A supine Snoopy opines in the last panel that he will *not* sleep comfortably for the whole night "with the cat next door laughing at me." The cat's ridiculing "Hee" thought-bubbles it's way onto the panel from the dark to its right. In the eyes of the cat (and the reader), Snoopy has become an object of ridicule.

In a *Peanuts* of 9 December 1984 Snoopy bangs on Charlie's door hoping for some cookies. Charlie tells him that yes, the cookies have been talking, but not calling Snoopy at all. Snoopy goes back to his doghouse perch thinking "I wonder if he was putting me on." Yes, Snoopy, he was. Charlie Brown actually outsmarted a dog. Charlie wins, you lose.

An *Archie* strip of 29 January 1984 finds Archie's dad in pain. His wife convinces him to call a doctor, whom Daddy is sure will never make a house call. But he phones a doctor who, miracle of all miracles, will make a house call. Unsure of himself, Daddy asks, "You're sure you'll be able to make it, Doctor." The last panel shows the "doctor" saying into the phone: "Absolutely! Just give me your address." The "doctor" is short, dressed as Napoleon, and has his right hand stuffed inside the left breast of his jacket. Daddy think's he has *won*, but he has *lost*, dreadfully.

Another *Archie* strip, this one from 18 March 1984, finds the high school principal discovering a plumbing leak. There is a pun ("drip" meaning both a leak and "Archie the drip," but that is a mere subplot of denigrating name-calling. Archie fixes the drip with chewing gum, but that is not good enough. Several adults try to fix it properly with tools and flood the school (an event always good for an innocent laugh). A week later Miss Beezly is seen headed somewhere with a big monkey wrench; she says there's a leak under the sink. The principal snatches the tool from her. The last panel has Archie under the sink and the principal saying to him, "Need more gum, Archie?" Score: Archie 1, Adults 0.

A third *Archie* has Jughead pleading the alibi for not having his homework as accidentally igniting it with his own telekinetic powers. The adults discuss Jughead's preposterous excuses for not doing homework; then he is sent to the space exhibit at the museum where he can actually experience "weightlessness." He is assigned to write a report on it. When he returns he explains why he wrote no report: "I started to...but my pen floated away." In *this* game it is *Jughead* 1, Adult 0.

In the *Momma* strip of 25 September 1983, Francis is complaining that "The country is in one rotten mess [but] there's nothing I can do about it." Momma, apparently of a Pollyanaish bent, explains that Francis can put *her* little corner of the country in order with a mop and bucket, a little picking up, a bit of sweeping and dusting, and so on. In the last frame Francis flattens Momma's optimistic psyche with the sarcastic, "How soon will the ripples from this reach Washington?" How sweet!

Two *Wizard of Id* (one of my favorites) strips use its famous town crier atop his crow's nestlike perch. In the cartoon of 18 March 1984, the crier screams "Halt who goes there!" only to be answered by "Ain't nobody here but us fog," a retort from a wisecracking smart aleck on the ground. In succeeding panels the crier calls out that the fog is thicker than pea soup—then thicker than cream of mushroom soup—then thick as potato soup—and finally as thick as vanilla pudding. In the last panel we have the midget-sized king in bathrobe and nightcap, carrying a candle, and demanding of his disgusted cook, "I'm hungry." Crier wins, King loses (to suggestion), and Cook loses (must fix snack in the early A.M. for demanding King).

The town crier in the 23 October 1983 strip poetically describes, panel by panel, "another magnificent sunrise..." In the last panel he has a stricken look on his face: "...either that or the woods are on fire!" The thrill of beauty dashed by the agony of arson!

A third "Wizard" has the King's agent handing down from the tower the latest rules for the peasants' returning refundable cans and bottles, ending with "No returnables will be accepted on weekends." A peasant raises his hand. His question, in the last panel: "What are weekends?" And once more we are reminded of the King's cruel treatment of his lowly peasants. All in fun, of course, but isn't all cruelty in comic strips "in fun?"

A dog character in *Boner's Ark* (6 January 1985) tells a penguin "Watch it, Buddy," advises another animal-like character to "Watch where you're going, fella!" He screams "Watch Out!" at a smaller dog character, tells a two-legged hippopotamus "Watch yourself, Buster!!" and nearly deafens a strolling mouse with *Watch It*!!" In the last panel our doggie says to himself with an oafish grin, "And they said I'd never be a good watch dog." A pun on the word "watch," certainly, but we also must conclude that this is a pretty stupid mutt!

In *Blondie* of 1 January 1984 we see the long-suffering gal dragging a sleepy Dagwood out of bed so that he can see a "fantastic sight" (newly fallen snow, icicles) outside. As she drags, pulls, shoves and lifts her limp husband and finally props his head on the window sill, she describes the utter beauty of the wonderful sight to begin the New Year. Assuring Dagwood that they will "go for a walk right after breakfast," Blondie hies to the kitchen and begins frying eggs with the self-satisfying assertion that "It's a wonderful feeling to be able to share a special moment like that with your husband." The last panel shows a never-awakened Dagwood sawing logs, his head still resting on the window sill. Score: Dagwood 1 (unconsciously), Blondie 0 (naïvely).

The *Bloom County* strip of 6 January 1985 is a lulu of "neutrality" and innocence. Steve Dallas, who consumed thirty-seven tequila "fannybanger" drinks six days ago on New Year's Eve, has hallucinated from his alcoholic stupor a host of weird beings; these creatures are using his phone in an attempt to get him an ambulance. They fear that alcoholic hallucinations like them hanging around for six days after the original raging drunk is pretty serious. During the telephoning poor Steve, dressed only in jockey shorts, a necktie, and an icepack topside, wanders soddenly into the room, spies his hallucinations, screams bloody murder, and dashes off. In the last panel one of his hallucinations is pleading with the emergency rescue people, "Can't you bring him some fresh, clean blood?" You would think that someone would have translated the theme of alcoholic delirium tremens into nursery rhymes for children by now, since they are so "innocent."

Ferro-Luzzi (1990) did not use so-called innocent or neutral humor in an empirical study, but argues that no *general* theory of humor can cover all cases of humor, a point in direct conflict with the main thesis of this book. He tries to make his point by using examples of "Tamil" humor.

He claims that the "superiority" theory (which my "win/lose" theory encompasses) is "falsified" by two examples. One involves a small boy with his father in an archeological museum who sees a human skeleton and asks his dad, "Was there famine also in those days, daddy?" This lad has obviously made a mistaken connection between the ancient skeleton and emaciated living beings he has witnessed; he makes the *mistake* of equating them. Remove the boy's mistake, you take out the humor.

The other example involves what Ferro-Luzzi calls a "tautology," but also admits that it is *a duel of wits* (emphasis mine).

> *Defendant*: Your honor said that I had been drinking when I drove the car, but this is wrong. I *was* drinking.
>
> *Judge*: In this case you need not go to jail for twelve months but only for one year.

The clever judge effectively squelches the defendant's obvious attempt to mislead through "doubletalk;" Winner: Judge. Loser: Defendant. Case closed on Tamil.

As I have said earlier, I have been seriously studying humor since 1955; in the process I have analyzed for "what-is-funny-about-this-piece" hundreds of thousands of jokes, cartoons, riddles, and so on. I have yet to find any truly funny humorous bit that this "laughter = winning" theory cannot explain. In this chapter I have deliberately sought out, occasionally with some difficulty, to find the examples of humor which other researchers have used under the [mistaken] labels of "nonhostile," "nonaggressive," "neutral," "innocent," and/or "nonsense." I think I have shown that, although these examples might rank quite low in aggressiveness, for instance, that none of them can be considered completely "innocent." As Koestler (1964) might put it, it may be difficult to taste the "salt" (of tendency) in the well-prepared dish (of humor), but without it, the dish would be tasteless.

Yet, contemporary writers continue to argue that the Hobbesian "superiority" approach cannot explain all humor. Hyers (1996) says that the Hobbesian view cannot cover the "play" nature of much humor (82), but he overlooks the *contest* nature of "play," the major point of this book. Davis (1993) argues, as do others, that *no* theory can encompass all humor (7). I hope that this latest effort of mine dispels that myth.

For years I have regularly challenged at our annual meetings my fellow members of The International Society for Humor Studies to provide me with a single example of humor that I could not render "dehumorized" by removing its *contest nature*. So far these colleagues in humor research have been unsuccessful. I now extend that challenge to any reader of this book.

James Randi (1980), a former stage magician who now specializes in exposing frauds who claim supernatural powers, made a standing offer of $10,000 for anyone who could produce, under laboratory conditions, a paranormal event or ability.

I do not have $10,000 with which to buy a certified check, as did Randi, but if anyone can successfully meet my own challenge, above, they will at least get a public recanting from me that I have been wrong for forty years.

References

Ainsworth, Catherine Harris. 1962. "Black and White and Said All Over." *Southern Folklore Quarterly* 26: 263–295.

Allen, V. L. and D.B. Greenberger. 1978. "An Aesthetic Theory of Vandalism." *Crime and Delinquency* 24: 309–332.

———. 1979. "Enjoyment of Destruction: The Role of Uncertainty." *Journal of Nonverbal Behavior* 4: 87–96.

Allen, V. L. 1984. "Toward an Understanding of the Hedonic Component of Vandalism." In *Vandalism: Behavior and Motivation,* edited by C. Leby-Leboyer. New York: Elsevier Science Publishers B.V.

Altman, Sig. 1971. *The Comic Image of the Jew.* Cranbury, NJ: The Viking Press.

Aman, Reinhold. 1983. "Kakologia: A Chronicle of Nasty Riddles and Nasty Wordplays." *Maledicta* 8: 275–307.

Annis, J. D. 1939. "The Relative Effectiveness of Cartoons and Editorials as Propaganda Media." *Psychological Bulletin* 36: 628.

Apte, Mahadev L. 1985. *Humor and Laughter: An Anthropological Approach.* Ithaca, NY: Cornell University Press.

Asher, R. and S. Sargent. 1941. "Shifts in Attitude Caused by Cartoon Characters." *Journal of General Psychology* 24: 451–455.

Baker, William J. 1988. *Sports in the Western World.* Urbana,IL: University of Illinois Press.

Banc, C. and Alan Dundes. 1990. *You Call This Living? A Collection of East European Political Jokes.* Athens, GA: University of Georgia Press.

Barclay, Andrew M. 1970. "The Effect of Female Aggressiveness on Aggressive and Sexual Fantasies." *Journal of Projective Techniques* 34: 19–26.

Barclay, Andrew M. and Ralph Norman Haber. 1965. "The Relation of Aggression to Sexual Motivation." *Journal of Personality* 33: 462–475.

Baron, Robert A. 1978. "Aggression-Inhibiting Influence of Sexual Humor." *Journal of Personality and Social Psychology* 36: 189–197.

Baron, Robert A. and Rodney L. Ball. 1974. "The Aggression-Inhibiting Influence of Nonhostile Humor." *Journal of Experimental Social Psychology* 10: 23–33.

Barrick, Mac E. 1980. "The Helen Keller Joke Cycle." *Journal of American Folklore* 93: 441–449.

Ben-Amos, Dan. 1973. "The Myth of Jewish Humor." *Western Folklore* 32, no. 2: 112–131.

Bergler, Edmund. 1956. *Laughter and the Sense of Humor.* New York: Intercontinental Medical Book Corporation.

Bergson, Henri. 1956. *Laughter.* Garden City, NY: Doubleday.

Berkowitz, Leonard. 1970. "Aggressive Humor as a Stimulus to Aggressive Responses." *Journal of Personality and Social Psychology* 16: 710–717.

Berscheid, Ellen. 1985. "Interpersonal Attraction." In vol. 2, *Handbook of Social Psychology*. 3d. ed. Edited by Gardner Lindsey and Elliot Aronson. New York: Random House.

Bill, Brigitte and Peter Naus. 1992. "The Role of Humor in the Interpretation of Sexist Incidents." *Sex Roles* 27: 645–664.

Bier, Jesse. 1979. "Sick Humor and the Function of Comedy." *The Humanist*, January/February, 45–49.

Blatz, W. E., K.D. Allen, and D.A. Millichamps. 1936. *A Study of Laughter in the Nursery School Child*. Toronto: University of Toronto Press.

Botkin, B. A., ed. 1944. *A Treasury of American Folklore*. New York: Crown Publishers.

Bradney, Pamela 1957. "The Joking Relationship in Industry." *Human Relations* 10: 179–187.

Brandes, P. D. 1970. "The Persuasiveness of Varying Types of Humor." Paper presented at the Speech Communication Association, New Orleans, LA.

Brett, Theodore H. 1990. *Don't Book a Judge by His Cover*. Santa Barbara, CA: Fithian.

Buchwald, Art. 1968. *Have I Ever Lied To You?* New York: Fawcett Crest.

———. 1979. *The Buchwald Stops Here*. New York: Berkley.

Burnam, Tom. 1975. *The Dictionary of Misinformation*. New York: Thomas Y. Crowell.

"Butz: A Tongue Out of Order." 1976. *Newsweek*, 11 October, 27.

Byrne, D. E. 1956. "The Relationship between Humor and the Expression of Hostility. *Journal of Abnormal and Social Psychology* 53: 84–89.

———. 1961. "Some Inconsistencies in the Effect of Motivational Arousal on Humor Preferences." *Journal of Abnormal and Social Psychology* 62: 158–160.

Cantor, J. E., J. Bryant, and D. Zillmann. 1974. "Enhancement of Humor Appreciation by Transferred Excitation." *Journal of Personality and Social Psychology* 30: 812–821.

———. 1975. "Enhancement of Experienced Sexual Arousal in Response to Erotic Stimuli through Misattribution of Unrelated Residual Excitation." *Journal of Personality and Social Psychology* 32: 69–75.

Cerf, Bennett. 1952. *Bennett Cerf's Bumper Crop*. 2 vols. Garden City, NY: Garden City Books.

Chambers, Cornelia. 1937. "The Adventures of Little Audrey." *Straight Texas* 13. Quoted in *A Treasury of American Folklore: Stories, Ballads, and Traditions of the People*, edited by B.A. Botkin. New York: Crown.

Chang, M. and C.R. Gruner. 1981. "Audience Reaction to Self-Disparaging Humor." *Southern Speech Communication Journal* 46: 419–426.

Chapman, A. J. and H.C. Foot, eds. 1976. *Humour and Laughter: Theory, Research, and Applications*. London: Wiley.

———. 1977. *It's a Funny Thing, Humour*. Oxford: Pergamon.

Chiarro, Delia. 1992. *The Language of Jokes: Analyzing Verbal Play*. New York: Routledge & Kegan Paul.

Christopher, Richard. 1984–85. "Ethiopian Jokes." *Maledicta* 8: 37–42.

Cohen, Sarah Blacher, ed. 1987. *Jewish Wry: Essays on Jewish Humor*. Bloomington, IN: University of Indiana Press.

Cooper, Eunice and Marie Jahoda. 1947. "The Evasion of Propaganda: How Predjudiced People Respond to Anti-Prejudice Propaganda." *Journal of Psychology* 23: 15–25.

Coser, Rose L. 1960. "Laughter Among Colleagues." *Psychiatry* 23: 81–95.

Crosland, Thomas William Hodgson. 1922. *The Fine Old Hebrew Gentleman*. London: T. Werner Laurie.

Culler, Basil. 1988. *On Puns: The Foundation of Letters*. New York: Basil Blackwell Inc.

Davidson, Jay. 1943. "Moron Stories." *Southern Folklore Quarterly* 7: 101–104.

Davies, Christie. 1990. *Ethnic Humor Around the World: A Comparative Analysis*. Bloomington, IN: University of Indiana Press.

———. 1990a. "An Explanation of Jewish Jokes About Jewish Women." *Humor: International Journal of Humor Research* 3: 363–378.

———. 1991. "Exploring the Thesis of the Self-Deprecating Jewish Sense of Humor." *Humor: International Journal of Humor Research* 4: 189–209.

Davis, Jay M. and Amerigo Farina. 1970. "Humor Appreciation as Social Communication." *Journal of Personality and Social Psychology* 15: 175–178.

Davis, Murray S. 1993. *What's So Funny? The Comic Conception of Culture and Society*. Chicago, IL: University of Chicago Press.

Dorinson, Joseph. 1984–85. "The Gold-Dust Twins of Marginal Humor: Blacks and Jews." *Maledicta* 8: 163–192.

Duncan, W. Jack. 1985. "The Superiority Theory of Humor at Work: Joking Relationships as Indicators of Formal and Informal Status Patterns in Small, Task-Oriented Groups." *Small Group Behavior* 16: 556–564.

Dundes, Alan. 1979. "The Dead Baby Joke Cycle." *Western Folklore* 38: 139–147.

———. 1985. "The JAP and the JAM in American Folklore." *Journal of American Folklore* 98: 456–475.

———. 1987. *Cracking Jokes: Studies of Sick Humor Cycles and Stereotypes*. Berkeley, CA: Ten Speed Press.

———. 1989. "Six Inches from the Presidency: The Gary Hart Jokes as Public Opinion." *Western Folklore* 48: 43–51.

Dundes, Alan and Thomas Hauschild. 1983. "Auschwitz Jokes." *Western Folklore* 42: 249–260.

Durant, John and Jonathon Miller, eds. 1988. *Laughing Matters: A Serious Look at Humour*. London: Longman.

Dworken, Earl S. and Jay S. Efran. 1967. "The Angered: Their Susceptibility to Varieties of Humor." *Journal of Personality and Social Psychology* 6: 233–236.

Eastman, Max. 1921. *The Sense of Humor*. New York: Scribners.

——— 1936. *Enjoyment of Laughter*. New York: Simon & Schuster.

Elephant Book, The. 1963. Los Angeles: Price/Stern/Sloan, Inc.

Ellis, A. and R.A. Harper. 1975. *A New Guide to Rational Living*. New York: Institute for Rational Living.

Esar, Evan. 1952. *The Humor of Humor*. New York: Horizon.

———. 1983. *Esar's Comic Dictionary*. 4th ed. Garden City, NY: Doubleday.

Espy, Willard R. 1975. *An Almanac of Words at Play*. New York: Clarkson N. Potter, Inc.

Evans, Bergen, ed. 1978. *Dictionary of Quotations*. New York: Avenel Books.

"Exit Earl, Not Laughing." 1976. *Time*, 18 October: 23,26.

Feinberg, Leonard. 1978. *The Secret of Humor*. Amsterdam: Editions Rodopi N. V.

Ferro-Luzzi, Gabriella Eichinger. 1990. "Tamil Jokes and the Poluthetic-Prototype Approach to Humor." *Humor: International Journal of Humor Research* 3: 147–158.

Fish, Lydia. 1980. "Is the Pope Polish? Some Notes of the Polack Joke in Transition." *Journal of American Folklore* 93: 450–454.

Freud, Sigmund. 1905. *Jokes and Their Relation to the Unconscious.* In *Complete Works.* Vol. 8. London: Hogarth.

Fry, William F., Jr. 1963. *Sweet Madness: A Study of Humor.* Palo Alto, CA: Pacific.

Garbarz, M. and E. Garbarz. 1992. *A Survivor.* Detroit, MI: Wayne State University Press.

Georges, Robert A. and Alan Dundes. 1963. "Toward a Structural Definition of the Riddle." *Journal of American Folklore* 76: 111–118.

Gibb, J. D. 1964. "An Experimental Comparison of the Humorous Lecture and the Nonhumorous Lecture in Informative Speaking." Master's thesis, University of Utah.

Goldstein, Jeffrey H. 1970. "Repetition, Motive Arousal, and Humor Appreciation." *Journal of Experimental Research in Personality* 4: 90–94.

Goldstein, Jeffrey H., Mantell, Madi, Pope, Brian, and Peter Derks. 1988. "Humor and the Coronary-Prone Behavior Pattern." *Current Psychology: Research & Reviews* 7 no.2: 115–121.

Goldstein, Jeffrey H. and Paul E. McGhee, eds. 1972. *The Psychology of Humor.* New York: Academic Press.

Gollub, H. F. and J. Levine. 1967. "Distraction as a Factor in the Enjoyment of Aggressive Humor." *Journal of Personality and Social Psychology* 5: 368–372.

Goodchilds, J. D. 1959. "Effects of Being Witty on Position in the Social Structure of a Small Group." *Sociometry* 22: 261–271.

Goodrich, Anne T., Jules Henry, and D. Wells Goodrich. 1954. "Laughter in Psychiatric Staff Conferences: A Sociopsychiatric Analysis." *American Journal of Orthopsychiatry* 23: 175–184.

Gordon, Harvey C. 1980. *PUNishment: The Art of Punning, or How to Lose Friends and Agonize People.* 2d. ed. New York: Warner Books.

———. 1981. *Grime and Punishment.* New York: Warner Books.

Graham, Harry. 1984. *Ruthless Rhymes.* London: Edward Arnold.

———. 1986. *When Grandmama Fell Off the Boat: the Best of Harry Graham.* London: Sheldrake.

Greig, J. Y. T. 1923. *The Psychology of Laughter and Comedy.* New York: Dodd, Mead.

Grotjahn, Martin. 1957. *Beyond Laughter.* New York: McGraw-Hill.

Gruner, Charles R. 1965. "An Experimental Study of Satire as Persuasion." *Speech Monographs* 32: 149–54.

———. 1966. "A Further Experimental Study of Satire as Persuasion." *Speech Monographs* 33: 184–185.

———. 1967a. "Editorial Satire as Persuasion: An Experiment." *Journalism Quarterly* 44: 727–730.

———. 1967b. "Effect of Humor on Speaker Ethos and Audience Information Gain." *Journal of Communication* 17: 228–233.

———. 1967c. "An Experimental Study of Editorial Satire as Persuasion." *Journalism Quarterly* 44: 727–730.

——— 1970. "The Effect of Humor in Dull and Interesting Informative Speeches." *Central States Speech Journal* 21: 160–166.

———.1971. "Art Hoppe vs. Capital Punishment." Paper presented at the Southern Speech Communication Association Convention, San Antonio, TX.

———. 1972. "Satire as a Reinforcer of Attitudes." Paper presented at the Speech Communication Association Convention, Chicago, IL.

———. 1978. *Understanding Laughter: The Workings of Wit and Humor.* Chicago, IL: Nelson-Hall.

————. 1979. "Dogmatism, Intelligence, and the Understanding and Appreciation of Satire." Paper presented at the Second International Conference on Humor, Los Angeles. ERIC document accession no. 178 981. Abstracted in *The Study of Humor*. Edited by Mindess and Turek. Los Angeles: Antioch University.

————. 1982. "Speaker Ethos, Humorous Self-Disparagement, and the Sense of Humor." Paper presented at the Third International Conference on Humor, Washington, D. C. ERIC Document Reproduction Service No. ED 220 879.

———— 1984. "Self- and Other-Disparaging Wit/Humor and Speaker Ethos: Three experiments." Paper presented at the Fourth International Conference on Humor, Tel Aviv, Israel.

————. 1985. "Advice to the Beginning Speaker on Using Humor-What the Research Tells Us." *Communication Education*. 34: 140–4.

————. 1987a. "More on Satire as Persuasion." Keynote paper presented at the Sixth International Conference on Humor, Part 1, Tempe, AZ.

————. 1987b. "Note on Editorial Satire and Persuasion." *Psychological Reports* 60: 884–886.

————. 1988a. "Prior Attitude and Perception of Satirical Theses." *Perceptual and Motor Skills* 67: 677–678.

————. 1988b. "Prior Attitude and Understanding of Editorial Satire." *Psychological Reports* 63: 54.

————. 1989a. "Measured Cynicism and Understanding of Editorial Satire." Paper presented at the Seventh International Conference on Humor, Laie, HI.

————. 1989b. "A Quasi-experimental Study of the Effect of Humor Preference and other Variables on Understanding/Appreciation of Editorial Satire." *Psychological Reports* 65: 967–970.

————. 1990. "'Humor Style'" and Understanding of Editorial Satire." *Perceptual and Motor Skills* 71: 1–2.

————. 1992a. "A Partial Replication Study of Factors Involved in the Understanding/Appreciation of Editorial Satire." Paper presented at the Tenth International Conference on Humor, Paris.

————. 1992b. "Satire as Persuasion." Paper presented at the Speech Communication Association Seminar on "Humor and Communication," Chicago, IL.

Gruner, Charles R. and Dwight D.L. Freshley. 1980. "Retention of Lecture Items Reinforced with Humorous and Nonhumorous Exemplary Material." Paper presented at the Speech Communication Association Convention, New York. ERIC Document Reproduction Service No. 193 725.

Gruner, Marsha W. and Charles R. Gruner. 1991. "Gender, Argumentativeness, and Response to Editorial Satire." Paper presented at the Ninth International Conference On Humor, St. Catherine's, Ontario.

Gruner, Charles R., Marsha W. Gruner, and Lara J. Travillion. 1991. "Another Quasi-Experimental Study of Understanding/Appreciation of Editorial Satire." *Psychological Reports* 69: 731–734.

Gruner, Charles R. and Virgie Nobles Harris. 1992. "Understanding/Appreciation of Editorial Satire." *Psychological Reports* 70: 850.

Gruner, Charles R. and William E. Lampton. 1972. "Effects of Including Humorous Material in a Persuasive Sermon." *Southern Speech Communication Journal* 38: 188–196.

Gruner, Charles R., Laura J. Pelletier, and Melanie A. Williams. 1994. "Evaluative Responses to Jokes in Informative Speech with and without Laughter by an Audience." *Psychological Reports* 73: 446.

Gruner, Charles R. 1995. "The Pun: 'First' and 'Second' Degree." Paper presented at the Thirteenth Convention of the International Society for Humor Studies, Birmingham, England.

Harlow, H. H. 1969. "The Anatomy of Humor." *Impact of Science on Society* 19: 225–239.

Harms, Ernest. 1943. "The Development of Humor." *Journal of Abnormal and Social Psychology* 38: 351–369.

Hartley, E. L. 1946. *Problems in Prejudice*. New York: King's Crown Press.

Harris, Sydney. 1972. "Belgian Jokes." *Athens (GA) Daily News* 10, May 8.

Helitzer, Melvin. 1987. *Comedy Writing Secrets*. Cincinnati: Writer's Digest Books.

Herik, Richie, ed. 1980. *The Psychotherapy Handbook*. New York: Meridian.

Hertzler, Joyce O. 1970. *Laughter: A Socio-Scientific Analysis*. Jericho, NY: Exposition Press.

Hetherington, E. Mavis and Nancy P. Wray. 1964. "Aggression, Need for Social Approval, and Humor Preferences." *Journal of Abnormal and Social Psychology* 68: 685–689.

Hitler, Adolph. [1940] 1974. *Mein Kampf*. London: Hutchinson.

Hobbes, Thomas. 1839–45. *The English Works of Thomas Hobbes of Malmesbury*, edited by Sir William Molesworth. London: J. Bohn.

Hofstadter, Douglas, Gabora, Liane, Raskin, Victor, and Salvatore Attardo. 1989. Synopsis of the Workshop on Humor and Cognition, Indiana University. *Humor: International Journal of Humor Research* 2: 417–440.

Hoke, Helen. 1958. *Puns, Puns, Puns*, New York: Franklin Watts, Inc.

Huxley, Aldous. 1932. *Brave New World, A Novel*. Garden City, NY: Doubleday, Duran.

Hyers, Conrad. 1996. *The Spirituality of Comedy: Comic Heroism in a Tragic World*. New Brunswick, NJ: Transaction Publishers.

"J.", Mr. 1976. *The World's Best Dirty Jokes*. New York: Ballantine Books.

Jones, J. A. and J.M. Vincent. 1984. "Mirth and Mourning: Interactions of Humor and Speaker Credibility in a Funeral Eulogy." Paper presented at the Fourth International Congress on Humor, Tel Aviv, Israel.

Jung, Carl G. 1970. *Psychological Reflections*. Princeton, NJ: University of Princeton Press.

Kahn, Samuel. 1975. *Why and How We Laugh*. New York: Philosophical Library.

Kaplan, R. M. and G.C. Pascoe. 1977. "Humorous Lectures and Humorous Examples: Some Effects upon Comprehension and Retention." *Journal of Educational Psychology* 69: 61–65.

Kass, Leon R. 1985. *Toward A More Natural Science*. New York: The Free Press.

Kennedy, A. M. 1972. "An Experimental Study of the Effect of Humor Message Content upon Ethos and Persuasiveness." Ph.D. diss., University of Michigan. Abstract in *Dissertation Abstracts International* 33: 2539A.

Kerman, Judith B. 1980. "The Light-Bulb Joke: Americans Look at Social Action Processes." *Journal of American Folkore* 93: 454–458.

Kilpela, Donald C. 1961. "An Experimental Study of the Effects of Humor on Persuasion." Masters thesis, Wayne State University, Detroit.

Klumpp, James F. and Thomas A. Hollihan. 1979. "Debunking the Resignation of Earl Butz: Sacrificing an Official Racist." *Quarterly Journal of Speech* 65: 1–11.

Knott, Blanche. 1982. *Truly Tasteless Jokes*. New York: Ballantine Books.

———. 1983a. *Truly Tasteless Jokes Two*. New York: Ballantine Books.

———. 1983b. *Truly Tasteless Jokes Three*. New York: Ballantine Books.

———. 1984. *Truly Tasteless Jokes IV*. New York: Pinnacle.

Koestler, Arthur. 1964. *The Act of Creation.* New York: Dell.

Kurten, Bjorn. 1972. *Not From The Apes.* New York: Pantheon.

Kurti, Laszlo. 1988. "The Politics of Joking: Popular Response to Chernobyl." *Journal of American Folklore* 101: 324–334.

LaFave, L. 1967. "Comment on Priest's Article: 'Election Jokes: The Effects of Reference Group Membership.'" *Psychological Reports* 20: 305–306.

Lamb, Charles W. 1968. "Personality Correlates of Humor Enjoyment following Motivational Arousal." *Journal of Personality and Social Psychology* 9: 237–241.

Landy, David, and David Mettee. 1969. "Evaluation of an Aggressor as a Function of Exposure to Cartoon Humor." *Journal of Personality and Social Psychology* 12: 66–71.

Leacock, Stephen. 1935. *Humor: Its Theory and Technique.* New York: Dodd, Mead.

Leak, Gary K. 1974. "Effects of Hostility Arousal and Aggressive Humor on Catharsis and Humor Preference." *Journal of Personality and Social Psychology* 30: 736–740.

Lederer, Richard. 1988. *Get Thee To A Punnery.* New York: Dell.

Legman, G. 1968. *Rationale of the Dirty Joke.* New York: Grove.

———. 1975. *Rationale of the Dirty Joke.* 2d Series. New York: Breaking Point, Inc.

Levy-Leboyer, C., ed. 1984. *Vandalism: Behaviour and Motivations.* Amsterdam: Elsevier Science Publishers B.V.

Lew, Robert. 1995. "The Role of Ambiguators in Linguistic *Verbal Jokes.*" Paper presented at the Thirteenth Convention, International Society for Humor Studies, 2 August.

Lewontin, R. C. 1974. *The Genetic Basis of Evolutionary Change.* New York: Columbia University Press.

Lipman, Steve. 1991. *Laughter in Hell: The Use of Humor During the Holocaust.* Northdale, NJ: Jason Aronson, Inc.

Long, Debra A. and Arthur C. Graesser. 1988. "Wit and Humor in Discourse Processing." *Discourse Processes* 11: 35–60.

Losco, Jean and Seymour Epstein. 1975. "Humor Preference as a Subtle Measure of Attitudes toward the Same and the Opposite Sex." *Journal of Personality* 43: 321–334.

Love, Ann Marie and Lambert H. Deckers. 1989. "Humor Appreciation as a Function of Sexual, Aggressive, and Sexist Content." *Sex Roles* 20: 649–654.

Ludovici, A. M. 1932. *The Secret of Laughter.* London: Constable Press.

Lull, P. E. 1940. "The Effects of Humor in Persuasive Speech." *Speech Monographs* 7: 26–40.

MacHale, Des. 1981. *The Bumper Book of Kerryman Jokes.* Dublin and Cork, Ireland: Mercier.

MacHovec, Frank J. 1988. *Humor: Theory, History, Applications.* Springfield, IL: Charles C. Thomas.

Mandler, George. 1975. *Mind and Emotion.* New York: Wiley.

Marino, Matthew. 1988. "Puns: The Good, the Bad, and the Beautiful." *Humor: The International Journal of Humor Research* 1: 39–48.

Markiewicz, D. 1972. "The Effects of Humor on Persuasion." Ph. D. diss., The Ohio State University. Abstract in *Dissertation Abstracts International* 33: 3986.

Martin, J. M. 1961. *Juvenile Vandalism.* Springfield, IL: Charles C. Thomas.

McCroskey, James C. 1966. "Scales for the Measurement of Ethos." *Speech Monographs* 33: 65–72.

McFarlan, Donald, ed. 1992. *The Guinness Book of World Records*. New York: Bantam Books.

McGhee, Paul E. 1979. *Humor: Its Origin and Development*. San Francisco, CA: W. H. Freeman.

Menon, V. K. Krishna. 1978. *A Theory of Laughter*. London: George Allen & Unwin Ltd.

Mendel, Werner M., ed. 1970. *A Celebration of Laughter*. Los Angeles: Mara.

Mettee, D. R., E.S. Hrelec, and P.C. Wilkens. 1971. "Humor as an Interpersonal Asset and Liability." *The Journal of Social Psychology* 85: 51–64.

Middleton, Russell, and John Moland. 1959. "Humor in Negro and White Subcultures: A Study of Jokes among University Students." *American Sociological Review* 24: 61–69.

Mikes, George. 1970. *Laughing Matters: Towards a Personal Philosophy of Wit and Humor*. New York: Library Press.

Miller, Frank C. 1967. "Humor in a Chippewa Tribal Council." *Ethnology* 6: 263–271.

Miller, Gerald R. and Paula P. Bacon. 1971. "Open- and Closed-mindedness and Recognition of Visual Humor." *Journal of Communication* 21: 150–159.

Mindess, Harvey. 1971. *Laughter and Liberation*. Los Angeles: Nash Publishing.

Mindess, Harvey, Carolyn Miller, Joy Turek, Amanda Bender, and Susan Corbin. 1985. *The Antioch Humor Test: Making Sense of Humor*. New York: Avon Books.

Mindess, Harvey and Joy Turek. n.d. *The Study of Humor*. Los Angeles: Antioch University.

Mintz, Lawrence E. 1986. In *Jewish Humor*, edited by Avner Ziv. Tel Aviv: Papyrus.

Morreall, John. 1983. *Taking Laughter Seriously*. Albany, NY: State University of New York Press, Albany Press.

———. 1987a. "Funny Haha, Funny Strange, and Other Reactions to Incongruity." In *The Philosophy of Laughter and Humor*, edited by John Morreall. Albany, NY: State University of New York Press.

———, ed. 1987b. *The Philosophy of Laughter and Humor*. Albany, NY: State University of New York Press.

———. 1989. "Enjoying Incongruity." *Humor: International Journal of Humor Research* 2: 1–18.

Morris, Desmond. 1967. *The Naked Ape*. New York: Dell.

———. 1991. *Babywatching*. New York: Crown.

Mottley, John. [1739] 1963. *Joe Miller's Jests*. Reprint, New York: Dover Publications.

Mueller, Charles and Edward Donnerstein. 1977. "The Effects of Humor-Induced Arousal upon Aggressive Behavior." *Journal of Research in Personality* 11: 73–82.

Munn, William C. and Charles R. Gruner. 1981. "'Sick'" Jokes, Speaker Sex, and Informative Speech." *Southern Speech Communication Journal* 46: 411–418.

Nevo, Ofra. 1986. "Do Jews in Israel still Laugh at Themselves?" In *Jewish Humor*, edited by Avner Ziv. Tel Aviv: Papyrus.

———. 1991. What's in a Jewish Joke? *Humor: International Journal of Humor Research* 4: 251–260.

Nilsen, Don L. F. 1993. *Humor Scholarship: A Research Bibliography*. Westport, CT: Greenwood Press.

Novak, William and Moshe Waldoks. 1981. *The Big Book of Jewish Humor*. New York: Harper & Bros.

O'Connell, Walter E. 1960. "The Adaptive Functions of Wit and Humor." *Journal of Abnormal and Social Psychology* 61: 263–270.

Orben, Robert. 1969. *2000 New Laughs for Speakers*. Hollywood, CA: Wilshire Book Co.

———. 1966, *The Joke Teller's Handbook, or 1000 Belly Laughs*. Hollywood, CA: Wilshire Book Co.

Oring, Elliott. 1992. *Jokes and Their Relations*. Lexington, KY: University of Kentucky Press.

———. 1984. *The Jokes of Sigmund Freud*. Philadelphia, PA: University of Pennsylvania Press.

Osgood, Charles E., W. H. May, and M.S. Miron. 1975. *Crosscultural Universals of Affective Meaning*. Urban, IL: University of Illinois Press.

Osgood, Charles E., George J. Suci, and Percy H. Tannenbaum. 1967. *The Measurement of Meaning*. Urbana, IL: University of Illinois Press.

Paglia, Camille. 1991. *Sexual Personae*. New York: Vintage.

Palmer, J. 1994. *Taking Humour Seriously*. New York: Routledge.

Panati, Charles. 1987. *Panati's Extraordinary Origins of Everyday Things*. New York: Harper & Row.

Peter, Laurence J. and Bill Dana. 1982. *The Laughter Prescription*. New York: Ballantine.

Philbrick, Kathilyn Durnf. 1989. "The Use of Humor and Effective Leadership Styles." Ph.D. diss., University of Florida.

Piddington, Ralph. 1963. *The Psychology of Laughter*. New York: Gamut Press.

Playboy. 1986. *Still More Playboy's Party Jokes*. Chicago, IL: Playboy Press.

Pokorny, Gary F. and Charles R. Gruner. 1969. "An Experimental Study of Satire Used as Support in a Persuasive Speech." *Western Speech* 33: 204–211.

Powell, Larry. 1977. "Satirical Persuasion and Topic Salience." *Southern Speech Communication Journal* 42: 151–162.

Prerost, Frank J. 1975. "The Indication of Sexual and Aggressive Similarities through Humor Appreciation." *The Journal of Psychology* 91: 283–288.

——— 1976. "Reduction of Aggression as a Function of Related Content of Humor." *Psychological Reports* 38: 771–777.

——— 1983. "Locus of Control and the Aggression-Inhibiting Effects of Aggressive Humor Appreciation." *Journal of Personality Assessment* 47: 294–299.

Prerost, Frank J. and Robert E. Brewer. 1977. "Humor Content Preferences and the Relief of Experimentally-Aroused Aggression." *The Journal of Social Psychology* 103: 225–231.

Priest, Robert F. 1966. "Election Jokes: The Effects of Reference Group Membership." *Psychological Reports* 18: 600–602.

Priest, Robert F. and Joel Abrahams. 1970. "Candidate Preference and Hostile Humor in the 1968 Elections." *Psychological Reports* 26: 779–783.

Priest, Robert F. and Paul G. Wilhelm. 1974. "Sex, Marital Status, and Self- Actualization as Factors in the Appreciation of Sexist Jokes." *Journal of Social Psychology* 100: 245–249.

Radcliffe-Brown, A. R. 1940. "On Joking Relationships." *Africa* 13: 195–210.

———. 1949. "A Further Note on Joking Relationships." *Africa* 19: 133–140.

Randi, James. 1980. *Flim-Flam: The Truth About Unicorns, Parapsychology, and Other Delusions*. New York: Harper & Row.

Rapp, Albert. 1951. *The Origins of Wit and Humor*. New York: E.P. Dutton.

Raskin, Victor. 1992. "Meaning, Truth, and the Sense of Humor." Paper presented at the November Speech Communication Association seminar on "Humor as Communication," Chicago, IL.

————. 1985a. Jokes. *Psychology Today* (October): 34–39.

————. 1985b. *Semantic Mechanisms of Humor.* Boston, MA: D. Reidel Publishing Co.

Redfern, Walter. 1984. *Puns.* New York: Basil Blackwell, Inc.

Rezwin, Max, ed. 1958. *Sick Jokes, Grim Cartoons & Bloody Marys.* New York: Citadel.

Reid, J. K. 1971. "The Effect of Humor on Perceived Attractiveness of a Speaker." Master's thesis, Oklahoma State University.

Roberts, A. F. and D.M. Johnson. 1957. "Some Factors Related to the Perception of Funniness in Humor Stimuli." *Journal of Social Psychology* 46: 57–63.

Rosenwald, George C. 1964. "The Relation of Drive Discharge to Enjoyment of Humor." *Journal of Personality* 32: 682–698.

Rosten, Leo. 1982. *Hooray For Yiddish!* New York: Simon and Schuster.

Rothcart, Mark K. 1976. "Incongruity, Problem-Solving, and Laughter." In *Humor and Laughter: Theory, Research, and Applications*, edited by A.J. Chapman and H.C. Foot. London: Wiley.

Rowley, Hon. Hugh 1866. *Puniana: Or, Thoughts Wise and OtherWise.* London: John Camden Hotten, Piccadilly.

Ruch, Willibald and Franz-Josef Hehl. 1988. "Attitudes to Sex, Sexual Behavior, and Enjoyment of Humor." *Personality and Individual Differences* 9: 983–994.

Russel, Roy. 1987. *Life, Mind and Laughter: A Theory of Laughter.* Chicago, IL: Adams Press.

Sagan, Carl and Ann Druyan. 1992. *Shadows of Forgotten Ancestors.* New York: Random House.

Saper, Bernard. 1991. "A Cognitive Behavioral Formulation of the Relation between the Jewish Joke and Anti-Semitism." *Humor: International Journal of Humor Research* 4: 41–59.

Schmidt, Casper G. 1984–85. "AIDS Jokes or, *schadenfreude* around an Epidemic." *Maledicta* 8: 69–75.

Schwartz, Steven. 1972. "The Effects of Arousal on Appreciation for Varying Degrees of Sex-Relevant Humor." *Journal of Experimental Research in Personality* 6: 211–247.

Schmaier, Maurice D. 1963–64. "The Doll Joke Pattern in Contemporary American Oral Humor." *Midwest Folklore* 13: 205–216.

Schultz, T. R. 1976. "A Cognitive-Developmental Analysis of Humor." In *Humour and Laughter: Theory, Research, and Applications*, edited by A.J. Chapman and H.C. Foot. London: Wiley.

Schutz, Charles E. 1989. "The Sociability of Ethnic Jokes." *Humor: International Journal of Humor Research* 2: 165–177.

Scoggin, Forrest R. and Michael Merbaum. 1983. "Humourous Stimuli and Depression: An Examination of Beck's Premise." *Journal of Clinical Psychology* 39: 165–169.

Simons, Elizabeth Radin. 1986. "The NASA Joke Cycle: The Astronauts and the Teacher." *Western Folklore* 45: 261–277.

Singer, David L. 1968. "Aggression Arousal, Hostile Humor, and Catharsis." *Journal of Personality and Social Psychology Monograph Supplement* 8: 1–14.

Singer, David L., Harry F. Gollob, and Jacob Levine. 1967. "Mobilization of Inhibition and the Enjoyment of Aggressive Humor." *Journal of Personality* 35: 562–569.

Smyth, Willie. 1986. "*Challenger* Jokes and the Humor of Disaster." *Western Folklore* 45: 243–260.

Spalding, Henry D. 1969. *Encyclopedia of Jewish Humor*. New York: Jonathan David.

Spencer, Gary. 1989. "An Analysis of JAP-Baiting Humor on the College Campus." *Humor: International Journal of Humor Research* 2: 329–348.

Stearns, Frederic R. 1972. *Laughing: Physiology, Pathophysiology, Psychology, Pathopsychology, and Development*. Springfield,IL: Charles C. Thomas.

Stein, Mary Beth. 1989. "The Politics of Humor: The Berlin Wall in Jokes and Graffiti." *Western Folklore* 48: 85–108.

Stocking, H. S. and D. Zillman. 1976. "Effects of Humorous Disparagement of Self, Friend, and Enemy." *Psychological Reports* 39: 455–461.

Strickland, John F. 1959. "The Effect of Motivation Arousal on Humor Preferences." *Journal of Abnormal and Social Psychology* 59: 278–281.

Sulloway, Frank J. 1979. *Freud, Biologist of the Mind*. New York: Basic Books.

Surlin, Stewart. 1973. "The Evaluation of Dogmatic Television Characters by Dogmatic Viewers: 'Is Archie Bunker a Credible Source?'" Paper presented at the April International Communication Association, Montreal, Quebec.

Sutton-Smith, Brian. 1960. "'Shut Up and Keep Digging': The Cruel Joke Series". *Midwest Folklore* 10: 11–22.

Tannen, Holly and David Morris. 1989. "AIDS Jokes: Punishment, Retribution, and Renegotiation." *Southern Folklore* 46: 147–157.

Taylor, Archer. 1943. "The Riddle." *California Folklore Quarterly* 2: 129–147.

Taylor, P. M. 1964. "Research Report: The Effectiveness of Humor in Informative Speaking." *Central States Speech Journal* 15: 295–296.

Thrasher, F. M. 1936. *The Gang*. Chicago, IL: University of Chicago Press.

Trice, Ashton D. 1982. "Ratings of Humor following Experience with Unsolvable Tasks." *Psychological Reports* 51: 1148.

Tucci, Ralph G. 1989. "The Effects of Self-deprecating, Aggressive, and Neutral Humor on Depressive, Acting-Out, and Normal Adolescents." Ph.D. diss., St. John's University.

Untermeyer, Louis. 1926. *Collected Parodies*. New York: Harcourt, Brace.

Verinis, J. Scott. 1970. "Inhibition of Humor Enjoyment: Differential Effects with Traditional Diagnostic Categories." *Journal of General Psychology* 82: 157–163.

Vidmar, Neil and Milton Rokeach. 1974. "Archie Bunker's Bigotry: A Study in Selective Perception and Exposure." *Journal of Communication* 24 (winter): 36–47.

Vincent, J. M. and A.J. Jones. 1983. "The Impact of Humor on Speaker Credibility in Funeral Eulogies." Paper presented at the International Conference on Culture and Communication, Philadelphia, PA.

Walker, Gerald. 1956. "Sick Jokes." *Esquire* (December): 151 ff.

Welford, T. W. 1971. "An Experimental Study of the Effectiveness of Humor used as a Refutational Device." Ph.D. diss., Louisiana State University. Abstract in *Dissertation Abstracts International* 32: 7120.

Wells, C. 1923. *An Outline of Humor*. New York: G. P. Putnam's Sons.

Wilde, Larry. 1979. *The Official Book of Sick Jokes*. Los Angeles: Pinnacle Books.

Wilson, Christopher P. 1979. *Jokes: Form, Content, Use and Function*. New York: Academic Press.

Young, Richard D. and Margaret Frye. 1966. "Some are Laughing, Some Are Not-Why?" *Psychological Reports* 18: 747–754.

Youngman, Henny. 1992. *Henny Youngman's Book of Jokes*. New York: Carol.

Youngman, R. C. 1956. "An Experimental Investigation of the Effect of Germane Humor vs. Non-germane Humor in an Informative Communication." Master's thesis, Ohio University.

190   The Game of Humor

Zillman, Dolf, Bryant, Jennings, and Joanne R. Cantor. 1974. "Brutality of Assault in Political Cartoons Affecting Humor Appreciation." *Journal of Research in Personality* 7: 334–345.
Zillman, Dolf and Joanne R. Cantor. 1972. "Directionality of Transitory Dominance as a Communication Variable Affecting Humor Appreciation." *Journal of Personality and Social Psychology* 24: 191–198.
Zillman, Dolf, Joanne R. Cantor, and Jennings Bryant. 1975. "Enhancement of Experienced Sexual Arousal in Response to Erotic Stimuli through Misattribution of Unrelated Residual Excitation." *Journal of Personality and Social Psychology* 32: 69–75.
Ziv, Avner. 1982. "Cognitive Results of Using Humor in Teaching." Paper presented at the Fourth International Conference on Humor, Tel Aviv, Israel.
——— 1984. *Personality and Sense of Humor.* New York: Springer Publishing Co.
———, ed. 1986. "Introduction." In *Jewish Humor.* Tel Aviv: Papyrus.
———, ed. 1986. *Jewish Humor.* Tel Aviv: Papyrus.
———. 1988. "Teaching and Learning with Humor: Experiment and Replication." *Journal of Experimental Education* 57: 5–15.
Ziv, Avner and Orit Gadish. 1990. "The Disinhibiting Effects of Humor: Aggressive and Affective Responses." *Humor: International Journal of Humor Research* 3: 247–257.

Index

Abrahams, Joel, 89, 187
Adam and Eve tale, 1
Addison, Joseph, 133
adultery jokes, 120
AIDS jokes, 58 ff.
Ainsworth, C. H., 179
All in the Family, 100, 129
Allen, K. D., 180
Allen, Fred, 41
Allen, Gracie, 154
Allen, V. L., 44, 179
Alperin, Mimi, 1–3
Altman, Sig, 179
Aman, Reinhold, 179
ambiguity, verbal, 25
America's Funniest Home Videos, 73, 94
American Jewish, 104
Andy Capp, 104
animal jokes, 117
Annis, J. D., 179
Apte, Mahadev L., 18, 179
Archie, 173
"Aristotle Contemplating the Bust of Homer," 80
art, of puns, 140 ff.
Asher, R., 179
Athens, Georgia, 36
Atlanta Braves, 36
Atlanta Constitution/Journal, The, 28
Attardo, Salvatore, 184

B.C., 171
Babywatching, 19, 186
Backus, Jim, 70
Bacon, Paula P., 186
Baker, William J., 35, 179
Ball, Rodney, L., 110, 179
Banc, C., 179
Barcelona Olympics, 28
Barclay, Andrew M., 114, 179

Baron, Robert A., 110, 111, 114, 179
Barrick, Mac E., 57, 179
BBC, 139
Ben-Amos, Dan, 93, 179
Bergler, Edmund, 137, 179
Bergson, Henri, 14, 179
Berkowitz, Leonard, 110, 166, 179
Berle, Milton, 93
Berman, Shelley, 92
Berscheid, Ellen, 19, 180
"Best of the Stan Freberg Shows, The," 161
Bier, Jesse, 81, 180
Big Nate, 54
Bill, Brigitte, 129, 180
Blatz, W. E., 10, 180
blonde jokes, 58 ff.
Blondie, 175
Bloody Mary's, 45 ff., 66
Bloom County, 175
Bloopers and Practical Jokes, 72
Boner's Ark, 171, 174
Born Loser, The, 171
Botkin, B. A., 180
Brandes, Paul D., 180
Bradney, Pamela, 163–164, 180
Brave New World, 34, 35, 184
Braves, Atlanta, 36
Brett, Theodore, 180
Brewer, Robert E., 110, 163, 187
Bruns, Ryan, 6
Bryant, Jennings, 14, 109, 165, 180, 190
Buchwald, Art, 89, 108, 180
Bunker, Archie, 100, 129
Burnam, Don, 159, 180
Burns, George, 154
"Button-Down Mind of Bob Newhart, The," 159
Butz, Earl, 86, incident, 78 ff.
Byrne, Donn, 110, 180